Just a small crown  ...ly world

The
Self-Sufficient
Princess

SANGUINE ADDAMS

Copyright © 2023 Sanguine Addams
All Rights Reserved

This book is subject to the condition that no part of this book is to be reproduced, transmitted in any form or means; electronic or mechanical, stored in a retrieval system, photocopied, recorded, scanned, or otherwise. Any of these actions require the proper written permission of the author.

sanguineaddams.com

Edited by Ethan Franzel
Cover art by Gan!
Illustration by Alicyn Q. Foti
Book interior design by Booknook.biz

ISBN 978-1961075337 (paperback)
ASIN B0C4GB2GSX (ebook)

*To Lorynn, Alicyn and Emylee.
My princesses, my dragons.*

Acknowledgments

I WOULD LIKE TO thank my daughters for giving me the inspiration for writing this book. I raised them to be strong and confident women. It is difficult in today's society to be unaffected by the burden of social media and the horrific strains that are placed on a young woman. Although it has been a struggle, they have each been a vessel of love. I'm proud and honored to be a part of their lives. Lorynn, Alicyn and Emylee… I love you with all that I am. Love! Love! Love! All the love!

Many thanks to Tom Moynahan for bringing my creation to life by narrating the audiobook and giving me pointers throughout the process. If that were all you had done, that would have been enough. You have been a dear friend and confidant for forty years. I owe you a debt that I can never repay.

Ethan Franzel took over proofreading and editing when my eyes were too tired to recognize a comma from a coma. Thank you for always lending a hand or a shoulder and for knowing which one I needed the most. Thank you, Seymour.

The great team at Sound on Sound Studios in Montclair, NJ. Tony and Dan took an inexperienced writer and narrator and led us through the arduous process of recording an audiobook. I couldn't ask for a more understanding and competent team of professionals. Top notch all around.

Maryann McFadden, an internationally acclaimed author and friend, helped instill in me the confidence to proceed and realize my dream was reachable. Someday, I pray that I may be able to write as eloquently as you.

Saria Fluellen, my dear friend and surrogate sister, has been there for all the nonsensical clerical work and a kind ear in times of need. I am truly blessed to have you in my life these past thirty-five years.

And lastly, thank you to my soulmate, Chris. Someone who keeps seeing something in me that I can never see. Someone who continues to unselfishly nudge me along as I climb for the stars. My love for you will never waver. I will never be able to tell you that I love you enough. Just watch my leap of faith, again and again, as I submit myself to you. I love you.

Contents

Acknowledgments	vii
Chapter 1	1
Chapter 2	11
Chapter 3	25
Chapter 4	39
Chapter 5	51
Chapter 6	61
Chapter 7	75
Chapter 8	87
Chapter 9	99
Chapter 10	111
Chapter 11	125
Chapter 12	137
Chapter 13	151
Chapter 14	167
Chapter 15	181
Chapter 16	197
Chapter 17	211
Chapter 18	227
Epilogue	245
About the Author	249

Chapter 1

IN THE LAND OF This-and-That, there lived a princess who... Listen, I understand that these types of stories usually begin with some beautiful rhyming scheme. That is not going to happen here. It is not that I'm a lazy narrator, it's just that the premise seems a bit pretentious, is all. So... moving forward.

In the land of... Look, it is just difficult, OK? As your narrator, I feel that the rhyming might take away from this brilliant story that I am about to tell. I mean, have you ever tried it? What rhymes with princess? I'll tell you what. Nothing. It's a pain, and if the rhyme isn't good, it seems like you're cutting corners. Britney rhymed "calling" with "warning" and Usher rhymed "floor" with "go", and that's just plain criminal. On to the story.

In the... I'm just asking that you cut me a little slack here. Narrating jobs are scarce enough as it is, and I don't need your high expectations undermining my gig. I've got bills to pay. So, let's just have a little fun, alright?

Thank you.

In the land of This-and-That, there lived a princess named Nightingale. Princesses are depicted as having hair of spun gold and eyes of violet-blue who flitter around in their castle, summoning wildlife through melodious caterwauling. They gallop through glens of green on a beautiful stallion named Chestnut or Champion or some other regal-sounding name, where they inevitably meet the Handsome Prince, Sir Whatshisface of Whatever. They chat about scones and dancing for about three paragraphs, and by Chapter Six, a beautiful wedding, happily ever after, the end. They have twenty-seven kids, all of them gorgeous, and none of their children suffer from anxiety. They can totally get into all the good clubs without calling ahead first. Nightingale was all of this and more, except the complete opposite.

Our heroine is short with average brown hair and average brown eyes. Our heroine hates her nose but has come to grips with it. Our heroine drinks power drinks and stays up all night playing online war games such as Scabs of Destiny. She routinely kills players with nicknames like PizzaBoi, DeathFist, and N00bmaster, who camp by spawning sites and deserve to be dispatched with reckless aplomb. Our heroine loves her high-speed ping rate and eats cookie dough ice cream for breakfast. She wears a hoodie, despises high-heeled shoes, binge-watches streaming services, and loves to sleep until the crack of noon. Take a moment to close your eyes to imagine this girl. I'll wait. Are you back? Good. That's EXACTLY what she looks like.

Nightingale enjoys her life. She lives in a tower, but not because she was cursed by a witch or hidden from the world by an evil stepmother. She lives there by choice. She comes and goes as she pleases. Her tower has satellite TV and a fantastic mini kitchenette. A comfy couch and throw pillows of all sizes and colors are littered about the main room. The bathroom has excellent water pressure, a claw-foot tub and is decorated with a few plants. The bedroom is cozy enough, with a princess-size bed and plenty of closet space to harbor the fancy gowns and shoes she rarely wears. Pictures of family and friends are scattered about on the walls and dressers, with silly frames for the friends and royal ones for her parents. Adorning a wall in the living room is a magic mirror named Reflexa, who is hooked up to her Wi-Fi and is ready to answer the worldly questions that may burden a princess, such as "when is Scabs of Destiny 2 being released?" and "what power drink pairs well with a robust cheese puff?"

The tower is your basic round, white stone type with a red clay tile roof and tendrils of vines and bean sprouts climbing high along its walls.

Chapter 1

A heavy red oak door faces a flower-lined path leading to the Woods of Nevermore, which begin at the edge of her glen. Set high, the tower has a window facing each direction, and they overlook the beauty that is the kingdom. One on the south side to the Woods of Nevermore and one west facing her parents' castle, Castle Beckett. The castle sits far enough away to feel comfortable yet close enough to feel… well, comfortable. Her bedroom window faces north, and the sea could be seen on most nights. The smell of the salt air rides the breeze into her bedroom, and the morning sun's reflection off the waves would dance along her ceiling. The bathroom has a small window, big enough to let in enough sun for the plants but small enough to stop her from imagining serial killers peeking in on her while she is in the shower.

Hopefully, I, the narrator, have painted a clear enough picture of the princess' domicile. You're going to have to meet me halfway if we're going to get this done, so use your imagination a bit and fill in whatever blanks you have. Wondering what color her comforter is? Figure it out for yourself. That is literally how reading works. Moving on.

Upon graduation from high school, (You had no idea that princesses attended high school, did you? Well, some do. Most importantly, this one did), Nightingale's parents asked her what she would like as a present. Our princess chose solitude. It wasn't that she didn't like the castle or that she had an issue with her parents. She just wanted to try it on her own. No parents waking her up, no expectations, no responsibilities. She would have to do all her own chores and cleaning and food shopping. In return, she would have peace of mind and the ability to try herself.

I don't mean to make it sound as if living on her own was an easy sell. Her parents didn't graciously give her the keys and kiss her goodbye. The pushback on the idea was formidable and caused quite a rift within her entire family. Nightingale is an only child, and the king and queen are very protective, which is what they should be. What seventeen-year-old lives on their own a month after graduating high school?

Her father, King Killian, was enraged and took the planned departure as a slap in his face. As protector and provider, the king felt slighted that his efforts weren't good enough for his daughter. Meticulously, he itemized every worst-case scenario he could find, including a massive flood and invasion by hostile forces. Her mother, Queen Evelyn, was concerned for her daughter's virtue and reputation. How would it reflect on her if her only child ran out at such a young age? Her rebuttals included health concerns and "invasions" by "hostile forces," if you catch my drift.

The debate continued for weeks, with many a slammed door and tears shed on all sides. Nightingale pleaded her case that the new living arrangements would help round her as a woman and that she was eager to face the world head-on. How would she eventually become the leader of a kingdom if she didn't experience being the leader of herself first? Surely, her parents had armed her with enough knowledge and maturity to withstand living alone. This was a chance to take all of that knowledge for a spin around the block.

Countless discussions were had between the king and queen when, finally, they succumbed to the idea. Nightingale would use an old tower just outside of the castle walls. It was once an outpost for sentries during harsher times, when the threat of said hostile forces was prevalent. The princess would stay in contact with her parents, and they promised to keep her bedroom handy in case she needed to retreat. The king was certain that this would only be a fleeting fancy and that after some scary nights alone by the woods, his daughter would return home safe and sound.

Queen Evelyn was much brighter than her husband.

Once the princess tasted her freedom, the queen knew she would never return. She was once a seventeen-year-old princess herself and knew how they thought and acted. It broke her mother's heart to see her go, but she swore to support her daughter in ways that her own parents never had. In the end, the queen convinced her husband to loosen the ties a little and let their daughter spread her wings.

For the most part, Nightingale was happy with her simple life. When she was lonely, she would call her friends to hang out or just to chat. Occasionally, she would ride over to the castle to see her mom and dad for a hug and a snack and to hear the latest gossip of the kingdom. Mom would tell her who had the pox and who was dating whom, and if they had the pox. Dad would ask about her friends and discuss who was champion of what and whether the crops had gotten the pox. Frankly, upon reflection, there was way too much talk about the pox.

Chapter 1

Today was going to be one of the days when she would ride over to the castle to see her folks. She had promised to help her mother bake some chocolate chip cookies for a charity event, and if her father was home, she would like to drop a hint or two about what she wanted for her upcoming birthday. Nightingale was turning eighteen in a few weeks, and she figured that now would be a good time to casually mention the new sneakers she had been eyeing up. They were low tops in marshmallow with a petite floral design and so adorable that she had to have them. If she didn't say anything about her gift preference, her father would bestow upon her something traditional, like another tiara or that horrific crossbow that she got for a tower-warming gift when she moved in.

Baking was a fun bonding time for Nightingale and her mom. The king would always find an excuse to leave them alone in the kitchen, where they could talk and relax without the constraints of the parent-daughter relationship to hold them back. Among the mixing bowls and measuring cups, they were two friends enjoying each other's company, and laughing and complaining filled the time between batches. Many a crisis was thwarted in that kitchen, and Nightingale was counting on the good council.

Sometimes, you need a mom, and sometimes you need a friend, and a good mother can sometimes figure out what role is needed at the right time. Nightingale was in need of both, and she was hoping that her mother would recognize that. Our princess was facing a monumental dilemma, and she thought that today would be a good day to address it. You see, our princess wasn't sure she wanted to be a princess.

Ever since she was small, Nightingale was groomed to take over the family business. That's one thing if your dad is a cobbler or a district supervisor in charge of mass production and distribution of eastern markets for future gains in accordance with sectional titles and regulations, or, you know, a cobbler. It was another if he was running a kingdom. There is a ton of responsibility, and actual lives are at stake. One misstep and people starve, or have no water, or end up in a war, or even lose their unlimited cell phone coverage.

In a princess' world, there are countless balls, events, and meetings with people who think fresh-smelling breath is a luxury. Itchy silk gowns and tortuous high-heeled shoes are displayed with the proper protocols and traditions. Fake smiles and laughing through your teeth while balancing a small chandelier on your head in the guise of a crown was commonplace. None of this was appetizing to Nightingale, and she wasn't sure if she wanted to try.

She was showered, dressed, and ready for the short ride to the castle. Peering at herself in the mirror, she practiced what she would say to her mother about her abdication. How she would lightly feather it into conversation with phrases like: "Hey Mom, what has two thumbs and doesn't want to be a princess? This gal." or "You know what would be cool? Not being a princess. All my friends are doing it so I thought I would give it a shot."

Then there came the noise. A noise that would change her life. Not a "pah-poom" or even a "wat-wahhh." This was a special new sound. A sound with a lemon wedge and unlimited refills.

It was a noise like a sail unfurling or someone shaking out a very large blanket. Before she could identify the offending sound, it was gone. Then, she heard it again. Nightingale crept to the window facing the sea and peered out into the afternoon sky. Nothing. Then she checked out the view overlooking the woods. Again, not a thing. The sky outside her window had darkened, but not all at once. First, the shadow was in the south window, then the east. Quickly to the north, the west, and then south again. Great winds fought the leaves in the forest across the small glen, rustling and protesting mightily. At once, the shadow and the wind were gone.

The princess stood in the center of her tower, unsure of what to expect. Curiosity had outwrestled nervousness in her mind, and once again, she walked to a window, the south one this time, and leaned out to get a solid look-see. Nothing seemed out of the ordinary. The sun was once again shining high in the afternoon sky. No shadows or winds as far as the eyes could see.

Nightingale pulled herself back inside.

Perhaps the wind was playing tricks with me, she thought as she scooped up her phone to call a coach to give her a ride to the castle. Before she could dial, the phone made a series of annoying chirps. It was a text:

CHAPTER 1

!!DRAGON WARNING IN YOUR AREA!!

FROM THE DRAGON OFFICES IN MT. HOLLY: A DRAGON WARNING HAS BEEN ISSUED FOR THE FOLLOWING KINGDOMS: TOURIN, WILDERLAND, NOWHERE, AND THIS-AND-THAT. DRAGON(S) HAVE BEEN SPOTTED IN THE AREA COMING FROM THE EAST. PEOPLE ARE ASKED TO SEEK SHELTER IMMEDIATELY AND NOT TO DO ANY UNNECESSARY DRIVING. WHERE AVAILABLE, HEAD TO A ROOT CELLAR FOR SAFETY. TRY TO AVOID SCREAMING AND RUNNING IN TERROR.

Well, she thought, *that would explain the noise.*

Nightingale had never experienced a dragon before, although she knew that it was an "occupational hazard." Princesses usually encountered a dragon during their lifetime in one manner or another. One princess she knew had a dragon living in her kingdom for weeks until she could finally shoo it away. Another princess employed a team of knights to ride out and beg it to please go home and stop squishing all the peonies. During their stay, dragons would often scorch crops and feast on livestock, causing quite a nuisance for everyone involved, especially the livestock. After a neighboring kingdom was infested with a dragon, the place reeked of brimstone for months, putting a huge damper on their annual Tex-Mex festival. This incident prompted a new rule of thumb amongst the kingdoms: *When inhabited by a dragon, never under any circumstances feed it chili.*

Nightingale grabbed a chair from her kitchen table and dragged it across the floor to her front window overlooking the woods. Sitting down, she could not help but wonder why a dragon had chosen to visit her. She had no evil stepmother, nor was she a captive in her tower. No witches had cast a spell in her direction, and there was a vacancy in the Prince Charming department.

Speaking of which, Nightingale hadn't had a steady boyfriend since a boy named Brenton in high school. In fact, the only remnant of Brenton was a couple of pictures and the ratty sweatshirt she stole from him and was presently wearing. Women have a marked propensity toward lifting a hoodie from their ex-boyfriends so if any boys are reading this, let that be a warning to you all. Once a girl gets your hoodie, it is magically theirs, and there is nothing you can do to change it.

Truth be told, if the stars aligned and the moon was in the proper house, she missed Brenton just a little. When Nightingale weakened, replete with memories and a pinch of self-pity, she would become angry and immediately cleanse herself with a mouthful of whipped cream straight from the can. Then she would play a few rounds of Scabs to destroy something beautiful. This process, repeated as often as need be, seemed to help her convalesce.

No amount of canned cream nor avatar mutilations was going to help her stay strong in the face of a dragon. Nightingale would need to summon all of her princessly powers to stay her chin from an occasional quiver. Surely you have read the same books and seen the same movies as our heroine. Dragons were rumored to be big nasty beasties. Breathing fire and whatnot. Smashing through castles and ravaging kingdoms. Melting thrones and icy walls and being decidedly awful dinner companions. Nightingale would rather eschew the rumors and judge for herself.

Having never seen a dragon up close, Nightingale was a little excited to see what the big fuss was about. Sure, they looked terrible in pictures, but how bad can they really be? Maybe they were just not very photogenic, or they might have been having a bad hair day. Had anyone ever sat one down and tried to take a good picture of a dragon? Probably not. All the ones that Nightingale had come across were always action shots, and they'd never come out good. Action shots are all sweaty and blurry, with strange facial expressions and awkward angles. She had learned that from her days on the high school archery squad. Her yearbook photos from archery were a disaster, with lots of squinting and matted hair.

She propped her feet up on the stone windowsill and waited for her uninvited guest. The sky grew eerily dark, and the sail/blanket sounds grew louder and louder. A flash of red and white raced past by in an instant, too fast for Nightingale to get a good glimpse of the monster as it glided past her window. The force of the wind that followed nearly took her breath away as it fled out of sight, releasing the sun from its shield. Then darkness shrouded the tower once again, followed by more wind and the far away flapping of wings.

Chapter 1

"I might be in a little trouble here," said Nightingale to no one.

She grabbed her phone and dialed 9-1- and kept hovering her finger over the remaining emergency digit. If it was the dragon, it had her undivided attention. Nightingale again leaned out of her window, eyes darting in every direction. No sign of the creature anywhere. She contemplated leaving the window, but curiosity had riveted her in place. Her father did not raise a coward, nor her mother a fool. With a deep breath, she embraced the inevitable and prepared herself to meet her visitor.

With a loud thud that shook the stone tower, the beast landed in the glen directly before her window. A dragon it was, and an impressive sight at that. Twenty feet tall if it was an inch. Its coloring was deep blood-red with white feet and stripes of white running from its feet to its long tail, which put the dragon's length at a good fifty feet. No scales like in the storybooks, but a fine fur covered its body. A high ridge of hair raced along its spine, thick and white like the mane of a horse. The head was enormous, easily the size of an ox, and it housed the eyes of a cat, but rimmed with a fiery glow. Beneath its chin sat a white tuft of a beard. The face pulled forward in a snout like an alligator that failed to keep a frightening number of teeth at bay.

If Nightingale weren't a princess, she would have piddled there and then. I almost piddled writing that last paragraph, and I am a grown-up narrator. But a princess she was, and she was not about to show fear no matter how magnificent a beast landed on her front lawn. Our heroine stared directly into the eyes of the massive creature, resolute and unbending.

Chapter 2

In the land of This-and-That, the dragon spread its wings and sent an ear-splitting roar toward the heavens. Nightingale watched without so much as a tremor of nervousness. Inside, she was scared witless, but outside, she remained cool as a cucumber, whatever that means. In fact, she was getting a bit annoyed at the obvious attempt to garner attention. Drama was not something that Nightingale stomached for very long.

Light puffs of pink smoke fumed from its nostrils as it eyed the tiny princess in the window. It stared for some time, first examining the tower, reexamining the princess, and then back to the tower. Its eyes had a hint of confusion and disbelief as it seemed to attempt to gather its bearings. A glance at the tower, up at the princess, a look toward the woods, then back at the tower. After a few rounds of this, Nightingale had seen enough and decided to get to the bottom of things.

"Can I help you?" she said, unsure if the beast could answer. Instead, it ignored her and continued searching for a clue as to where it was, as befuddled as ever.

She tried again. "Hey, Dragon, do you mind telling me what you're doing on my lawn?"

"Sorry," it responded, "just trying to make sure I'm in the right neighborhood. They all look alike from down here."

Nightingale was slightly startled by the pleasant voice from the dragon. Not nearly as terrifying as she would have expected. *Well,* she thought, *that's what I get for being presumptuous.*

"Who are you looking for? Maybe I can help you."

With a puff of pink smoke, a large pair of reading glasses appeared and were perched on its formidable nose. A piece of paper the size of a bed sheet was unfolded, and the dragon traced over the words with a long, black claw, looking for information. With a gasp of recognition, it found what it was searching for.

"Ah! Here it is. Princess of This-and-That, edge of the woods of Nevermore... large tower... near the sea... east of Castle... named... Nightingale. Is she in?"

"You're looking at her," said Nightingale.

"Are you sure? I'd hate to be in the wrong place."

"Of course, I'm sure. She's me. I am Princess Nightingale."

"Well, you'll have to excuse me. You don't look very princessy. Any chance I can trouble you for identification? License? Major credit card?"

"And what, may I ask, is a princess supposed to look like?"

Nightingale had heard this before, and every time she did, it irritated her a little. Just because she didn't wear frilly gowns and have bluebirds circling her butt didn't make her any less of a princess.

"Well," answered the dragon, "usually, they have a frilly gown and bluebirds circling their butt."

"I guarantee you I am one hundred percent princess."

"Just to make sure, though..." the dragon said, "let's revisit the paperwork, shall we? Father is King Killian the Stout-hearted, and mother is Queen Evelyn the Just?"

"That's Mom and Dad," answered Nightingale with a tired sigh. "And who might you be?"

"OH! Very sorry. Where are my manners?" The dragon cleared its throat, and the glasses disappeared in another puff of smoke. It stood on its hind legs, spreading its vast wings, and roared with such force that the pictures on Nightingale's wall vibrated and rocked on their hooks. Winds swirled around the beast, and dark smoke filled the air. It was an

Chapter 2

attention-getter, to say the least, and, might I add, a bit intimidating. The dragon bellowed with an otherworldly voice:

"I AM WRATHNAROK! SLAYER OF VILLAGES! DEVOURER OF HOPE AND TORTURE TO ALL WHO LAY BEFORE ME! HARBINGER OF DOOM AND—"

"Hang on!" interrupted Nightingale. "My mom's calling me."

Wrathnarok slumped over, defeated that the grand entrance was rudely interrupted by the princess. With all that was going on, Nightingale completely forgot that she was holding her phone, and the thought of making cookies with her mom had become a distant memory.

"Hey, Mom." Nightingale answered the phone and looked at Wrathnarok with a shrug as if to say, "what are ya gonna do?" The dragon responded with a silent eyeroll.

"Hey, honey. Just wanted to let you know that I'm running a little late due to the Dragon Warning in effect, so if you get there before me…"

"Mom, it's here."

"What's there, hon?"

"The dragon. From the warning. It's here. Apparently, it's my dragon."

"Excuse me," interrupted the Dragon. "It's SHE, not IT."

"What's that now?"

"Although I abhor labels, Wrathnarok is a decidedly feminine name. I am a female dragon, complete with feelings that you have insensitively trod upon."

"Yes, of course. A girl dragon. A beautiful, wonderful, symbol of feminine magnificence."

"Don't patronize. It demeans us both."

"I'm just saying that it was wrong of me to presume. Apologies," said the princess. The dragon continued to look away, ignoring her completely. Way to go, Princess. You're off to a great start!

"Honey! Are you OK? Should I call your father?" The queen answered nervously.

The last thing the princess needed was for her father to think she was in danger. This would be an excuse to have her return home, and she needed to show that she could handle herself.

"Mom, no. Don't call Dad. It's under control."

"I can't believe you've got a dragon. Ok. Stay calm. Does it have the pox? Ask if it has the pox."

Nightingale leaned out the window to see the Dragon drawing pictures in the dirt with a claw and waiting patiently.

"Hey! Grassandrocks! Mom wants to know if you have the pox."

"It's Wrathnarok, and no, I don't."

Nightingale returned to the phone. "No, Mom. She said no pox."

"Oh, thank goodness!" exclaimed a relieved queen. "You can never be too sure nowadays. Old Lady Jenkins just got over the pox, and Sir Reginald the Rank had it and didn't tell anyone. No one knew because he smells so bad that no one would get close to him, which is a good thing because…"

Nightingale cut her mother off. She knew that once her mother started off on a tangent there was no stopping her.

"Mom, I'm going to go. I don't want to keep the dragon waiting. I'll give you a call later, OK?"

"Of course, dear. Be safe, and call if you need anything. Remember, your dad bought you that crossbow in case the dragon gets a little cheeky. Love! Love! Love!"

"Love! Love! Love!" Nightingale replied and hung up the phone.

She liked that her mother gave her enough space to try to deal with things on her own. She also liked knowing that, if things got out of hand, she could call her parents to help her out. What she did not like was the realization that she had returned the crossbow to the store the day after she had been given it and traded it in for a sweet pair of jeans.

Wearing an apologetic smirk, she peered back out the window. The dragon was inspecting her long black talons, digging around at little bits of dirt under the nails.

"Sorry, hon. You know how moms are. So where were we?"

"I was introducing myself," said the dragon. Once again, she hopped onto her hind legs and, spreading her vast wings, let out a roar.

And once again, Nightingale interrupted.

"Yo! Pop'n'lock! I think the moment is gone. You want to just move on from here?"

"Fine," said the dragon, a little disappointed that she would not make her grand introduction but realizing that the moment had indeed left them. "And it's Wrathnarok, and you know it."

Nightingale giggled at being caught.

"So, what brings you to these parts? I'm not sure I am in the market for a dragon. I mean, I'm not here against my will, and there's no evil spell or valiant princes trying to rescue me."

"That's where you're wrong, smarty. Princes ARE coming to rescue you. Your birthday is coming up, and tradition says you will wed soon. Right here on the invoice, it says…"

Poof. Magic smoke. Reading glasses. Paper.

Wrathnarok cleared her throat again and proceeded to read with a very regal and rehearsed tone. She seemed to clear her throat an awful lot. Maybe it was all the magic smoke choking her.

She read:

"Princes come from far and wide,
To seek the hand and take a bride.
At eighteen, so tells the tale,
The princess known as Nightingale."

Puff. Smoke. Glasses and paper gone.

Nightingale stared at Wrathnarok for what seemed like a lifetime. She was sure that her mouth was hanging open by the look on the dragon's face. No words would form in her brain as thought after thought raced around, screaming as if there was a tiger chasing them and the tiger was on fire. She tried to speak, but each sentence pushed the other out of the way and left her mouth moving but saying nary a word.

"You OK, kid?" asked the dragon. "You look like a puppy trying to bite a football."

Nightingale was not OK. In fact, she was about 86 miles to the left of OK. In all her reasoning for trying to place a correlation between her and the dragon, marriage wasn't even a wisp of an idea. Surely this can't be true. Her parents would have mentioned some archaic ritual where their daughter would be sold off to the highest bidder. When she finally snapped back to reality after a moment or two, all she could manage to utter was:

"Um… WHAT?"

"Yes. It's all true. Men are traveling from distant lands to woo the sweet Nightingale and win her hand in marriage. You turn eighteen in a few weeks, and as archaic ritual would have it, you are ripe for a wedding."

"Well, they are wasting their time because I have no intention of getting married."

"Yeah, I gathered all that when someone hit your mute button a minute ago. Yet come they will. May I suggest a quick shower and perhaps set out tea and sandwiches before they arrive? Speaking of sandwiches, I am a bit hungry. I was going to snap up a farmer on the way over here, but they are notoriously stringy from standing in a field all day, so I didn't. I'm beginning to regret my decision."

"I'm already showered, thank you," said the princess. "By the way, what part do you play in all of this?"

"I am your dragon. I stay here and keep an eye on things in case any of the princes turn out to be jerks. If so, I usually swoop down and eat them. If you find a suitor, I leave you be until the wedding. Then your dad gives me a treasure in gold, and I go home. If no gold, I usually start eating wedding guests until I get paid."

"That's extortion!" smiled the princess.

"That is a capitalistic society, missy. I don't make the rules."

"You don't look much like a dragon. You look more like a griffin," said Nightingale.

"I guarantee you that I am, in fact, one hundred percent dragon. Just take a gander at the tail," said the dragon.

"I've seen dragons. They're all leathery and mean-looking. They have two hind legs and wings for arms. You look a little blow-dried to be a dragon."

"Ah. You watch too much TV. No, see, they are what is known as a wyvern. They look like hairless cats with umbrellas taped to their backs. Griffins are a half lion, half eagle hybrid and reign in Greece, Egypt, and some parts of Rhode Island."

"I'm just saying that you ain't exactly fairytale caliber."

Chapter 2

"And you ain't exactly Meghan Markle, but here we are."

"And you really eat people?" asked the princess. She was beginning to regret returning the crossbow, but the jeans were so worth it.

"What am I? A monument to justice? Yes, I eat people. I am a dragon. It kinda comes with the territory."

Nightingale had heard enough. Though calm and collected on the outside, inside her stomach was a Gordian knot of nerves. She would need a few moments to process all of this. Maybe readdress it in, say, ten years or so. Stick a pin in it and table it another time. I don't know, pick a cliché and use that one. She was not about to get married and was not dealing with a farmer-munching dragon. All she wanted was a spoonful of cookie dough and a chat with her mom. She did not sign up for the extended princess warranty. *Time to put this to bed*, she thought.

"Listen, all of this doesn't work for me," Nightingale said. "I am not a big fan of the eating people thing, and I am definitely not a fan of getting married. I got a good gig here. I'm relatively happy. I have a nice room. I come and go as I please. I have all the major streaming services. I'm set!"

"Can't help you, honey. It's going to happen," said the dragon. "Meanwhile, I'll be here if you need me."

"Oh, I definitely won't need you. I can handle this myself. I'm not some weak little princess running away from my problems to some igloo or sleeping my day away waiting for some stranger to smooch me up. I'm good. I got this."

"Fantastic. Glad that's settled. Very cool," the dragon said, rolling her enormous eyes again. "But I'm here until I get paid, and that's that. Did I mention that I'm hungry? Maybe you can point me in the direction of the nearest cattle ranch, and I'll step out for a bit."

"No eating cattle or sheep or sheep herders until I figure this all out. If you're staying, I have a ton of questions for you, so I need you to stick around until we're done."

The young princess was perplexed. She had so many questions, and concerns, the most pressing of which was how to keep this monster from terrorizing the countryside and eating livestock like jellybeans. She needed to keep an eye on her somehow but feeding her was an issue. She tried at a compromise.

"It's a pity you couldn't come inside. I would whip you up some Mac and Cheese," said the princess.

"That depends. What kind you got? Powder or liquid cheese?"

"I have both. Take your pick."

"Well, I could shrink down and come inside if you'll have me. How small do you want me? Doberman pincher? Toy Poodle? Danny DeVito?" asked the dragon.

"Let's go with Kevin Hart. Think you can handle that?"

"Ooo! I like him. That man is hysterical!" said the dragon.

With a puff of pink smoke, the crisis was averted. Wrathnarok had shrunk down to border collie size. She walked to the door and waited to be let in. Nightingale sped down the spiral staircase to the front door, and with a loud creak, the door opened, and they were finally face to face. The shrinking had altered Wrathnarok's appearance quite drastically. The white fur was still there but blended with the red, making her look a bit pink in hue. Her wings had shrunk drastically, and now, instead of covering most of her back, they had become quite tiny in comparison. Her alligator face seemed softer and, with her teeth tucked in, less intimidating. Most noticeable were her feet. The white fur made it seem as if she was wearing little socks and gloves. She was, to coin a phrase, adorable. This did not get past the princess.

"Oh my goodness! Look at your little wings!" Nightingale purred and leaned down to give her a hug.

"Well, it's chilly out here. Don't get smart, princess, remember... I still have teeth, you know."

"And they're so cute!" said the princess, playfully pinching her cheek. "Come on upstairs, and I'll make us some snacks. I'm getting a little hungry as well."

As they climbed the stairs, she remembered the words that her mother had always said: *Trust your gut. If something doesn't feel right, then it probably isn't.* Nightingale did a gut check. All seemed well. The dragon was now puppy dog-sized, and hadn't she said that she was there to protect her? Surely there was no harm in keeping her inside. Besides, it would be easier to stop her from eating the neighbors if she kept her small and well-fed. Plus, it would be nice to have a little company for a while.

Chapter 2

Living alone in a tower was great, but it did have its drawbacks. Getting homesick and lonely was, without a doubt, near the top of the list.

"Make yourself at home while I cook us up some food," Nightingale said as they reached the living room. Wrathnarok plopped herself on the couch in front of the television right next to a pair of dirty socks. Living alone had made the princess lag in her housekeeping skills. She wasn't dirty, but she let herself be too comfortable, and it may have gotten a little out of control. The dragon pinched them up with two claws and, with a nauseated grunt, flung the socks onto the floor.

"Don't mind the mess," Nightingale said as she recognized the sign of disgust coming from the living room. It was the same one her mother made when she visited unannounced. She waited for the water to boil and removed two boxes of Mac and Cheese from the pantry. She went with the powdered type since archaic traditions were the theme of the day.

While she was cooking, Wrathnarok sat upright on the couch with her wee hind legs dangling off the edge. As Nightingale tended to the macaroni, she tried to make her guest feel at ease. It was one of those princessy things that she was accustomed to doing.

"Do you like my digs?"

"Very cozy. Warm, too. I like the deco you've chosen. Urban Laundromat is an underutilized theme in most households." Wrathnarok winced as she pulled a bra from between the couch cushions and laid it on the coffee table.

"Sorry about that. Haven't had much of a reason to clean lately."

"Do you know what a good reason to clean is? Being clean. It's a fantastic reason." The dragon scratched at a brown stain on the arm of the couch with her claw.

"Been in many houses, have you?" asked an annoyed princess.

"Not really, no."

"I can see why. You're a fairly rude houseguest. If you want, I can make this order to go."

"I'll consider it," said the dragon. "Don't you have people who do this sort of thing for you?"

"No. I'm on my own here. I do what I please when I please. I don't need to be taken care of. I'm a grown woman who enjoys her independence. If I don't want to clean, I don't. If I want to cram a dirty pair of underwear under the couch, I do that, too."

"Did you cram a pair of underwear under the couch?"

"I'm not sure. When I clean, it's like a scavenger hunt. New treasures hiding in every corner."

Awkward pause. Not exactly a pregnant pause but a pause that has been on a few fun dates. Finally, Wrathnarok tried to break the ice.

"So, you're out here in the woods all by yourself? That sounds scary."

"I am. And don't get any crazy ideas about eating me. My dad got me a crossbow for my graduation," said the princess.

"Please. If you had a crossbow, it would have been in my face the minute I hit the ground. All kings get their daughters a token of violence, and they always trade it in for a sweater or purse or something. One princess parlayed a set of daggers into tickets to an EDM festival in Michigan. What did you get?"

"A pair of jeans. They were so choice."

"Very cool," said the dragon. "So, Princess, what do they call you? Do you go by Nightingale or Gale or Nighty or something? Nightingale is a bit of a mouthful."

"My folks and friends call me Gale."

"Do you have a title? Like Princess Nightingale the Slovenly or something of that nature?"

"What do you mean?" asked the princess.

"Well, your parents are Killian the Stout-hearted and Evelyn the Just. I just wondered if you had a title as well. I'm fairly old, so I have a bunch of titles which you would have known if I wasn't so rudely interrupted during my intro," the dragon said, tongue in cheek.

"Yeah, sorry about that. No, I don't think that I have one. Usually, it's given to you, right? The people of the kingdom gave my parents their titles. I don't think I know enough people to get one yet."

"I'm sure you have one. You just might not know about it."

"Well, that's a bit concerning," said the princess. "What if it's something that I don't like?"

"It's not up to you. You just get one. People might be calling you Nightingale the Putrid as we speak."

Chapter 2

"Not sure that I like that. Not a big fan of labels. Do you like being called the Harbinger of Boogers or whatever it is that you were going on about?"

"It's Harbinger of Doom, and if I don't eat soon, you'll know it first-hand," said the dragon.

Nightingale walked in with two bowls of food and placed them on the coffee table. She gave Wrathnarok a fork, although she wasn't sure if dragons used utensils or if they just wolfed down their food. She wanted to be polite to her guest since, after all, she was a princess.

Wrathnarok picked up the fork and ate it. Then she grabbed the bowl filled with Mac and cheese and ate it all in one gulp, bowl and all.

"Hey, you sleaze! My bowl!"

A sheepish grin crept across the dragon's face as she quietly spit out the fork and empty bowl into her paws. She tried to hand the spit-covered place setting to Nightingale, but the look in her eyes made it understood that it was not the right idea. She daintily placed them back onto the coffee table, using a cup of the discarded bra as a coaster.

"Are we done playing games?" Nightingale asked with a chuckle in her voice.

"Sorry, kiddo. Sometimes I forget myself. I am a dragon, after all."

"See? None of us are perfect," said Nightingale. She realized her guest felt a little uneasy, so she tried comforting her.

"There's plenty more. Grab your bowl and go in the kitchen and get some. And this time, try the fork. It's all the rage."

"Noted," said the dragon as she hopped off the couch and made her way into the kitchenette.

"Any chance I can call you Gale?" Wrathnarok blurted nervously. "It would be nice since we're going to be together for a while, and Nightingale is a bit much, don't you think?"

"Only if I can call you something other than Wrathnarok."

"Fine. But only when I'm small. When I'm big, I need the name back. I must keep up appearances, you know. How about Tallulah? No, that's too long. Aloysius? No. Apple? North? Canada?"

"I think Canada's taken," laughed Gale.

"Rocky? Or maybe Rocco! It's a play on Wrathnarok, get it? I kinda like that one."

"I was thinking maybe… Mittens?" Gale said with a hopeful grin.

Silence flooded the room like a belch of baloney as the dragon slowly turned from the kitchenette to face her host. The look on the dragon's face was of complete disgust. Gale kept her smile in place though the weight of the moment made it difficult. She stared at the princess for a long time. Like a really long time. Like too long. Then finally…

"You've got to be kidding me!"

"Hey, pal, you just ate my bowl. You owe me."

"No."

"Come on! I promise to only call you Mittens when you're small!"

"Absolutely not."

"Pleeeeeaase? I can't help it! You're way too cute when you're small. And your little paws look like little mittens," Gale said in a cutesy baby voice.

"They're not paws. They're talons of terror. And still no."

"Please, oh please, oh please, oh please? I'll be your best friend!"

The dragon drew a deep breath and let out a long sigh of defeat.

"Fine," said Mittens. "But only when I'm small."

"Deal. Can I pet you?"

"Can I use your throw rug as a Piddle Pad?"

"No!" said Gale.

"Well, there's your answer," said Mittens.

Mittens hopped back onto the couch, scooped a big mouthful of Mac and Cheese onto her fork, and ate it with a smile. After a moment, the dragon spoke without looking up.

"I've never had a nickname before. I kinda like them," Mittens mumbled.

"Me too, buddy. Me too," said Gale. The princess looked at her guest as she struggled to clamp the fork between her talons. Though she was struggling with her food, the great and powerful dragon looked at ease for the first time since they met. Honestly, Gale felt relaxed for the first time in a long time herself. Another gut check was made, and Gale found herself comfortable.

Chapter 2

Thus began the tale of Gale and Mittens. The new names certainly helped the narrator, who had become tired of typing Nightingale and Wrathnarok. It's quite tedious and hard on the fingers. They are very long names, and since it is their story, it was going to be a hassle. I only wish they would have done this somewhere around page four.

Gale and Mittens spent the night swapping stories about the trials and tribulations of princess-dom and the life of dragons. They carried on as if they had known each other for years. They spoke of people that had been met and people that had been lunch. Reflexa was asked to play some easy-listening background music, and the air was littered with the melodies about nameless horses and southern crosses.

While scarfing down a few bags of microwavable popcorn, it was decided that a trip to her parents' house was in order for the morning, and as midnight introduced itself to the evening, Mittens curled up on the couch with a pillow and blanket and Gale retired to her room. Both were pleased with the new friend that they had made. As Mittens drifted off to sleep, Gale couldn't help but wonder about what, or more to the point, whom, the new day would bring.

Chapter 3

IN THE LAND OF This-and-That, the sun rose as it normally does as this is its only job and is generally considered a good work ethic. Birds chirped and fluttered about, announcing the dawn of a new day filled with wonderful opportunities and hopes of greatness. People began their daily routines. Bakers baked, farmers farmed, barbers barbed, and narrators narrated. The bright, beautiful morning stretched out its arms and was embraced by the entire kingdom. Save for the princess and the dragon, who went to bed after midnight and were not about to embrace anything even remotely resembling a routine.

We'll check back in on them in a bit.

Meanwhile, take a moment to do some things that you've been avoiding. Get a head start on that laundry that has been piling up, or maybe call a friend that you haven't spoken to in a while. Really, you have plenty of time. I know Gale, and she's not about to wake up anytime soon. Even if she does, she won't be active for some time. She likes to mull about, put something mindless on the TV as background noise and shuffle about nursing a cup of tea and scratching her head for at least an hour before even thinking of becoming productive. We've got time, so go do something, and we'll check back later.

Still nothin'.

Chapter 3

… Any minute now.

OK, they're up. Let's try it again.

In the land of This-and-That, the princess rose to meet the afternoon. She left the warm comforts of her bed and shuffled out to the living room, scratching her head where she saw Mittens still curled up on the couch, remote in hand, mindlessly flipping through channels.

"There's nothing on," said Mittens when she heard the princess scrape by. "If I see one more castle flipping show or hovel renovation, I swear I'm going to fly to the studio and eat the lot of them!"

"I know," she said, "TV is a disaster. I usually play a game or put on some movie that I've seen a thousand times until I can muster the strength to actually *do* something. Want breakfast? I'm making waffles."

"Is this some slang I should be aware of?" asked the dragon.

"No. I'm actually going to make waffles."

"Then I'm in," said Mittens. "When are we heading over to see your parentals?"

"Later. I was thinking we'd get there before dinner and horn in for a good meal."

Gale opened the freezer and pulled out several boxes of frozen waffles and a bag of frozen sausage. She had honestly considered making fresh waffles, but after bearing witness to the eating machine that was Mittens, she thought better of it. She wasn't sure that the dragon actually *tasted* her food since it was more of a shoveling operation. The six empty bags of microwavable popcorn from last night bore strong evidence of this. She half considered counting the throw pillows to see if one or two had been ingested in the dead of night.

As she put the kettle on for some much-needed tea, she heard a loud thumping noise. A rhythm of low beats from far off, growing louder. And louder. And louder still. Gale looked at Mittens, who seemed unfazed by the noise, continuing to flip through channel after channel with a glazed disinterest. Still, the beats grew louder and closer. Gale plopped some waffles into the toaster and walked into the living room.

"You hear that?" she asked.

"Yup."

"Does that concern you at all?"

"Nope." Click… click… click went the remote.

Chapter 3

Now the beats were so strong that the pictures and Reflexa were bouncing to the rhythm. Gale felt the noise in her chest thumping and thumping. Her eardrums were thumping as well. The noise was so loud that she almost didn't hear the whistle on her kettle. She went back to the kitchen, poured herself a cup of tea with honey, threw the freshly popped waffles onto a plate, and grabbed the syrup. She carried it all to the living room and plopped the plate and syrup onto the coffee table for Mittens. Still, the beat went on. It was a bit early in the afternoon for surprises, thought Gale, but after Mittens landed on her doorstep, the princess felt as if she was prepared for just about anything.

"New dragon?" she shouted to Mittens. It wasn't a bad question, remembering Wrathnarok's volatile entrance the day before.

"New suitor," yelled Mittens as she crammed a syrup-laden waffle into her mouth.

"You have got to be kidding me!" she yelled back.

Mittens pointed to the window as if to say, "go look for yourself," and Gale walked over to do just that. Outside her door in the glen where Mittens had landed the day before was a horse-drawn carriage led by a team of four white stallions. The coach was sleek and white with a crest on the door and seated very low to the ground. Beneath the carriage were blue lights as an accent. Gold trim was on every corner and door handle. What was exposed on the wheels showed spinning rims also plated in gold. Sticking out of the rear of the coach was the origin of the distasteful thumping: two huge speakers, all in black but trimmed once again in gold. Painted onto the screen of the speakers was the same crest that was on the door. All the windows were tinted black.

Remember that song you heard about the girls in the club? The one about dancing on the floor and then going back to his place? It was that song. Followed by yet another song about girls in the club on the dance floor. The volume was so loud that Gale doubted that the girls in the song would have been able to remain upright, let alone dance on the floor. Gale was known to play her music a bit on the loud side, but this was borderline dangerous. The entire planet seemed to vibrate. If Gale was one of those princesses with birds flying around her butt, she had no doubt that they would have been in peril of imminent explosion.

The Self-Sufficient Princess

No one was outside the carriage except the coach driver. He was decked out in white pants and a white button-down shirt, a gold chain clinging to his tree-trunk-thick neck. He was an enormous specimen, easily six and a half feet tall, with arms and a chest that his shirt strained to keep at bay. A pair of dark aviator sunglasses covered his eyes, and his bulbous bald head seemed to erupt from his shoulders just to glisten in the afternoon sun.

Upon noticing Gale in the window, the coach driver leaped from his perch and walked to the carriage door. His beefy mitt grabbed the handle and swung it open. From inside, a blue light matching the light under the carriage bled out, and from the light appeared two men, also decked out in white. They were not as impressively built as the coach driver. Reaching beneath the carriage stairs, they grabbed a gold rope braid that was hidden there and pulled. A metallic gold runner came with them and lay shimmering about ten feet on the ground.

The men flanked the runner and began to speak. The only problem was she couldn't hear them over the loud thumping of the song. Gale placed a hand to her ear as if to symbolize that she couldn't hear. Again, the men spoke but tried to speak louder. Gale shrugged her shoulders and shook her head, pointing at her ears. Now the men cupped their hands and appeared to be shouting but to no avail. It became rather evident that the pair were not on the bright side. The princess made a downward-pointing motion. Finally, the coach driver realized the obstacle and produced a small remote control from a pants pocket. He lowered the volume enough so that the announcement could be heard.

"Yo, Princess! This is the moment you've been waiting for. You are about to meet the Prince of Pleasure. The Duke of Desire. The future King of Everything. The one. The only. Sir Chadwick the A-MAAAZ-INGGGG!"

On cue, out stepped the prince. Sir Chadwick was tall and thin with a mop of dyed-grey hair. He was dressed in black leather pants and a black leather sports jacket with no shirt. Tattoos covered his chest, and sitting around his neck were at least ten gold chains of various sizes and weights. Every finger had a ring, and each fingernail was painted a shiny black. Eyeliner surrounded a pair of pale blue eyes, and his face held a hang-dog expression. Your narrator isn't exactly sure what that means,

Chapter 3

but I'm sure that's the right word to use. Hop on Google and give it a look-see if you must. I can't do all the heavy lifting here.

"So… How does Sir Chadwick the Amazing look?" asked Mittens, still surfing through channels.

"Pretty darn amazing!" exclaimed Gale.

Mittens put down the remote and made her way to the window. She stayed low so as not to be noticed and peeked out of the window to see the spectacle that Gale had labeled impressive. Mittens quickly agreed.

"This guy is a smoke show but I prefer my men not to walk among the undead," whispered Mittens.

"He does give off a vampire vibe. Must be all the late-night partying. Is he hot, though? I'd hate to think my time out of the dating pool has skewed my radar."

"Nope. You're good. Definite hotness."

"Right? You know, I might actually get used to the whole suitor thing," said Gale.

Sir Chadwick stood in a jaunty pose for a minute, looking around—but in a disinterested manner as if to say that he was above all the show-boating that he obviously was responsible for. Finally, he cast his gaze up to the window and addressed the princess.

"'Sup?" mumbled the prince. And nothing more.

Nightingale had been a princess her entire life. She had spoken with kings and fools, poor farmers, and wealthy dignitaries from around the world. Although she was a bit shy in public, Gale was able to hold her own in conversation. Nothing in all those meetings had prepared her for a "'sup."

"How can I help you, Sir Chadwick?"

Instead of Chadwick responding, he continued to look around, disinterested. Instead, one of the other men spoke. The one on the left. For narrating's sake, we'll call him Lefty.

"Yo, yo, Princess, check it out: Sir Chad wants to know if you want to hop into this sweet ride and maybe head out to a club or something," said Lefty.

"I may. Does Sir Chad speak?"

"Yo, yo, Princess, Sir Chad doesn't like to address people directly. In fact, if you weren't such a stone-cold fox, Sir Chad wouldn't appreciate you even looking at him," said Righty. Evidently, they spoke in stereo surround sound.

"Ah, well, if Sir Chad has anything to say, I suggest he start talking because I'm too busy for this posturing," said Gale. She directed her next comment at the prince. "Yo, Sir Stringbean, do you speak, or are you going to stand there and let the human bookends do all your talking for you? And if you could ask Muscles to cut the music, I might not have to shout."

Gale was getting irritated. Though it was close to one in the afternoon, it was way too early for the freak show that was playing out on her lawn. She thought the prince was good-looking, but not everything that glitters… well, you get the idea. Still, she tried to give him a chance. She was a princess, after all.

Muscles looked at the prince for approval, and with a nod from Sir Chad, the music was cut off. Gale grabbed her tea and walked away from the window. She asked Reflexa to bring up Gracebook, the social media site that connected all the kingdoms. Slipping on her flip-flops, she made her way to the door.

"Where ya going, princess?" asked Mittens.

"I'm going to head down for a closer look."

"Want company?"

"Nope. I got this," said the princess. "While I'm gone, you're gonna search this guy on Gracebook and let me know what you find. How do I look?"

"Like a stone-cold fox," Mittens said with a chuckle.

The princess sarcastically flipped her hair over her shoulder and made her way downstairs. Upon her arrival, she smelled a distinct scent that filled the glen. A smell that took her back to her days in high school. It took a moment to realize what it was, but after that moment, it was sadly clear. These men used Battle-Axe body spray. And a ton of it. Like all the spray. She was grateful for the lack of open flames available because the ensuing fireball caused by these men would wipe out the forest.

The princess figured that, upon her emergence from the tower, maybe, just maybe, someone would have the common decency to acknowledge her existence. They all were standing on her lawn in her kingdom, after

Chapter 3

all, and she thought perhaps a simple "hello" might be in order. Instead, the crowd just stood there. The massive coach driver stared off to the right, the prince off to his left. Each of the bookends stood dead-eyed, gazing at, I don't know, a random brick in her tower? A fanciful shrub? Anything but the tea-sipping figure on her doorstep.

Gale wondered if this posing was rehearsed, and if so, why? Did they find it attractive to stand around trying to resemble a movie poster? If this was how this meet-and-greet was starting, Gale didn't see it ending well. Still, like a car crash, she could not look away. Intrigued, she stepped down and began to approach the group. The bookends saw this as a threat and snapped into action, holding up their hands and telling the princess to step away. Princesses do not step away.

"Relax, Rosencrantz and Guildenturd. Stand down. I just want to talk. Tired of shouting down from the window." Gale sipped at her tea casually and looked again at Sir Chad. *Even better close up*, she thought. *Well, let's see what's under the glitz.*

"Hi, Chadwick. I'm Nightingale, Princess of This-and-That. I'm sorry that you came all this way, but I am not interested in getting married, so if you want to head on out, I completely understand."

"You ain't gotta call me Chadwick. I got plenty of nicknames if you want. There's Chad, Sir Dude-a-Lot, Big Sexy, Chaderino, the Chadster…"

"Let's stick with Chad, shall we?" said Gale cutting him off. "I go by Gale. Sorry about my appearance, but you did come by unannounced in a totally non-creepy way."

Sarcasm was lost on this man as he proceeded to nod again at nothing. It was as if a friend was hiding away in the woods, urging him on.

"'S cool. Not looking to get married either. Wanna go to the club or something?"

"Hang on. I'm confused. You rode all the way out here, and you don't want to get married? So why are you here?"

"Yo, look, like, my dad? He's a super-rich king or something, so I just kinda ride around going from club to club looking for a party. You wanna party, Princess?"

As he spoke, The Chadster bobbed his head like a pigeon. He also sucked in his cheeks when he was done in an attempt to look even more anemic than he already did. If this worked to impress other women, it wasn't working on Gale. Chad the Amazing was getting less and less amazing by the syllable.

"It's one in the afternoon. Do I look like I want to party? I'm standing here in sweatpants and flip-flops."

"'S cool. So, you wanna shower or something 'cause you look like, I dunno, a dumpster fire or something."

The boys laughed at this joke way too hard to be taken seriously. Gale shot them a dirty look and looked at the coach driver. He didn't laugh and gave the princess a look that said, "Hey, I just work here." Smart man.

"So, you just comb the world looking for a party. Must be nice." Gale said, sipping at her tea.

"Yup. Me and the crew just living our best life. Going to clubs, scooping up witches, having a good time."

The bookends proceeded to whoop it up and high fived about six times. Muscles stood motionless, having seen this play out before. Gale was motionless too. She couldn't believe her ears. This clod had no respect for women whatsoever, and his lackeys were just as wrong. Normally this would have been the end of the discussion, and Gale would have dismissed this whole debacle for what it was and gone back upstairs to play Scabs online. But, alas, poor Yorick, she had been insulted. Calling her a witch was not a good idea.

"And you think I'm a witch."

"Yo, like, yeah. Witches. I call girls witches. You gonna shower or something? I wanna go to the club. You wanna go to the club, Princess?" Chad stood there smiling and nodding what appeared to be an empty head. The bookends high fived a dozen more times while whooping and laughing. Muscles did nothing.

"What possibly made you think that I was looking to 'go to the club?'" Gale asked, using air quotes where I had placed them.

"Well, since you're getting married or something, I thought you'd be up to party. You seem like you're desperate for a good time. Thought I'd take you to the club, get to know you better or something."

"Yeah, I think I know what the 'or something' is that you have in mind." Again, Gale used air quotes where I had placed them. The boys

Chapter 3

high fived forty-seven more times and yelled things like "You know it, baby!" and "Allllllright!" Muscles said nothing.

"Hang on a sec, won't you, precious? I want to check something out," Gale said, and she made her way back to the door. She shouted up the stairs to Mittens, "What do you got?"

"Well, according to Gracebook, Big Sexy over there comes from a kingdom about a day west of here. His dad is, like, a rich king or something. He's also in a relationship with three other princesses. Oh, I'm sorry. Witches. The guy's got almost a hundred problems."

"But this witch ain't one," said Gale, furious, as she walked outside.

This is where the fun begins. Gale had enough ammo to dispatch this loser without any added info. Now she had confirmed that he was a complete pig and in desperate need of a beatdown. She mentally took off her crown. For the next few minutes, she was not a princess. Not a princess at all.

"So, Sir Sad. It seems like you've been busy. Gracebook said that you're in a relationship with three other princesses. Is that true?"

"Yo, like, I never said I was, like, exclusive or something. Like, the Chad has to roll, ya know? Wanna roll with the Chad?"

More incessant bobbing followed. Gale was almost positive that she could hear a rattle every time he did this.

"No. I don't want to roll with the Chad. I don't know anyone who would want to roll with the Chad. Frankly, you're abhorrent. Normally I would feel sorry for you, but you're just too pathetic to give a second thought. You're in a relationship or relationships, and you want to get to know ME better? What's wrong with you?"

"Why you trippin' Gale? I just wanted to have a good time. You ain't gotta get all up in my face about it. You don't know me. I don't take any of those girls serious." Chad had an angry and disgusted smirk on his face and sucked at his teeth. He was not accustomed to being disrespected in this manner. So instead of being smart and riding away, he continued to fight back.

"Yo, witch, you ain't even worth my time. My dad's like a rich king or something. I don't need you. I wouldn't even take you as a side witch. You couldn't even be like my number three witch."

The bookends whooped it up and high fived a hundred and sixty-four times. Muscles said nothing but looked a bit uncomfortable to be part of this altercation.

Gale had a full head of steam at this point.

"You have no respect for women at all, do you? You *number* them like things that you collect? Did you ever think that maybe they took it seriously? Maybe the other girls have enough self-respect to deserve better than a place in your group? You disgust me, both physically and emotionally. You need to take a good look in the mirror and sort yourself out because this, whatever this is, doesn't last. You're useless. And take a shower because you smell like a funeral bouquet. An entire can of body spray isn't single serving. You guys are a walking fire code violation."

The bookends said nothing. Laughter echoed from the top of the tower as Mittens couldn't help but lose it over the verbal undressing that she had just witnessed. Muscles tried with all his effort not to smile. But he failed because, as we know, there is really no way to work out your face. So, he weakened under pressure.

"So," asked a completely clueless prince, "Is someone goin' to the club with me or what?"

"NO ONE IS GOING TO THE CLUB WITH YOU, YOU BUF-FOON!" Shouted a princess who was completely and utterly done with the clueless prince.

"Yo, man, witches be trippin'. Forget you, Princess!" Chad dismissed her with a wave of his hand.

"Oh, and that word. You keep using that word. I don't think it means what you think it means," Gale replied.

From the top of the tower shouted Mittens, "Whoa! You go, girl!"

Chad squared his shoulders and smirked. "And what word is that? Come on, Princess, you're so tough. What word is that?" He hung his thumbs on his belt and leaned back in a futile attempt to look cool.

Her eyes narrowed. "You know exactly what I'm talking about," she said.

In a few steps, Chad was in her face, trying to intimidate the much smaller princess. He was way too close for comfort, and for a moment, she thought she might be in over her head. The prince towered over her,

Chapter 3

leaning down into her face, his arms spread wide as if expecting a fight. *Neither a coward nor a fool,* she thought as she looked the Chad dead in the eyes. There was no fear in her face and no quiver in her lip as she stated her ultimatum.

"Call me a witch… one more time."

"What are you gonna do about it? Huh? Sic your bodyguard on me or something?"

"Or something," she said, eyes locked on his.

"I don't sweat you. My dad…"

"Is a rich king or something. Yeah, I heard. We all heard. So, tough guy. Is there something you wanted to say before I head back upstairs and throw my head back in laughter?"

"Yup. You ain't nothing but a spoiled… stupid…"

"Don't do it," warned the princess.

"… witch."

He did it.

The telltale sail/blanket sound came from the rear of the house as Mittens—sorry, Wrathnarok—used the bedroom window to make her entrance. The sky above them grew dark quickly as a blood-curling roar filled the air, much louder than any song that Muscles could summon up with his remote. While we are on the topic of Muscles, he had smartly fled down the path upon the dragon's arrival, driving the coach at a breakneck speed. All that was left were the prince and the bookends, who were busy looking skyward and screaming like little girls on a rollercoaster, and the princess, who suddenly had a craving for waffles.

Run, run, run, as fast as you can, thought Gale as she walked inside, closing the door behind her.

She calmly sipped at her tea as she made her way to the kitchen. Two frozen waffles were plopped into the toaster as the sounds of terror and wing flapping made their way up from the glen. She popped a few links of sausage in the microwave and listened with a satisfied grin at the begging and pleading that the Chad and his minions had begun. Gale guessed that the answer to their pleas was no and that there was a chase going on since the roars and screams and smell of body spray were all getting more and more distant.

The princess made a sandwich out of the waffles and the sausages and headed over to the couch to await the return of her dragon. She picked up her phone to shoot her mom a quick text:

Running a little late. I'll explain later. Love! Love! Love!

The silence outside of her tower was deafening. Surely her dragon had chased the prince and his idiot friends away by now. Gale took a healthy bite from her sandwich and walked over to the window where she had first spoken to Sir Chad. All that met her were a few chirping birds and a light breeze from the sea. Slowly, a tiny wrinkle of worry and self-doubt made its way into her stomach. She returned to the couch and tried to bury it with another bite of the sandwich.

For just a moment, a tiny sliver of a moment, she worried about the prince. Maybe she was a little harsh. Maybe letting Mittens-sorry, Wrathnarok—chase him away wasn't the best of ideas. Gale sat and waited for the dragon's return. She prayed that she wouldn't regret it.

Chapter 4

IN THE LAND OF This-and-That, the concerned princess thumbed at the TV remote and tried desperately not to panic.

A quick loop of the channels yielded nothing. She finished scarfing down her breakfast and contemplated taking a shower. Mittens had been gone for what seemed like an eternity, and Gale was beginning to worry. Worry about the prince, worry about Mittens, worry about what, if anything, she herself was responsible for. She was contemplating calling her mother for advice when there was a knock at the door. Peeking out the window revealed a tired Mittens standing there patiently. Gale had forgotten that she couldn't get back in.

"Coming!" she yelled as she raced down the spiral staircase.

When she flung open the door, she couldn't help but wrap her arms around her friend. Gale was so relieved to see her that all of the knots in her stomach seemed to melt away.

"Easy, Princess. Don't get all emotional on me. You'll wrinkle my wings," Mittens said with a smile and walked up the stairs to the living room.

Gale plopped back on the couch, and Mittens joined her.

"So?" asked Gale.

"So what?"

"You jerk. Tell me what happened!" Gale said as she threw a pillow at her.

"Well, after you left, we all had a nice quiet discussion about how the word 'witch' was inappropriate terminology and a derogatory term for women. I asked them politely to stop, and they agreed that it would be in their best interests."

"Try again. And this time, no lying, or you'll get the pillow again. Let's start with Muscles. How did he make out?"

"Ah, Muscles. You saw him peel out the minute I showed up, right? He was racing down the road at top speed. The poor horses were running as fast as they could. At one point, he had the carriage up on two wheels. I swooped down and gave him a thumbs-up to let him know that he was OK. He waved and pulled up on the reins a bit. I figured he was harmless in all of this. I would have hated for him to have escaped those dreadful idiots only to break his neck in a carriage accident. Plus, I think the carriage was a rental. Maybe Chad's rich daddy wasn't footing the bill anymore, and the kid had to make do on his own."

"Good. I'm glad he is OK," said Gale. "He looked a little embarrassed to be there. Poor guy."

"The bookends didn't get off the hook that easy," said Mittens a little too sheepishly for Gale.

"You didn't eat them, did you? Please tell me you didn't eat them."

"Oh no," said Mittens. "I did not eat them. Laurel and Hearty Hand Slap started crying and begging for their lives. They tried very hard to throw Big Sexy under the bus, saying it was all his idea and that they didn't even like the prince very much. I spit a little fire at them to show that I didn't believe them, and they fled into the woods. You'd think they'd be smart enough to hide, but they were not. Want to guess how hard it was to find two guys dressed in white in a forest? Go on, guess."

"Not very, I'm sure," answered Gale.

"It was embarrassingly simple. They were standing there like two snowmen contemplating their next move when I swooped down and snatched Lefty mid-sentence. I introduced him to some lake outside of Bradenland. I think the twenty-foot drop into the center of the lake might have given him the life lesson he so richly deserved."

Chapter 4

"Wow! Twenty feet? I hope he can swim," said Gale.

"If not, it'll be another life lesson. See, I try to enrich the community as a whole by gifting my knowledge to the poor ignorant youths in the area," joked Mittens. Her joke was met with another airborne pillow.

"Yeah, you're a real pillar of virtue. What about Righty?"

"I flew back to the spot where I left him, and he was still standing there. Can you believe it? He was texting someone. I really hope it wasn't Lefty. No amount of rice was saving his phone, I can assure you. So, I scooped him up as well. Righty looked like the woodsy outdoorsy type, so I took him on a hiking trip in Wilderland."

"You just left him there?" asked Gale.

"Yup. Just left him."

Gale paused and waited for more. The dragon sat, tight-lipped.

"Just left him *where*, exactly."

"I figured he needed better cell phone reception, so I found the highest tree on the highest cliff and sat him on the top. When I flew away, he looked like the angel on the Christmas tree in Rockefeller Center."

"Outstanding. That'll give him some time to think, I'm sure. Maybe he'll find an eagle to practice high fiving with until he meets up with Lefty again," joked Gale.

"The guy's a dope, Princess. I don't think he could find sand if he fell off a camel. It'll take him a lifetime to find Lefty again. You know, I should carry some Change of Address cards around with me. It'll be helpful to the poor youths that I relocate. Just helping the community and all," Mittens said as she batted her eyelashes in an attempt to look innocent.

Gale got up to put the kettle on for some more tea.

"Now for the big finale. What became of the Chad? Did you drop him off in Antarctica or something?"

"Or something," said Mittens as she picked up the remote to flip through the channels.

"C'mon, Mittens, spill it. You told me what happened to the Funky Bunch. What became of Jerky-Jerk?"

Mittens said nothing. She just sat there trying desperately to avoid Gale's gaze and continued flipping through the channels.

41

Gale was not having it. She stared at the dragon and waited for her to speak when suddenly, it hit her like a cloud of body spray.

"Holy Panini! You *ate* him??" Gale said, covering her mouth in amazement.

"I'm sorry, Princess, but it had to be done."

"You actually... *ate*... him. Like ate. You ate him. How could you do that?"

Gale was now pacing frantically around the kitchen. This would not do. Her dragon cannot go around just eating whoever displeases her, no matter how much of a jerk he is. Granted, Chad probably deserved to be punished for threatening her, but that seemed a bit on the extreme side.

"See? This is why I don't want to be a princess. For exactly this reason." Gale was now pacing about like an expectant father in an old cartoon.

"If it makes you feel any better, he tasted terrible. All that body spray was disgusting. It was like licking wet paint. I'm never gonna get this taste out of my mouth."

"Good. I hope that he makes you sick. Serves you right. I explicitly stated my stance against eating people. And worse off, that's on me! You're *my* dragon! What you do reflects on me. How could you do that?"

"Well," said Mittens, "I just kind of yeeted him up in the air and caught him like a peanut."

"No, you moron!" yelled Gale, "How could you do that at all!"

Gale was yelling now, and it made Mittens feel quite uneasy, which is extremely difficult to do to someone holding the title of "Harbinger of Doom" in her intro. Her hands were little balls, and she kept squeezing her thumbs in a fit of nervous energy.

"I can't believe you purposely disobeyed me! What kind of friend does that? Not a good one, I assure you. All the things I have going on right now, what with the party and the denouncement and the creepy wannabe husbands..."

"Wait a minute!" said Mittens. "Go back a bit. What did you just say?"

"The party?"

"No, come forward, just a smidge."

"Husbands?"

"Back it up a bit."

"... The?" asked Gale, knowing exactly what Mittens was asking about.

"You know exactly what I'm asking about," said Mittens, reinforcing my stellar narration.

"Yes. It's true. I'm thinking about denouncing the throne," said Gale, sounding a bit defeated.

"I thought you said something about not wanting to be a princess before, and I let it slide, but now I see you are serious. You are serious, aren't you, Gale?" asked the dragon.

"I don't know. Some days I am. Some days I'm not. If being a princess makes me responsible for people getting eaten by dragons, then yes. I don't think that I'm cut out for this."

"OK, then let's pretend for a second that I didn't turn Sir Schmuck into a canapé. You would still think about not being a princess?"

"Absolutely."

The air was still and heavy for a moment as the weight of the statement lingered. Mittens looked at the princess, who, for the first time, appeared frail and worrisome. Gale was really just a little girl in a big world, and the look on her face showed an overwhelming fright. All the smart-talking and posturing that Gale could muster didn't hide that her life was a little much. Even a princess doesn't have a perfect life. And if a princess didn't have one, then nobody does.

"Want to talk about it?" asked Mittens.

"No. Just leave me alone," said Gale as her eyes turned glassy and distant. She was determined not to cry in front of her dragon. Usually, when this type of incident played out with her parents, the princess would have stormed off and locked herself in her room. This was Gale's house and Gale's sanctuary, and she was not about to duck and cover under her own roof.

Mittens stood there feeling guilty to an extent. She truly felt bad about eating Sir Jerk-Face, but remember, this was not her first princess. Mittens had experienced many a confused and scared girl in her day, and she knew how to handle this very situation. Best thing to do for a troubled friend is to be accessible. Second best thing? Shut up and listen.

The Self-Sufficient Princess

So, there they stood, saying nothing. Mittens shuffled her feet, and Gale stifled her tears. Minutes felt like days, that felt like weeks, that felt like minutes again because that's what they are.

"Well, Princess, I'm here if you want to talk," said the dragon.

"Sure! Let's talk! Let's talk about how I distinctly told you not to eat anyone. Let's talk about how I am now guilty of murder to some extent and how I will be perceived as a heartless killer amongst my people. They'll call me Princess Nightingale the Bloodthirsty. Nursery rhymes will be written about me. Ever hear a happy nursery rhyme? Never. Know why? 'Cause there are none."

"Ring around the Rosie!" said a confident Mittens.

"Rumored to be about the plague."

"Sing a Song of Sixpence?"

"Dissolution of monasteries."

"Little Miss Muffet?"

"Mary Queen of Scots."

"Really? That's disheartening," said a startled dragon.

"All rumors, though. And stop trying to shift the topic. You defied me. You broke my heart," said Gale, still swallowing her tears.

"Maybe I can get a second chance? You can be Nightingale the Merciful."

"How's about Nightingale the Dragonless. Nightingale the Lone Wolf. How's about Nightingale the Friendless? You've been here less than a day, and already you've hurt me. Where can we go from here? Do you have any idea how many sycophants and plastic friends I have? Dozens. I have, like, two cousins that I kind of trust, and they're older and never around. All my friends are too busy or too wrapped up in themselves to be true friends. They make plans and skip out or only call when they need something. I just was hoping that you were different, is all. I should have known better."

"Gale, I'm really sorry," said Mittens. Her sincerity was so thick that it dripped from every word.

"I don't blame you. You're just like the others. I blame myself. I thought I had made a friend. I need to remember that this is just a business arrangement."

"Those words hurt, Gale," the dragon muttered.

Chapter 4

"Listen. I appreciate you coming to help me get rid of the trash that came to annoy me. I probably could have handled it myself. But I didn't stop you. I don't know if I could have if I tried. That's scary, Mittens. I don't like being scared."

"Neither do I," said the dragon. "Seeing that broomstick lean his face into yours alarmed me a bit. So, I did what I do. I protected my princess. I guaranteed that no further harm would come her way. I made sure there was no future vindication or provocation. It's literally my job."

Mittens was trying to sound apologetic, but she wasn't sure if the words were coming out right. The intent was there, but the intonation was lacking a bit. Like when you text someone, and they can't tell if you're being serious or not. Word to the wise: never have a serious discussion while texting. It never comes across right.

"Yeah, well, your job is stupid," Gale said while wiping an escaping tear from her cheek. "See, this is why I like being by myself. No drama. I rely on me, and I rarely disappoint me."

"That's a crappy way to go through life, Gale."

"Maybe. But for right now, it suits me. I don't need anyone. I don't need you. I don't *need* you to be my friend. But I *wanted* you to. I really did. And that's what hurts so much."

"Is that why you don't want to be a princess? You don't want to need or be needed?" asked Mittens.

"Kinda. I'm good right here. No pressures. No problems. No pox or famines, or diplomacies. No stupid dinner parties. No posturing. No princess. I did not ask to be a princess. I should be given the choice, don't you think?"

"I agree. Is this a choice you need to make right now? Couldn't you put it on the back burner for a while?"

"No. I legally become a ruling figure on my birthday. And I don't want to."

"Can't you just put it off for a few years?"

"You saw how that went with the whole marriage thing. Nobody cares what I want. These princes or knights or whatever are going to keep coming. You said so yourself. You can't hide from your future. It is coming anyway."

"Maybe I can help you?"

"What are you gonna do? Eat everyone? I've already seen how you handle adversity. With a side of disco fries. No. I have to figure this out on my own. Adulting is hard, and I am not a coward or a fool. I just want to be left alone."

Gale was trembling from head to toe. She was done talking. She was done with the dragon and Sir Chad and with everything. Gale decided to go on to the castle and ask her father for enough gold to send Wrathnarok away and denounce her crown. She did a gut check on her decision. No good. Waffles and sausages were trying to sandblast their way out of her stomach.

With her head hung low, Mittens made her way to the stairs. It was evident that the conversation was over and that nothing was resolved. If the princess needed to be alone, the dragon would grant her solitude.

"Where do you think you're going?" asked Gale.

"You said you wanted to be left alone. You got upset when I didn't listen, so I thought it would be best if I left."

"You're not *leaving,* leaving, though. Are you?"

"Not until it's time."

"And when is that?"

"You're the only one who knows that, Gale."

Anger and animosity had filled the small room, and when that happens, there is little room for anything else. Especially wee dragons. As we said earlier, this wasn't Mitten's first princess, and she knew how to handle such things. She knew that it would all be OK and that Gale shouldn't be concerned with the crown, the party, or for that matter, even Sir Chad. She also knew that any other princess needed to figure it all out on her own. But, alas, Gale wasn't any other princess.

"If you still want me to go to your parents with you, I'll be outside. If not, I'll stay outside." Mittens made her way down the stairs.

Once the dragon was out of sight, Gale collapsed into an ocean of tears. She sat on her kitchen floor and tried not to sob as she wept, but it was too hard to hold it in. Being strong was difficult, and sometimes you lose the struggle. It's OK to cry, folks. Tears are a wonderful oil that helps turn the gears in your heart and mind.

Chapter 4

As she sat and rocked and cried and sobbed, she looked toward the stairs and saw Mittens peeking guiltily from around a corner.

"What?" Gale said between sobs. "Why are you back?"

"My little hands can't work the doorknob, and I didn't want to bother you."

"Did you try eating it? I bet that would have done it," said Gale, a bit too harshly.

Without responding to the dig, Mittens quickly hopped up on the windowsill and jumped out into the glen with a little sail/blanket action to ease her fall.

After a few more tears and sobbing, Gale composed herself enough to make her way to the shower. Showers were a great place to solve the world's problems, and she had plenty. She liked the water as hot as she could possibly take it, so as the steam filled the room, she sat on the tub's edge and tried not to cry. Everything was happening a little too fast for her. She missed her simple life. Just a day ago, her biggest issue was some laundry that needed folding. Now there were dragons and suitors and weddings and edible princes.

She was beside herself with what to do with Mittens, too. She really liked having her around, but this... this was something completely different. Would she really have stood up to Chad if the dragon wasn't here? Probably. The outcome might have been a totally different story. Things are frightening for any girl nowadays, let alone a princess living on her own in the woods.

After her shower, she dressed in a white top and the new jeans she had traded the crossbow for a while back. Minimal make-up was applied: a little eyeliner and lipstick, nothing fancy. Her hair was thrown up in a scrunchy, and a pair of gray knitted boots completed the outfit. Not exactly a frilly gown, but she was only heading home to see her parents. Gale liked to look neat when she went home so that her parents didn't worry about her living by herself.

Slipping on a lightweight navy-blue jacket, she walked to the mirror to see how she looked. Hopefully, the shower had knocked some of the puffiness out of her face from the crying that had taken place. It hadn't.

She looked tired and drawn, which was appropriate since she felt like she had been hit by a runaway cart.

"Reflexa, how do I look?" she said as she adjusted her hair in the mirror. Reflexa chimed to life but said nothing.

"Reflexa, how do I look??"

Again, the mirror chimed to life. Again, no response.

"Reflexa, don't make me say it. I'm not in the mood."

Another chime and nothing.

"Fine. Mirror, Mirror on the wall, does this girl look good at all?"

"You look good. Mom and Dad will be happy to see you," replied the mirror.

"Reflexa, can I ask you something?"

"Ask away. It's what I'm good at."

"What do you know about dragons?" she asked.

"Searching dragons. According to sources, dragons are creatures with long tails and wings. They can range anywhere between fifty to one hundred and fifty feet in length and can possess a myriad of powers, including but not restricted to shapeshifting, making objects appear and disappear, juggling, and pottery. Dragons are known to hoard gold and protect princesses, both incarcerated and otherwise. Their means of defense are usually fire breathing, tail swatting, or the devouring of their enemies whole. Would you like to hear more about dragons?"

"Does it mention where the dragons don't follow their friends' wishes?"

"File not found."

"Yeah... yeah. Blah blah blah."

"People who searched dragons also searched trebuchets."

Pictures of trebuchets appeared on the screen in all different shapes and sizes.

"Would you like to add one to your cart?" asked the mirror.

"No, thank you."

"Ok, adding trebuchet to your cart. Is there anything else I can help you with today?"

"I said no to the trebuchet."

"Ok. Adding trebuchet to your cart. Is there anything else I can help you with today?"

Chapter 4

"Reflexa, I said no trebuchet."

"OK. Adding trebuchet to your cart."

"Reflexa!" shouted Gale.

The mirror went blank and gave a little laugh.

"Just trying to cheer you up, hon. Any other questions?"

"Reflexa, I don't know what to do about Mittens."

"That's what moms and dads are for, Princess. Talk to them. Then the rest is up to you."

"Well, what would you do if you were me?"

"I am not a princess, but I might think about giving her the benefit of the doubt. She is a dragon, and that's what they do. I don't believe it's a reflection on you at all. Reflection! See what I did there?" Reflexa asked with a giggle.

"Mirror humor. Lovely."

"I try. Do you remember the story of the Frog and the Scorpion?"

"I do," said Gale. (If you don't, then look it up. It's pretty cool.)

"Well, it's kind of like that," said the mirror.

"If I recall, that story didn't end well for either of them. That's a terrible analogy."

"Hey, I told you to speak to your parents. Not everything that comes out of my mouth is a nugget of wisdom, you know. Don't shoot the direct messenger."

"Noted. I'm also a bit confused about the whole suitor thing. I'm definitely not ready to marry, and I often think about getting back into the dating world, but I don't know. If all the guys out there are like Chad, I'm going to be alone for a long time. I hear other horror stories from my friends, and the internet is filled with tales of bad dates or bad guys, or worse. Aren't there any nice guys out there anymore?"

"Patience, Nightingale. Try a little patience," the mirror answered.

"Thanks, Reflexa. I know. I'll try."

"OK. People who tried patience also tried a trebuchet. Would you like to see *Trebuchet trials near me?*" Reflexa giggled at the recommendation.

"You're all full of jokes today, aren't you?"

"Just trying to cheer you up, sweetie. Have fun by your parents. Send them my best. And try not to be too hard on Mittens." With a chime, the mirror turned off.

So, dear reader, the freshly showered princess grabbed her purse and walked down the stairs to head to her parents. Gale shot them a quick text to say she was on her way. She had six new messages from friends asking if she saw the dragon today, and a few even took some pictures of Wrathnarok soaring through the afternoon sky. They were, of course, blurry action shots, and she looked terrible in all of them.

Gale opened her door, fully expecting to see Wrathnarok breathing fire and scratching at the ground. She had a full intent to "discipline her dragon," which kind of sounds like the title to an old Bruce Lee kung-fu movie, but I can assure you it is not. Instead, what she found was Mittens sitting on the stoop waiting for her princess. Gale reached down and scratched her playfully between the ears. Mittens looked up hopeful.

"We good, kid?" she asked as she stood up to greet her.

"I'm not sure yet. But I'll promise to let it go until I am."

"That's very nice of you. I appreciate it." Mittens said with all the sincerity that a dragon could muster.

"I know. I said I'd try," she said. "I'm a princess, after all. That's what we do."

Then quickly, she added, "But don't get your hopes up."

A coach had arrived to bring the pair to the castle. After hopping inside, Gale stared out the window and silently wished everything would just go away. She just wanted her life back to the way it was, and this extra stress was a nightmare. Acting like the strong princess was her forte, and usually, she could, but now her head was swimming with thoughts of doubt and regret. So, of course, the worst thing to do was to add even more ingredients to the mix. And add, she shall.

They rode off to see her parents.

Chapter 5

Your narrator would like to take a moment to discuss the events thus far. First point that needs addressing is the eating of the prince. Now, although Gale is having a bit of a struggle in digesting the digestion that happened under her watch, I feel that it must be remembered that we are knee-deep in a fantasy story about a princess and a magical dragon. The story is filled, quite comically, I might add, with funny anecdotes and familiar references to keep the audience riveted to every word. No one was actually harmed, and no one condones the eating of people. Rumor has it that we are a bit chewy and crunchy and doughy in places.

I'd also like to point out that there was a story a while back about an ogre who won his bride by facilitating a dragon to eat his wife's husband. No one complained, and they made countless sequels about the life and struggles of said ogre. If any of you have a law degree and are feeling a bit litigious, smack that idea out of your head right now. I have very little money, and you'd be wasting your time trying to get blood from a stone. No, "Blood from a Stone" was not a Bruce Lee kung-fu movie, either.

As for the prince's names, they may seem a bit heavy-handed in the cliché department. Chad was obviously an example of symbolism, and I must admit that there will be more. I have no idea what the princes' real names are, but trust me, they are quite tedious. Can you see me writing

Lord Cumberbatch Buttslapp of the Kingdom of Kringleberry, who bravely battled a head cold, who once fought a galloping horde at a Black Friday sales event, who hath prayed for seven days following a trigonometry exam, who once blardy blardy blar. See, no one cares. I couldn't even finish making up a phony title because I was so bored. So, let's all pretend that this is going well and just crack on.

In the land of This-and-That, a beautiful horse-drawn wagon pulled through the towering wooden gates of Castle Beckett. The walls surrounded the castle, and directly down the center was a wide paved path that led directly to the palace. On either side of the main road lay dozens of shops and businesses that supplied the residents with everything from pizza to nail salons. Off the road branched other smaller roads that led to condos and other housing for the city folk. Farmers lived outside the walls toward the outskirts of the kingdom, providing various farm-like industries that kept the people fed.

There are a host of castle terms, like crenels and merlons and machicolation. They are decidedly boring and dated, so we won't bother ourselves with them. Instead, we will concentrate on gates and walls and courtyards. Much easier on the tongue, and it's really all that we need to know to continue. Trying to make it simple for you guys.

The Palace Beckett rises high and wide and is a bit pink in hue. Great towers spring up throughout, and in the front lies a massive expansive courtyard that would be the focal point of Gale's coronation and birthday party. It leads to a set of wide stairs that brings you to a patio area and then to the main entrance of the palace. A path surrounds the palace: to the left, it leads to the livery and stables, and off to the right is an entrance to bring you to the rear courtyard.

The courtyard in the back is easily the size of three football fields. Green grass and hedges decorate the walkways that lead out to the sea. In the distance are a few docks where the Royal Fishermen use the Royal Boats to catch some Royal Fish. Again, stairs and a patio that match the front entrance are in the rear, which is mostly used by people who work in the palace and our princess.

Gale wasn't a fan of coming through the front door when she visited her parents. She tried to avoid fanfare at all costs, and arriving from the

Chapter 5

back gave her an opportunity to see some of the workers that she had known all of her life. They were all like an extended family to her. The cooks and seamstresses and chambermaids were like aunts and cousins, and the knights and stable hands were like uncles. They always treated her warmly, and Gale returned the love.

Plus, the added shock of arriving with an unannounced wee beastie wasn't fit for a front-door arrival. There was a buzz going about the kingdom regarding the princess' new friend, and not all of it in a positive tone. Some people had a strange opinion of dragons due to slanderous propaganda or personal experiences, and Gale figured it best to keep Mittens out of sight for now.

Before the doorman could reach the carriage, Gale and Mittens popped out into the courtyard at the base of the stairs. She thanked the driver for the ride and promised him a five-star rating. Although it didn't show on her face, Gale was glad to be home. She felt the tension leave her shoulders as she looked at the familiar surroundings.

"C'mon, Mittens. Let's go meet the folks. Try not to eat anyone along the way," Gale said as they made their way up the grand rear entrance steps.

The ride to the castle was a little tense, and very few words were spoken. Mittens asked questions about points of interest, and Gale only looked out the window and mumbled a response. The dragon looked as if she started to regret her decision to join them for the evening. Mittens' eyes darted every which way, either taking in the sights or planning her escape. Good dragons don't just run out and leave when the going gets tough. Neither do good friends, and Mittens was trying to be both.

Upon reaching the top, Mittens stopped next to a gonfalon and looked at Gale. She could tell that the princess was still a bit out of sorts, and she thought it would be best if she met with her parents alone at first.

"Do you mind if I stay out here and look around for a bit?"

"Sure, if that's what you want. Try to stay out of sight, though. I'd hate to freak out the natives. They're good people, and they don't need any added excitement."

"Not my first joust, Princess. I got it."

Gale left her on the steps and walked toward a heavy wooden door that was usually open but not today. That was a sure sign that the queen

53

had given the staff the night off. She rather enjoyed alone time with her parents, and having the staff puttering about preparing meals and such was a distraction. It also meant that pizza was probably on the menu, a notion that made the princess smile. Her mom really had a knack for knowing what to do when things got a little harried. That was how the queen came to be known as Evelyn the Just.

Pulling on the giant iron ring, she opened the door and walked inside. There was a stone hallway that led to the kitchen, and Gale had just begun to navigate it when she heard a rushing of familiar footsteps. She stopped and waited for the coming assault and tried to hide a smile from her face. She could not, for she knew that out of the shadows would appear a very large and very loud man.

"Gale!" exclaimed the king. His arms were opened wide, and he engulfed his daughter with a hug that only a father could provide. She left her feet as he swung her around and around. A kiss on the cheek was immediately administered, and all at once, Gale felt at home. Her harrowing day seemed to melt in his arms. A younger Gale would pretend to dislike this embarrassing display, but her father never stopped. On a day like today, she was glad that he didn't.

He was a big man, not too tall but robust of build. His arms were strong though his belly had softened over the years. His hair had greyed and thinned, but there was still a youthful fire in his eyes that seemed to put everyone he was in contact with at ease. Yet don't be fooled by his gentle demeanor. As a little girl, one look from those eyes could freeze her to the bone, and she would stop whatever foolishness she was in the middle of doing. She had seen her father set that stare on a knight or dignitary and would try not to chuckle at seeing someone else wither in the face of disapproval from the king. As she got older, those moments were fewer and farther between and she became more of a peer and less of a silly schoolgirl. She loved him dearly, and so did most of the kingdom.

"How are you, sweetie? You look fantastic. Are those new jeans?" asked the king. Gale quickly changed the subject, remembering the crossbow.

"Yes, thanks. And where are you off to? Didn't Mom tell you I was coming?"

Chapter 5

"She did, but I thought you could use a little 'mother-daughter' time, what with the new dragon and all. I'm heading off with the knights for a while. We had a long day, and I thought I'd treat them to dinner."

"Long day? What happened?"

"There is a poor family who had a farm boy named Weasel or Nestley or something not too far from our kingdom. Evidently, there was some drama involving the daughter. I didn't get into it with them, but apparently, he left to join the Navy or something like that. Anyway, they needed a little help until they could find a new farm boy, so the knights and I rode out to give them a hand. I came home to wash up and change."

"That was very sweet of you," said Gale.

"I try, I try. All in the name of the kingdom and all that. Afterwards, we're going to see Sir Knoxville's new trebuchet. He's been flinging melons with it and getting pretty good at it. One night he himself climbed in it, and the boys shot him into the Sea of Weeman! It must have been quite a sight!"

"He's a jackass," Gale said.

"Yes, he is, but he's a good man. Come on and walk me out. The knights would love to say hello. With any luck, they'll be here shortly. You are missed around here, little girl." The king grabbed her by the hand, and out the back door, they went.

Before he opened the door, the king stopped and turned to his daughter. A look of slight concern crossed his face. Gale realized in that look that he wasn't seeing her as a princess or a mature woman living on her own. It was the concern from a father for his little girl. She guessed that she would always be his little girl in one way or another, and she was fine with that.

She had wanted to mention the afternoon that she had to her father. The words sat in her throat and begged to come forward, but the princess held her tongue. If she was going to ask for gold to pay off Wrathnarok or ask for some kind of aid in dealing with her newfound troubles, this was a perfect opportunity to speak up. But, after all, she was a princess, and the words stayed put. Keeping an expression of worry off of her face was another matter.

"You OK, kid?" he asked softly.

"Yeah, I'll be fine."

"You know that if you ever need me that I'm always here, right?"

"Yeah, Dad. I know," Gale said with a smile.

"OK. Glad we got that squared away. How do I look?"

The king stood in front of Gale for inspection, arms spread and spinning in a circle.

"Maybe untuck the shirt," said Gale.

He quickly pulled his shirt out and brushed it down to flatten some of the wrinkles. With a mighty meaty hand, King Killian pushed the heavy wooden door open, and both he and Gale gasped at what they saw. Mittens was surrounded by four knights who had drawn their swords and were circling the dragon slowly, seemingly ready for battle. Mittens had reverted to the Harbinger of Doom as smoke puffed from her nostrils, her wings raised in defense. The dragon kept her massive head low, looking each knight dead in the eyes.

Any thoughts that Gale had about asking for gold and dismissing her dragon were quickly replaced with fear. She knew these men, and they were all skilled swordsmen. She also knew that Wrathnarok might see them as less of a threat and more of a buffet. None of this was what we, in the narrating field, call good.

"NO!" screamed Gale as she raced down the stairs, arms waving. Pleas of stopping came from her with every step.

"Men! Sheath thy swords! This beast is friend, not foe! She shall remain unharmed by order of the king!" King Killian stood at the top of the staircase to make this proclamation, and as the words echoed through the back courtyard, all the knights put their swords away and stood to look at their king.

"Sorry, King. We were just joking around," said Sir Knoxville.

"Yes, my liege, we have missed being tested in the battle for so long. The gracious and mighty Wrathnarok agreed to parry us for amusement," said Sir Reginald the Rank, obviously free of the pox and as smelly as ever.

"Ah, just a farce! Very amusing! I would hasten a guess this was the folly of Knoxville?"

"Indeed, M'Lord," answered the knight.

"Always full of pranks, that one," smiled the king as he lumbered down the stairs.

The men bowed to the princess in unison. All of them begging forgiveness for startling her with their little game.

"Cut it out with the bowing. You're all a bunch of idiots, you know that? You almost gave me a heart attack!" said Gale as she approached each of them for a hug.

The first she approached was Sir Robert, a short, bearded man who resembled the king quite a bit. During some turbulent times in the kingdom, Robert would often pose as the king if there was any chance of danger. A few years back, her father even sent Robert to act as a dignitary to quell some dispute on his behalf. It took some convincing for everyone at the meeting to believe that Robert wasn't the actual king.

"My princess!" said Robert as he enveloped Gale in a hug. "How are things in the new place? All settled in, I hope."

"I'm getting there. Still a few boxes to unpack. Kid stuff, mostly. I tucked them into storage for the time being."

Next came Sir Knoxville, a tall, lanky man with a shock of white hair. He carried himself with a pronounced limp from years of stupid and selfless antics. Call it stupidity, call it bravery; Knoxville never dipped his lance in fear. Give the man any task, and he would attempt it without a moment's hesitation.

"M'Lady. Still a vision, I see," said the knight.

"Knoxville! Dad told me about the stunt with the trebuchet. You're gonna get yourself killed one of these days if you're not careful."

"I just like to entertain the men. By any chance, did he mention my recent stint as a bullfighter? Wonderful animals! They're dangerous at both ends and crafty in the middle. I didn't know!"

"Yeah? Well, you're stupid," Gale teased.

"Remember me?" Sir Hunk asked as he pushed Knoxville aside to get his hug. Knoxville met him with a little lighthearted but good-natured resistance. Sir Hunk embraced the princess warmly and gave her a gentle squeeze. His real name was Ray, but he received the playful moniker due to his scarecrow-like physique.

The Self-Sufficient Princess

"My princess," said Sir Reginald the Rank. Whether due to his pox or his stench, the knight kept his distance and deeply bowed before Gale. A thick, scraggly black beard fell from his chin, and long greasy black hair rested from his head to his shoulders. Though his monstrous size could intimidate, he carried a smile that was gracious and inviting. He was her father's oldest and dearest friend. There was not a time in her life when Sir Reg was not around. He was the king's right-hand man, and they were nearly inseparable.

"You guys! Stop! I've only been away for a month or so," Gale said with a blush.

As we mentioned, the princess hated a fuss or drama. Now, due to the events of the last few days, she rather enjoyed the attention. Seeing the knights and her father among familiar surroundings relaxed her and made her feel safe and back in control of things. There is nothing like going home again. Thomas Wolfe must not have had a family like Gale's. I'm almost sure he wasn't a princess either, though I would have to check.

The king approached Wrathnarok, and the dragon spread her wings and bowed before him. For a huge animal, the dragon was quite graceful and seemed at ease in the face of royalty. It made Gale wonder exactly how many princesses were in her past. She would have to remember to circle back to that conversation later.

"Rise, great dragon. I must thank you for not besting my men on this day. Although they have fought valiantly, I can see that you were truly the victor," said the king as he smiled playfully at his men. A roar of disagreement rose from the knights, all claiming that they were the winners.

"May I have your name, brave and conquering dragon?" asked Killian.

"Wrathnarok, my Lord."

The king, placing a hand on the dragon's massive head, leaned in and said quietly, "Take care of our girl, would you?"

"She doesn't need any help, believe me," Wrathnarok answered with a wink.

"Don't I know it! She's just like her mother," said the king.

"Standing right here! Hello?" said Gale. "And maybe you can stop with the grandiose 'kingspeech?'"

Chapter 5

"King's Speech? I didn't stutter, did I?"

"No, not *The* King's Speech. 'Kingspeech'. That whole 'Gather, men, and we shall vanquish a foe' thing. It's just us out here. No reason to sound official."

"But the men love when we speak of the olden days in olden ways. Right, men?"

"Huzzah!" The knights all cheered.

"See?" said the king as he elbowed his daughter.

"Uff! You guys are ridiculous. Get going and stay out of trouble," said Gale as she kissed her father and waved at the knights.

"Come, men! You must all pay dearly for embarrassing me on the battlefield today," said the king as they walked to their horses.

"Meaning what?" asked Sir Reginald.

"Meaning you have to buy the first round at the pub!" said the king as they laughed and joked their way out of sight.

Mittens had returned to a more manageable size and stood by the princess. She was smiling, thinking about how Gale ran to protect her. Maybe Gale was going to give her a second chance after all. Let's hope so. It'll be a short book if she doesn't.

"The king seems nice. Cool knights, too. Maybe someone can slip Reginald a bar of soap for his birthday? That guy is in dire need of good hosing down," said Mittens.

"Yeah, they're all pretty cool. They're like uncles to me. My dad's got some pretty good friends. And I wouldn't be pointing any fingers at Sir Reginald, either, O Harbinger of Halitosis."

Mittens did a quick breath check that resulted in the stench of body spray and regret.

"So, did your father have anything to say about, you know, the whole Chad incident?" asked Mittens.

"I didn't say a thing. I wanted him to meet you on a level ground since you're going to be staying for a bit." Gale stared at the dragon to make sure she was aware of the gracious second chance that was allotted to her. Mittens picked up on it and nodded in agreement, trying to suppress a happy smile.

"I don't need him to start the protective-dad routine. He needs to learn that I can handle things. Seems to be a familiar theme today," said Gale, giving the dragon a sideways glance.

She wished she could stop herself from throwing little verbal barbs at Mittens, but often her brain works too fast, and things just pop out of her mouth. It was considered immature and definitely not a princess-like quality, but Gale had come to grips with the fact that these flaws didn't define her, and she was OK with them. All princesses are a work in progress, and there were plenty of construction signs and safety cones posted around Gale.

The visit with the king was sweet, albeit brief. Normally, she'd feel a little sad about not seeing her father for long, but he is a king and has responsibilities. She'd been dealing with that annoying fact for most of her life. Many times, she had reached for her father and found a king in his place. Today was different, and she was glad that the king was heading out, and although she often leaned on the king for certain issues, right now, Gale needed a mother's advice without any fatherly interference.

Nervous energy took over as they walked through the huge door that led back into the castle. How would her mother react to her tale of this afternoon's events? Would she be understanding or disappointed in her? More important than either of those questions was whether or not she had ordered pizza. Gale was getting nervous, and nervousness made her hungry. She decided to tackle the situation head-on.

"C'mon, Mittens," she said, "Let's go meet the queen."

Chapter 6

IN THE LAND OF This-and-That, the princess and her dragon made their way through the labyrinth of halls and rooms that made up the palace. They passed ballrooms and kitchens and libraries and halls and conservatories and billiard rooms and studies and lounges until, finally, they arrived at the dining room.

Before they entered, Mittens did another breath check. Brimstone and body spray. Not really the first impression one wanted to make when meeting a queen. She poofed a pink smoke cloud that produced a fistful of white and red cellophane-covered peppermints. Mittens crammed the entire cache into her mouth and began to chew. Gale stared at the performance with disapproval. The princess made a mental note to work with Mittens on her eating skills.

Mittens reached a claw into her mouth, pulled out a half-chewed, still-wrapped mint dripping with pink saliva, and offered it to Gale.

"Want one?" she asked.

"Ewww! No! That's disgusting. And no amount of mints can cover up that disaster. Now, try not to embarrass me in there. I need to talk to Mom without any dragon drama. Think you can manage that?"

A loud gulp was followed by a burp that echoed down the stone hallway as Mittens finished her mints and wiped her mouth.

"I make no promises. Ready?" she asked.

Shaking her head, Gale tugged at the large door that led to the dining room. As they entered, they saw the queen placing at least ten pizzas on the large table. A stack of plates and napkins were nearby, along with various types of beverages. Queen Evelyn was tapered and tall for a woman her age. A palette of differently shaded hair framed a pretty face and eyes that matched her daughter's. She was dressed casually in stretchy pants and a white tunic, but still carried an aura of elegance. Gale often wondered how her mom did it and hoped that she would have the same talent as she got older.

"Hey, honey, who's your friend?" asked the queen as she made her way over to Gale for a hug.

"Mom, this is my dragon, Mittens. Mittens, this is Mom."

The dragon bowed again, as the queen nodded with acceptance. Queen Evelyn pointed at the chairs and began handing out plates and napkins. "Help yourselves," she said as she popped open a pizza box or two.

"You expecting company? This is a lot of pizza," said Gale as she reached for a slice.

"Not my first dragon," the queen replied as she looked at Mittens and handed her an entire box of pizza. "You just missed the delivery boy. Kind of cute and around your age, Gale. Seemed very nice."

"Just what I need. Another suitor," Gale said as she pulled a cheesy bite from a slab of pepperoni.

They ate as the queen discussed the latest news of the kingdom and the preparations for Gale's birthday party. It was just a few weeks away, and the kingdom was alive with plans and arrangements for the upcoming gala.

The princess wasn't in the mood for a big party bash. She did enjoy a party but preferred it more when she wasn't the main attraction. The dragon and the princes had put a damper on the whole thing, and she asked her mom if they could kind of keep it low-key.

"You can do what you wish, but I'd like it if you at least made yourself slightly available. There will be over seven kingdoms coming to pay their respects. You know how these things are, hon. Show your face briefly, then sneak away to do whatever you want."

"I don't want to embarrass anyone by not being around," said Gale.

Chapter 6

"It's your birthday, dear. Celebrate it however you want. Besides, as you age, you'll realize that birthday parties are less for you and more for the people who throw them," said Evelyn.

"Do I have to get all princessed up?" she asked, referring to the frilly gown and circling butt-birds.

"Very casual. Shorts and a tee shirt are fine for the party, but I will be sending over the seamstress to fit you for a presentation gown," replied the queen.

The presentation gown was meant for when she would announce to the planet her engagement plans and her acceptance into the royal family as an acting head of the kingdom. You know, all the things that Gale had traveled here to ask her mom to forget about. She had been here for five minutes, and things were already getting dicey for Gale.

"So," said the queen wiping her hands and mouth, "Are we ready to talk about your day?"

Gale pointed at Mittens and gave her a stern look indicating that it was her story, and she was not to say a word. The dragon put her hands in the air in surrender and grabbed another box of pizza. The watershed moment that Mittens had about her out-of-shape physique was lost among the scent of garlic and oregano.

The princess told the tale of Prince and the Resolution, trying hard not to embellish as she spoke of the horrible human garbage that was the prince. She mentioned the intimidation she felt, the disgusting innuendos that were tossed about, and the general attitude surrounding her first encounter with a supposedly potential suitor. She even included the barbs that she threw back to show that she was not a victim during the altercation. As she went on, she could feel her pressure rise, and the tone of her voice heightened. By the time she was near the end describing the unsightly occurrence of the Harvest Formerly Known as Prince, Gale was practically shaking with anger.

The queen rested her hand on her chin and gave her daughter the undivided attention that she so desperately needed. When Gale had finally finished, Queen Evelyn looked at the dragon, now polishing off the last piece of olive pizza in the box and remained emotionless. She stayed quiet for some time and finally stood from her chair.

"Mittens, my dear, do you think there may be something on the television that would entertain you for a while?" the queen asked.

"Nah. Nothing but garbage lately. One more real housemaids show, and I promise I'll give back all the pizza that I ate," she responded.

The queen continued to look at the dragon with a raised eyebrow until she finally realized that Mom wanted to be alone with her daughter.

"OH! Right! Forgive me, your highness. It's been a long day, and I'm a bit slow on the uptake."

Mittens excused herself from the table and made her way toward the door that led to the remaining living area. Halfway there, she did an about-face, scurried back to the table, snatched another box of pizza, then made her way out again. Finally, the mother and daughter were alone.

"She's a good dragon. You could have had worse," stated the queen.

"I know, I know, it's just that I can't have her eating everyone I disagree with. I can handle things myself, Mom."

"Surely you can, but you can't be afraid to ask for a little help now and then."

"Mom, I had it under control. At least, I thought I did. That still doesn't excuse Mittens from using the prince as a Pu-Pu platter."

"Yes, but you can't tell me you weren't a little relieved to see her come to your aid," said the queen.

"Maybe. It's just all a little confusing. All of it. OK, maybe a lot confusing."

"Yes, it is. The whole world is a confusing place filled with things we don't agree with. But dragons eat people. Princes know this when they set out to seek a princess' affection. They know the risk of rejection. They battle the dragon and hope for the best. Many a prince or suitor won't even try because they know the risks. And many a man's arrogance or ignorance has been his demise."

The queen walked over to Gale and sat beside her. The poor princess looked troubled and torn, and it hurt her to see her this way.

Well, Gale thought, *it's now or never. Time to break my mother's heart.*

Each question was a difficult one to ask. Gale struggled to decide which bomb to drop on her mother first. Should she lead with the denouncement or the marriage? If she leads with the denouncement and her mom gave her

Chapter 6

blessing, wouldn't that handle the whole wedding business? Or would the queen expect her to marry anyway? Maybe she would put more pressure on a wedding if she wasn't a princess.

A quick gut check revealed only pizza and soda.

She decided to start with the lesser of the two evils. At least, she hoped it was the lesser one. Honestly, both conundrums were a Thanksgiving Parade of evil so, hey, flip a coin.

"Mom, am I supposed to get married? Mittens said that when I turn eighteen that I'm supposed to, and I don't want to." Gale blurted it out in a nervous bleat.

"Absolutely not," said the queen.

"Really?" Gale nearly collapsed with relief. "There isn't some stupid law that says I have to get hitched by a certain time?"

"If there was, don't you think your dad would have changed it the day you were born? He is the king, you know."

"True. But you got married young. Was there something that said you had to or lose the kingdom or something?"

"I only got married early because I met your father at the right time. I grew up in a different world than you did, Gale. Times were much more traditional then. I had been told all my life that I would be married at eighteen, and I was ready for it."

"Do you ever regret it?" asked Gale.

"I'd be lying if I said that I didn't. I was still a child at eighteen. I hadn't really done anything with my life, but I was a princess, and at the time, that was enough. I did what was expected of me. I had a family and went into the family business, so to speak. I surely wasn't prepared for all of it. But that was me, and those were my choices to make. I stand by them and sometimes think of the good things I would have missed if I had waited. Your life is your own, hon. You do what's natural to you. Understand?"

"Yes," said Gale. "I just don't want to be a disappointment."

"If you want to disappoint me, then change. I'm very proud of my daughter as she is."

"Thanks, Mom. Sometimes I don't know what's expected of me."

"No one ever does, Gale, so you try your best. That's all you can do."

"Good. So, no more suitors, then. That's a relief!"

"I never said that. They will still come. There's nothing you can do about that."

Plopping her head onto the table, Gale let out a groan of frustration.

"Nope, you're stuck with that until after your birthday. Once we announce to the people that there will be no wedding, the flow of suitors should turn into a trickle. You can move into your old room if you want until it's over."

"Can't you just tell them now? Post something on the kingdom's website saying I'm off the market? Maybe I can change my relationship status on Gracebook?"

"It won't do any good. They will still come with visions of glory. To battle the dragon and win the princess. Not all boys are stupid, Gale. But not all boys are smart, either," said the queen.

"Did you have a dragon when you met Dad?"

"I did. Adhemar the Merciless." The queen's eyes brightened at the memory. "Big green dragon with yellow stripes and a huge tail. He was something to behold. Absolutely magnificent."

"Did you let him sleep inside?"

"Your grandmother forbade it, but I'd sneak him in at night if it got too cold. Again, times were much different back then," said the queen.

"I'm guessing he was there to protect you, too?"

"Yes, he was. I had a bunch of princes chasing me back in the day. Adhemar would weigh and measure them, and if he found them lacking quality, they were quickly dispatched."

"Any of them get dispatched as a prince pâté?" asked Gale.

"Well, back in my day, princes didn't roll up in a carriage with an entourage. They rode on horseback in full armor, prepared to do battle and save the fair maiden from the dangerous beast that kept her 'captive.' A bit romantic if you think about it."

"I'm a little more pragmatic," stated Gale.

"As am I. They would ride up and profess their love of me to my father and ask permission to battle the dragon. Your grandfather was a bit of an ass, so he'd grant them permission. Then they would battle Adhemar for some stupid, macho reason. They would either flee or, well, pâté."

"That's terrible!" exclaimed Gale.

Chapter 6

"Again, different times."

"How did Dad defeat Adhemar?"

"I never told you the story? It's quite funny if you think about it. Your father rode in on his horse, and instead of armor, he was decked out in the finest fashions."

"I can't see Dad getting all dressed up in the latest threads. All I ever see him in are kingly robes or casual dad-clothes," said Gale.

Gale sat on the edge of her seat, trying to imagine her father dressed in the leather suit that the Chad had worn earlier. The thought of it made her giggle. Her dad would never wear eyeliner and all those garish rings. She was beginning to wonder if her mother's memory was slipping just a bit or if the hands of time had altered the story.

"Oh yes. He was quite the handsome prince and dressed to match."

"So, what happened?"

"Well, every day, he would ride in from This-and-That to our castle with the finest gifts he could muster and present them to my parents. First, it was sweets from the chocolatier. Boxes and boxes of them. Next, it was crates of fish and shells from the sea. Lobsters and seashells and starfish and even a small shark if I remember."

"*That's* what won you over?" Gale asked in disbelief.

"Absolutely not," said the queen. "It was merely a distraction. After he dropped off the gifts, he would ride around to my window and talk to me all night. We spoke for hours. Not the silly professions of love and 'Oh, your beauty is radiant in the moonlight' crap. We really talked. What interests I had, what music I liked, everything you could think of. He really wanted us to get to know each other."

"Adhemar didn't gobble him up, obviously."

"No, he was still being weighed and measured. This went on for quite a while. I was beginning to fear that he would run out of things to bring. I found myself looking forward to his visits more and more, but I couldn't risk leaving my room at night. Princess virtue and all that. So, I waited."

"That must have sucked," said Gale.

"Yes, it did. But it worked. I was slowly falling for your father. It was fun. None of this instant gratification that your generation is accustomed to. Real old-school romance."

"There is something to be said for both, you know. No judgey."

"I don't judge. Anyway, on the last day, when your dad felt he was ready, he came with one last batch of gifts. Only they weren't for my parents."

The queen changed the subject as she got up and walked toward the kitchen.

"You want me to make some tea? I could go for some tea right about now," said the queen.

Gale was up instantly, following her mother to the kitchen like a dog looking for a treat.

"MOM! You're killing me! What did he bring? Was the gift for you? Finish your story!"

Gale was practically begging at this point. Evelyn filled a kettle and put it on the stove. Then she grabbed some cups and a box of chamomile out of a cupboard. One thing Gale knew, the woman could keep you on the edge of your seat.

"Mom!" yelled Gale.

"Oh? Did you want to hear the rest? I didn't want to be a bore," teased the queen.

Leaning on the counter, Gale stood with her arms crossed and stared at her mother.

"How did Dad defeat Adhemar. What did he bring you?"

"The gift wasn't for me. It was for Adhemar. It was barrel after barrel of beer. He called out to Adhemar and offered a toast to the wonderful princess. The dragon couldn't refuse such a toast, so they drank. They drank well into the night right outside my window. Your dad explained his intentions to the dragon, and after a while and a few jokes, your dad charmed the dragon."

"So, Dad got Adhemar drunk?"

"Dragons don't get drunk," said a voice from the door. It was Mittens still gnawing on a pizza crust. "Sorry to interrupt, but I thought I'd check in to see how it was going. Was getting a little boring in there," she said.

"Dragons don't get drunk?" asked Gale.

"Nope," said the queen. "But the gesture seemed to work, and that night, Adhemar let me leave my room, and I gave your dad his first kiss. We announced our wedding about a few months later."

"That's so cool," said Gale.

"Here's the kicker, and don't tell your dad that I told you. The beer was a specialty that This-and-That was famous for back then. It was a stout beer. So, when the story got out, as they always do, about how your father won my heart by using stout beer, your dad earned the title of Killian the Stout-hearted."

The kitchen filled with laughter at this revelation. The queen poured some hot water into the cups and handed one to Gale. Her mother's story was warm, and she loved that she confided in her. Gale would keep her mother's secret safe.

"Do you ever hear from Adhemar?" asked Mittens.

"We keep in touch, but not like we should. Age slows you down, and it becomes a comfort just knowing he's out there," said the queen.

"I heard he retired," said Mittens.

"Yes, he did. His last princess was some actress out in Hollywood, and when he saw what a complete disaster the in-laws would be, he ran out of there as quickly as he could. Didn't even wait to get paid."

More laughter bounced along the kitchen walls because they all knew the story of the Hollywood princess and her horrid in-laws. Gale was hoping that was a battle that she wouldn't have to face. With her parents' guidance, she wouldn't have to deal with that for a while, if ever. For the first time in days, Gale felt OK again.

"I don't think that I'll ever get married. I just can't see it," said Gale.

"Never say never, hon. But there is no rush. Relax and enjoy life. It's better to be alone for the right reasons than in a relationship for the wrong ones," said the queen.

"Please. I don't even know how to find a guy if I wanted one. Do I get all dressed up and go out clubbing like some of my friends do? Do I just wait and see what happens? Do I actively search for someone online on one of those stupid apps?"

"Well, if you pretend to be someone else, then he'll fall in love with a stranger. Just be you. Are you happy being you?" asked the queen.

"I think so. Sometimes. I don't know."

"Again, that's everybody. There's nothing wrong with self-improvement but changing yourself to fit in is just silly. If your cat had kittens in a stove, would they be muffins?"

"Let me say that I have no idea what that means," said Mittens.

"Eat your pizza," Gale said, and she walked out to get yet another slice.

The queen approached Gale and took her in her arms. She gave her a hug that only a mother could give. After the embrace, Evelyn moved a few strands of hair away from her daughter's face and looked at her. Her daughter was so grown, but Gale could tell that she would always be her little girl in one way or another. And Gale was okay with that.

"I hope that I helped you a little bit. Even as a queen, I don't have all the answers, and some things you're going to have to figure out for yourself. Meanwhile, I'm always here. Want to move back in for a little while? Your room is always ready for you."

"No. I'm good, Mom. Really. I'll be fine, I promise."

"Good. That's my girl. Try to control your dragon. But remember, it's a dragon that you're trying to control," said the queen.

They stayed for a bit longer and spoke of the days when Gale was just a little princess. Mittens made sure to leave a few slices for the king in case he needed a nosh when he returned. When the evening had played itself out, Gale rose with a stretch and announced the night had ended.

"Time for bed, I think. What do you say, Mittens? Ready to hit the road?" she asked.

Mittens nodded and rose with a stretch from her head to her tail.

"I'm getting up early," said Queen Evelyn. "I'm meeting with the decorators for the party bright and early and running some things by the caterers right after."

"Nothing too crazy, all right, Mom?"

"I promise," said the queen.

The queen walked them to the door and with a light-hearted "Love! Love! Love!", Gale and Mittens walked back down the stairs and into the rear courtyard. In the darkness, Mittens began looking around for something.

"Where's the coach? Did you call for the coach?" she asked.

"I thought you'd fly us home."

"What on earth gave you that idea?"

Chapter 6

"Well, there was a TV show where this girl had some dragons. She used to ride them all the time," said Gale.

"Do you see these wings, sister? Where are you gonna sit?"

"I can sit on your neck and hold on," said Gale.

"Not gonna happen. How about I hold on to your neck, and YOU jog us home."

"If you don't think you're up to the task, just let me know," chided Gale.

"Ask Lefty and Righty if I was up to the task. If you fall off, we're going to end up with a Nightingale omelet. Your mom can serve that at the party," said Mittens.

"Looked pretty cool on the show, is all I'm saying."

"Yeah? Remember how that ended for the girl? That part looked pretty cool, too. Meanwhile, maybe stop watching so much TV. It's rotting your brain. Scoop up a book or something…"

As Mittens continued her rant, a coach swung its way into the courtyard to pick them both up and return them to the tower.

"I called before we left. Hop in," said Gale with a smile.

"Ah! Princess got jokes! I see what's going on here."

As the coach pulled onto the road, Mittens figured she should try to find out where she stood with the princess. If the talk went well, she would hopefully be back on the couch. If not, she'd be crawling up on the lawn for the rest of her visit. Mittens was not a fan of the lawn. It was cold and damp, and she had a bit of an allergy. As we all know, there is nothing worse than a dragon with a head cold. A stuffy nose and scratchy throat make for a very messy dragon, and when last I checked, no one was making bed-sheet-sized tissues.

"The parentals seemed nice," Mittens said.

"Yeah, they're pretty cool. I'm glad you all got along."

"Consider yourself lucky. I have been around for ages, and I have seen some strange moms and dads. Lots of fights and misunderstandings. Not everyone communicates the way that you guys do."

"It wasn't always like this. We had our fair share of rough spots when I was growing up. Mom was a little old school and wanted me to act a certain way. Dad was a little strict. Running the kingdom was really beating on him for a while. The land went through a real rough patch, and he seemed so angry all the time. Plus, I was in the middle of my rebellious stage, and there were more than a few quiet dinners and then yelling and slamming doors. Did you ever try to slam a twelve-foot solid oak door? It ain't easy."

"That's hard to believe after meeting them. You guys look so tight," said Mittens.

"Mom even took me off the Archery team, and I was first string. My grades were slipping, and I was a mess. But here we are. We still don't see eye to eye on everything, but we get along for the most part." Gale shrugged. "I used to envy the other girls who weren't royalty. Some of them seemed so happy and lived these perfect lives. Then you hear things, and you see that no family is perfect. My dad used to say that there was a secret behind every door, and I found out he was right."

"What got you past it all? I'm sure that growing up helped. Moving out must have helped too."

"Lots of compromise and listening. I stopped looking at my parents as just parents and tried to look at them as people. They stopped treating me like a helpless little kid, and sooner or later, it works itself out."

"Or it doesn't," said Mittens.

"Or it doesn't," agreed Gale. "I think most people love their family, and the hardest thing is trying to figure out how to do it."

"True. Did your mom give you any dragon advice?" asked Mittens with hope in her voice.

"Yes, she did. She said I need to get you to behave."

"And what did she have in mind?"

"Swatting you on the nose with a rolled-up newspaper."

"Still with the jokes. We good, Princess?"

"Yeah… we good," said Gale.

"Well, then, to celebrate the moment, you may pet me. Just this once, and we never speak of it again. Deal?" asked Mittens.

"Deal," said Gale. Mittens laid her head on Gale's lap, and she scratched her behind the ears as the carriage rocked its way back to the tower.

"By the way, I don't believe you mentioned the denouncement to your mom, now did you?" asked Mittens.

"By the way, shut your stupid mouth and enjoy the scratching," replied Gale.

They rode on in silence all the way to the tower. Gale scratched Mittens' head to show there were no hard feelings, and Mittens shut her stupid mouth and enjoyed every scratch.

Because that's what good friends do.

Chapter 7

In the land of This-and-That, the princess slowly crept through the woods. Strapped to her back was a newly acquired crossbow, the BFC9000. On her right hip was a full broadsword, sheathed but prepared for battle. On her left was a tiny dagger that she named Trouble. It was good for throwing and even better for slitting a throat in close combat.

Crouching behind a tree, she checked behind her to see if she was followed. No one was nearby. Next, she surveyed the area. Far off in the distance was a large boulder about twenty yards from an abandoned farmhouse. For an instant, she thought she saw a flicker of movement. She waited patiently, eyes fixed on the rock for another sign of life. Patience was truly a virtue.

There! Another brief but detectable flash of blue, and then it disappeared again behind the boulder. Without a sound, Gale readied her crossbow. She took aim at the spot where the blue flash was seen just a moment before. When it reappeared, she would be ready.

After what seemed like an eternity, the mark revealed itself from behind the rock. That rock of protection was about to become its tombstone.

"Shhh..." she whispered, "Go to sleep."

Gale let fly a bolt from the crossbow and took the breath from her target. She raced ahead to find her kill. There laid a man, dead as a result of her keen marksmanship. She took whatever gold he had from his fresh corpse and rushed back to the woods.

"PizzaBoi! You are terrible at this game!" Gale said into her headgear.

"How did you find me? I was well covered." His voice crackled through her earphones.

"Not well enough! You can't just camp there all the time. You've got to keep moving," Gale laughed.

Her team was winning by a sizable margin, and she had been making a regular feast of PizzaBoi all game. She could hear the frustration in his voice as he respawned and headed back into the fray. Scabs of Destiny was a great way for the princess to relax a bit, and she had missed playing with all the recent events. She sat cross-legged and as close to the TV as she could without climbing into the set, a bowl of pretzels at her side.

"Hey! Tell DragonSlayr that I find his name demeaning and insulting," said Mittens from the couch.

With a toss of Trouble, Gale dropped the offensive adversary and then ran to retrieve her dagger and whatever gold she could find. Soon a screen appeared announcing that hers was the final kill of the match and that her team had secured an easy victory.

"How was that?" Gale asked.

"Good job, Princess. You would have made a great dragon. You're ruthless!"

"I try. I play way too much, but that's the only way to get any good. I'm still nowhere close to most of the guys online, but I hold my own."

"Except for PizzaBoi. That guy has no killer instinct."

"Yes, he is pitiful, but at least he keeps trying," said Gale.

Whenever the princess played Scabs of Destiny, she found herself looking for PizzaBoi to see if he was online. He was pleasant and always asked Gale for help and advice, even if he was on an opposing team. She tried to help when she could and even enjoyed giving him tips, regardless of whether he applied the knowledge or not. Many of the other players had a bit of a nasty streak, cursing up a storm and slinging vulgar comments at anyone within earshot. PizzaBoi never joined in with the name-calling. He was just there to have fun, as was Gale, and his demeanor radiated through the game and made it all the better.

Chapter 7

Gale put her controller down and grabbed a fistful of pretzels from the bowl. Cramming them into her mouth, she got up to stretch while the next round was loading. Mittens was sprawled on the couch, watching the princess play and trying to learn how it was done.

"Want another soda?" she asked as she walked to the kitchen.

"Nope. I'm good. Are you going to give me a shot at playing soon? You are a controller hog," said Mittens.

"Oh, do we think we're ready?" asked Gale.

"Please. I'm a massively intimidating tool of despair. This will be child's play."

"You can barely handle a fork. I have a question before I let you play. Can you work a zipper?" chuckled the princess.

"Why do you ask?"

"No reason. But I've seen you get stumped by a doorknob a time or two, and I was measuring your dexterity level."

"Alas, more jokes. We'll see who's laughing after I take over the leaderboard. Besides, I got a bone to pick with DragonSlayr."

After a few button presses, Gale set up the dragon with an avatar and sent her off to play. The round began, and Mittens was quickly dispatched by none other than N00bMaster. Whoever that kid was, he had to be cheating. He was the best player the princess had ever seen. After a respawn, Mittens was again wasted by N00bMaster, this time with a lance from behind.

"Oh look, I've been impaled!" said the dragon. "Someone attacked me with a pointed stick!"

"It's called a lance," said Gale.

"My dear, I have seen many a lance in my day," Mittens said as she tried desperately to make her character jump but only succeeded in producing tiny bunny hops.

Gale laughed at the feeble display and tried to give her friend a few pointers. The dragon respawned yet again but was immediately beheaded. N00bMaster proceeded to play soccer with the avatar's bloody head. Then he stabbed it with a pike and stuck it in the ground as a monument to futility.

"Stupid N00bMaster! I swear he's just camping by the spawn site," said a frustrated Mittens.

"I don't think so. That guy is just really, really good. Maybe you need a tougher-sounding name?"

"What's wrong with 'RokCandy?'"

"It sounds a little frilly, don't you think?"

"No. It makes me sound like a killer."

"No, it makes you sound like a stripper," laughed Gale.

"You're just jealous that you didn't think of it first." Mittens sounded a little wounded as she said this. The game was new to her, and Gale knew that she was trying her best. She knew that she should be supportive of her friend. At least Mittens was showing an interest in something that Gale enjoyed.

"Well… not like a bad stripper. Like a stripper with a heart of gold. Like in the movies," Gale said, trying to sound supportive.

"… Now watch out for that guy on your right. He looks like he's gonna assault you with a stack of dollar bills!" laughed Gale. Supportive but not too supportive.

Things had been less tense between them since the visit with her parents. Gale took her mother's advice and tried to give Mittens the benefit of the doubt, provided she promised not to turn any more suitors into a fruit snack. When they got home after the visit, the girls had a heart-to-heart drawing up some boundaries and expectations. They resolved to be more respectful of each other's wishes and to limit their brownie intake to one night a week.

The other problem that remained was how Gale did not have the nerve to mention her renouncement to either of her parents. The princess was sure that they would back her whatever her wishes would be, but actually professing that wish was going to be a problem. She would hate to be a disappointment to them. But in protecting the king and queen, she would undoubtedly be a disappointment to herself.

Also hanging in the balance was her indecisiveness. The princess wasn't one hundred percent sure that she wanted to give up the throne. There were aspects of her post that she enjoyed. She loved to interact with the people. She enjoyed the casual manner in which she could act and speak. After all, until she became a "Royal," as the citizens of the kingdom called them, she was one of the common folk. Gale had no

Chapter 7

desire to change any of that. People's views of her would undoubtedly change the moment she made the announcement, or so she believed.

Plus, Gale had spent a lifetime under the scrutiny of the kingdom. Bad behavior was immediately reported to the king and began the chins wagging all over town. Think for a moment about something embarrassing that you may have done in your past. Maybe you ripped your pants or pooted while you sneezed in class like your narrator did in the fifth grade. Now imagine if it became headline news. "Princess Poots in Shop Class Nightmare, A Nation Mourns," or something to that effect.

Forget about trying something frisky or risky. Stealing her first kiss was a terrible and utterly unromantic disaster. While her friends were sneaking out at night and going to parties, or planning clandestine liaisons with a secret crush, Gale would not dare to stretch her boundaries for fear of getting caught and disgracing her family. It's stunting to a growing girl, and it was a focal point of her commandeering the tower. She had needed some alone time, not just from her family, but from her world.

"Are you hungry? I could use a sandwich or three," said Mittens, her tiny claws still fumbling with the controller.

"I'm still stuffed from last night's pizza. You can eat if you want."

"That pie was sooooo good! How many slabs did you have?"

"Three. Maybe four. Way too many if you ask me, and I'm paying for it," Gale said as she extended her stomach and gave it a robust slap.

"Three?!?" exclaimed a shocked dragon. "Those are rookie numbers."

"Why? What did you eat?"

"Eight."

"Eight pieces? You little piggy!" said Gale.

"No. Eight whole pizzas. Maybe eight and a half, I'm not sure. It was all kind of a blur."

"You're unbelievable," said Gale.

"I am a machine," said the dragon. "Maybe you can scoot off the couch and throw some salami on some bread for me, huh? You good kid." Mittens stayed fixated on the screen, trying to use her body language to guide her player, but her attempts were fruitless.

"Fine, I'll do it. Try not to die in the thirty seconds that I'm gone. And you have to hold the right button down to jump. Tapping it just makes you look like you're doing a river dance."

"Maybe I am. It's the dance of my people. We call it 'victory!'" said Mittens as her character caught a flying boulder with her face, killing her instantly.

"And keep an eye out for enemy trebuchets! They're easy to dodge if you'd stop dancing for a moment."

"Respect the dance, Princess. It's a newly added part of the dragon culture."

Gale pried herself from the comfort of the couch to make her way to the kitchen. The pizza still sat heavy on her stomach, and she envied her friend's cast iron gullet. Popping open the fridge, Gale pulled a package of salami out of the deli drawer and made a quick inspection of supplies. There were enough fixings for a decent taco dinner if the dragon hadn't gobbled up the chopped meat. A peek inside the freezer revealed a few pounds of beef, and she removed them to defrost for her Mexican snack to be prepared later.

As she was shuffling the bread and the salami together for her houseguest, the princess felt as if she was being watched. Everyone knows about the five senses that people have, but there are so many others. Sense of humor, sense of distance, and in this case, a sense of awareness. Something, somewhere, was amiss.

Slowly, she crept to the window to take a look outside. Seeing what was out there startled our heroine, and she let out a little gasp and clutched her chest. She shook her head in disbelief at her unfortunate circumstance. *I cannot wait for this to be over*, thought Gale. *I don't have to worry about a renouncement. At this rate, I'm either gonna have a heart attack or a nervous breakdown before I even get to the party.*

Because, dear readers, outside of her front window was standing a man. A huge man. A man that made Sir Chad's chauffeur look like one of Santa's elves. This guy was so big, the sun had to shine on him in shifts. So big that when he went swimming in the ocean, people waited until he was done using it. His shoulders had their own time zones. To give him a hug, you had to change planes in Atlanta. We're talking big.

On Gale's lawn stood Sir Flex-a-Lot. Not really sure if he was a prince. You can ask him if you wish, but I won't bother him. This man was a

Chapter 7

specimen of human form. An Adonis in Adidas. The veins in his arms were thick as rattlesnakes. His biceps were easily the size of Gale's waist. Legs as thick as redwoods. This guy hasn't been to a gym. He IS a gym.

Gale looked again and couldn't help but stare. You'd stare too if a mountain just walked onto your lawn. He had a deep tan and was sporting a tee-shirt with no sides or sleeves. A pair of purple gym shorts cut high on the thigh tried not to cut off the circulation to the rest of his body. Sneakers with no socks finished the ensemble. His thick blonde hair was cut in a fade that seemed to accentuate the muscles in his forehead. Coating his entire body was a sheen of sweat, cocoa butter, and tanning oil. In one hand, he held a warrior's helmet of polished steel sans face mask. In his other, a gallon jug of water.

"Mittens! Get a load of this lug," Gale said.

She hopped off the couch and peeked out the window.

"Wow! I see Scabs of Destiny 2 is out. Looks like you got the home version," said Mittens.

"Maybe he's a LARPer," said Gale. "You know, Live Action Role Playing."

"Whatever he's playing, I bet he's winning. He's a beast. What do you think, Princess?"

"I'm going to go take a peek under the hood. You stay here, OK? And please, behave yourself," warned Gale.

"Dragon's honor," Mittens replied, holding up three fingers. She waltzed into the kitchen to grab a sandwich as Gale made her way down the stairs. The princess had given up concerning herself with appearances since these guests were unannounced but regretted not brushing her teeth when she woke up. C'est la guerre.

Opening the door revealed Sir Flex. He was even bigger than expected, his muscles twitching and rippling this way and that. His every movement was a display to accentuate his chiseled physique. As Gale walked outside, Flex lifted the water jug to his lips to take a swig, producing a bicep larger in circumference than Gale's head.

"Hi, I'm Nightingale. Princess at large. Who might you be?"

"Princess, I am Sir Flex-a-Lot, and it is an honor to stand before you."

The Self-Sufficient Princess

Flex bowed deeply, making sure that his thighs were tight as he did. As he rose, he stretched in a manner that showed off his gargantuan back.

"Well, Flex, I was kind of hoping that news of my aversion to getting married had spread. I am not entertaining proposals at this time, so if you want to bounce, I fully understand."

Flex drank from his jug before responding, large glugs emitting from the bottle.

"Hadn't heard," he managed to mutter, wiping his mouth with his massive forearm.

Not exactly the response Gale was anticipating. She was hoping for a nice thank-you and a speedy exit but saw none coming. Instead, Flex just stood there, slack-jawed and glassy-eyed. She decided to take another whack at it.

"Well, now you have. I don't have any parting gifts or door prizes, so maybe we can call it a day?"

Another gulp from the water jug as Flex seemed unfazed by any of her polite attempts at escaping.

"Is there anything else that I can help you with, Mr. O-Lot?"

"Dear Princess, I would be honored to escort you somewhere nonetheless."

This was an answer that Gale wasn't prepared for, and her surprise was evident. She was sure that he would think he was wasting his time and hurry off into the woods. She wore pajama bottoms and an old tee shirt with a hole near the neck, which was not exactly her best look. Gale figured that this outfit would have made less of an impression, let alone getting a date offer. Yet there he stood. She really had to admire his tenacity.

"That's very kind of you. What do you have in mind?"

"I'm not sure."

Gale waited for a continuation of thought, but none was coming. Just a nice, thick, awkward pause.

"Really thought this out, huh?" asked Gale.

Here's a dating tip, guys. If you ask a young lady out, try to have a destination in mind. A movie or a meal, or some public event. It makes the girl feel special and can help her decide if she would like to join you. The princess was not feeling special at the moment.

Chapter 7

"I think me and you have a lot in common," grunted Flex.

"Such as?"

"I'm not sure," said Flex.

Another bark-covered, deep-grained awkward pause rolled through the glen. Gale did not want to assume that Sir Flex was just another stereotypical "dumb jock." He didn't look like a moron. He just seemed out of his element. Some guys just have a hard time talking to girls. She thought she'd help him with the details in her typical princess-like manner.

"Do you like movies?" she asked.

"Yes."

"Fantastic! What's your favorite?"

"I'm not sure. Maybe Pumping Iron. There's one with that guy who did that thing that time. I kinda liked that one."

She waited to see if he would ask about her favorite, but no such question passed through his lips. Just the application of more water to an obviously hydration-concerned Flex.

"Yeah, I like that one too. I also like the one with the girl who had that thing. It may have been the sequel."

"Never saw it."

"Do you have a favorite actor?"

"I like Arnold and Bautista and Johnson."

"Of course you do. How about books. Like any books?"

"Print is dead."

"That's one of my favorites as well," said Gale. Flex missed the joke. Instead, he took this time to apply more water, wiping his chin with his forearm when he was done. Another awkward pause caught the A Train through the meadow.

"Dear Princess, I would like to escort you somewhere nonetheless," Flex said finally.

"Oh! Ok… umm… I'm obviously not ready now. What are you doing tomorrow?"

Glug, glug, glug went the water bottle.

"I don't know. What day is tomorrow?" he asked.

"Tuesday."

"Chest. I do chest on Tuesday." Glug. Glug. Glug.

"Maybe when you're done?" asked Gale.

"I hit the gym around ten-thirty and don't finish until seven. I'm usually pretty beat by then." Glug. Glug. Glug.

"Wednesday?"

"Back. I do back on Wednesday."

"Thursday??" Gale said, still trying to give him a chance.

"Shoulders. You don't want to do shoulders too close to chest day. You see, the chest activates the shoulders, so they need to rest. Otherwise, you pull a delt. You work out, Princess?"

As Flex described the muscle workout, he pointed to and flexed each group that was being discussed. His colossal chest flapped around, and Gale was almost sure they were creating a breeze.

"Nope. Can't say that I do."

"You don't do crunches? Why would you even get out of bed unless you did two-hundred crunches?"

"I have no idea. What was I possibly thinking?" asked Gale.

"You should totally come to the gym. I could whip you into shape." Glug. Glug. Glug.

"You don't like the way I look now?"

"No, you look fine, I guess. I'm just saying that there's room for improvement. Maybe some squats to lift that butt and a triceps regimen to tighten up those bingo wings."

Bingo wings? thought Gale. *Slow down, cowboy! A girl can only take so many compliments.*

"Do you have any spare time that doesn't require a membership?" Gale asked.

"Hmm…" Glug. Glug. Glug.

Pause.

Glug. Glug. Glug.

Pause.

Glug. Glug. Glug. After some serious consideration, Flex came up with a solution.

"I could probably squeeze you in around eight forty-five on Sunday. I usually tan, but after, I'm free for a bit. Really, Princess, you should hit me up at the gym."

Chapter 7

Gale was understandably done with this dolt. She was not someone who needed to be "squeezed in" to someone's life. She deserved better. Granted, she wasn't very demanding and had her own life, but she would like to at least be a consideration. This side of beef had no time or thoughts for anyone but himself. That's a lifestyle choice that Gale did not want to be a part of, even if it came with a free water bottle and access to a sauna.

"Eight forty-five on a Sunday? Boy, you're really sweeping me off my feet. I wouldn't have pegged you as such a romantic. Are you thinking a late dinner?"

"I know this great place. Lots of protein and limited carbs. The guy who works there gives me extra grilled chicken on the house." Flex-a-Lot said, brimming with pride.

"Sounds enticing. Do I need to bring my own gallon jug, or will a trough be provided for me?" asked Gale.

"Funny. I like a girl with a sense of humor. No, they got plenty of water there. I think. I don't know. I usually bring my own."

"Well, a girl's got to stay hydrated."

"No lie," said Flex as he glugged down a few more gulps. "So what do you think, Princess? Do you think you'd like to give me a shot?"

"I'll tell you what. I appreciate you coming and asking me out. It was very sweet. I'm going to go upstairs now and pretend like this was enjoyable. Is that OK?"

"So, that's a no, then?"

"Wow. You shouldn't waste your talents at the gym. You should be scouring the earth for crimes and mysteries to solve. You've got a knack. Anyway, have a good night, Sir Lacks-a-Lot."

"That's fine. I get it. That's a hard no. Now, if you would show me this dragon I keep hearing about, I'd like to get down to business." Flex stood there, flexing and stretching. He was doing lunges and twisting at the hips.

Gale stopped dead in her tracks.

"What are you doing?" asked Gale.

"Getting ready to fight the dragon. I don't want to pull a glute."

"But I've already said no. You don't need to fight anyone," said Gale.

Happiness is fleeting, folks. For a brief instant, Gale thought she was successful in retiring without any drama. She had handled a slightly awk-

85

ward situation on her own, and no harm came to anyone. If only this mountain would make his way back to the range, it would be over. But instead, he stayed there, stretching and cracking his knuckles.

"Sorry, Princess. I came here to woo a princess and fight her dragon. The first part is over. Now on to the main course," said Flex.

"I really don't think that's a good idea. Have you ever seen a dragon before?"

"Yeah," said Flex. "I've seen some blurry pictures online. No big deal. Can you go get him, or do you need me to find him for you?"

"I don't think you understand. She's a bit busy at the moment. Maybe come back in a few decades?"

"Cool. Chick dragon. I'm totally into the whole feminist movement thing."

"Yeah, I figured that when you said the word 'Chick.' Really, though, can't you give a girl a break?"

"Sorry, sweetheart. No can do."

Gale would need to hammer her point home. This dope couldn't catch a hint with both hands.

"Listen, stupid. She breathes fire. She is about two tons of molten terror. I'm asking you to please just leave."

Gale did not know how to get the information through this guy's muscle-bound skull. Maybe if she poured her words into a gallon jug, he would drink it. He knows she's not interested in anything he has to offer, but he still stays. Now he is insisting on fighting her dragon. Her friend, the dragon. Again, Gale felt her world spinning out of control.

"Flex, please. Just let it go. No need to prove anything to me or anyone else. I'm asking you as a princess. Just go on home. I'm sure there's a lonely weight bench out there missing the warmth of a man of your caliber."

"Princess, this story ends with me fighting a dragon. Now, either go get her, or I will."

That's when she heard it. That telltale sound of sails unfurling. Gale looked up to the sky in time to see the sun disappear. Her heart sat firmly in her throat.

Chapter 8

In the land of This-and-That, with a rush of air and the shuttering of trees, Wrathnarok landed with her patented earth-shaking thud. The dragon was in full battle mode and lowered her head to size up her foe. This was no game like the display at the castle. Wrathnarok's eyes were fixed on her target with an icy golden glare.

No matter how large and impressive a man Flex-a-Lot was, he was nothing in comparison to the full-grown dragon. Gale watched in horror as Wrathnarok approached Flex, eyes narrow and set. Her enormous tail raked against the trees sending leaves cascading in her wake. Claws were bared, and teeth were revealed beneath a hideous grin that almost turned Gale's stomach.

"You rang?" asked Wrathnarok.

"Now that's what I'm talking about," said Flex.

The princess wanted to shout, but no sound came out. Every hair on her neck stood at attention as the dragon circled their visitor. Still, Gale refused to panic. When confronted with a seemingly winless situation, it's best to take a moment to assess. The Marines have a saying: Improvise. Adapt. Overcome. These are wise words whether you're a Marine or not. It also applies if you're just a headstrong princess.

Retreating a bit from the vicious maw of his foe, Flex pulled off his tee shirt and tossed it aside. If anyone could explain to me why some guys peel their shirts off before fighting, I'd like to hear it. Just contact the publisher and send the answer 'care of the narrator.' I have never taken my shirt off in a fight. I don't even take it off in the pool. I'm a bit overweight, and no one needs to be subjected to such harsh punishment as seeing me topless.

Gale needed to think fast. She saw that she could not control the situation, so she opted to control her friend instead.

"Rocco! Alive!" she yelled at Wrathnarok.

"Hey! You called me Rocco!" said the dragon. "Much better than Mittens, don't you think?"

"You told me I can't call you Mittens when you're big and angry."

"True. You are supposed to refer to me as Wrathnarok, Harbinger of Doom…"

"Yeah, still not a good time for introductions. We do have company, you know."

"Well, I refuse to do battle with someone that I haven't been introduced to."

"Fine," said an exasperated Gale. "Sir Flex-a-Lot, this is Wrathnarok."

Flex stood there, confused as ever. He took another swig from his water jug and tried to figure out what was happening. The words finally seeped into his concrete head, and slowly Flex began to laugh.

"Wrathnarok? What kind of a name is that?" laughed Flex.

"It's an old Gaelic name. It means 'the last thing you'll ever see,'" said the dragon.

"No, it doesn't," said Gale.

"I assure you that it does," countered the dragon.

"No, it doesn't. It's German for 'not gonna eat anyone,'" Gale said firmly, hands on hips.

"How about it's Romanian for 'mind your own business.'"

"Maybe it's Russian for 'sleeps on the lawn?'"

"No. It's Finnish for 'these 'Gale' force winds are starting to irritate me.'"

"Maybe it's Swedish for 'is this a game to you? Or Italian for 'make your own stupid sandwiches!'" shouted Gale.

Chapter 8

Flex saw this bickering back and forth as an opportunity to make his move. Quickly, he leaped onto Wrathnarok's neck, pulling and punching in a flurry of mighty fists. He tried to wrap his massive arms around the dragon to choke her but to no avail. Sitting upright, Flex pounded the back of Wrathnarok's head with blow after mighty blow. The sounds of each punch echoing through the glen.

The dragon pointed at her back and looked at Gale.

"Do I have something on me?" she asked.

"Other side," Gale corrected.

"Oh, sorry," said the dragon as she plucked the man from her back like the dirty socks from the couch. She gently placed him on the ground before her.

"Had enough?" asked a winded Flex.

"Pal, if you hit me, and I find out about it, I'm gonna get very upset," was the answer.

Flex reared back with a right hook and punched the dragon squarely in her eye. Then he grabbed hold of some beard hair with both hands and yanked it right out of Wrathnarok's chin. In the blink of an eye, the mighty dragon took wing and flew around the tower, getting higher and higher until she was finally out of sight. Gale and Flex stood and squinted upward at the sky, watching the dragon disappear.

Grabbing his water jug from the lawn, Flex sat down and took a few much-needed gulps.

"Well," said Flex, catching his breath. "I guess she couldn't take it. I don't see what the big deal was about. She wasn't so bad."

"Yeah, about that. Sir, I'm going to ask you to stow away your tray table and return your seat to its upright position. Have a nice flight. Buh-Bye, now," Gale said in a condescending tone and gave Flex a condescending wave.

"What's that supposed to mean?" Flex asked.

He never saw it coming.

A streak of red flashed past the princess, and just like that, Flex was gone. Wrathnarok flew him high above the Woods of Nevermore, and as she watched them sail away, she hoped that her dragon would heed her warning. With any luck, she would return in a moment after dropping

89

off her opponent in a cactus patch or something of that sort. Gale went back upstairs and wondered how the chopped meat was defrosting.

Honestly, she had done all that she could to defuse the situation. Her instructions were firm and pointed. The rest was up to Mittens. Either she would value their friendship enough to respect the princess' wishes, or Gale would be done with her. Her dragon would either return with a story that didn't involve any chewing, or she would turn her opponent into beef-on-Flex.

Opening the fridge did not inspire her as she hoped it would, but she saw that she had the defrosted ground beef that needed to be utilized. Did dragons eat tacos? She had no idea, but she thought she'd brown the beef anyway. As she was cooking, she waited patiently for Mittens.

Time passed slowly, and she caught herself racing to the window at the slightest sound outside. The meat was finished and placed in a bowl and back into the fridge. Still no sign of the dragon. A wave of doubt started at Gale's toes and slowly made its way to her head. She couldn't control a dragon. She couldn't even fold a fitted bed sheet, no matter how hard she tried.

An hour passed, and then another. Gale found herself nervously cleaning her tower, wiping off counters, and gathering laundry to be washed. She cleaned her bathroom, which was a chore that she dreaded, but she would do anything to keep her mind off the thought of Flex-a-Lot becoming another tossed peanut into her friend's mouth. She played over the day, again and again, looking for answers.

Surely, she was not responsible for whatever happened to Flex. He had brought this upon himself. Gale had practically begged him to leave while he still had the chance. She wished she knew why boys needed to fight to prove something. It just seemed silly to her. Does that make them think that they are more of a man? Does it prove that they can protect her if the need arises? It seemed barbaric and childish, and she would not be a part of it. If Mittens—sorry, Rocco—had gone against her wishes, that would be the end of their relationship.

Flipping through her phone, Gale tried not to concentrate on her missing dragon. Nothing could hold her interest for long. Silly memes and short videos usually kept her occupied for hours, but today her heart

CHAPTER 8

wasn't in it. Scrolling through her contacts for someone to talk to was fruitless. She wanted to talk to someone, but no one drew her interest. She checked online for PizzaBoi, but he had signed off of Scabs. Frustrated, she tossed the controller onto her carpet.

"Reflexa? Are you busy?" asked the princess.

"Never too busy for you," replied the mirror with a chime. "What's on your mind?"

"I'm sure you heard everything that happened out there."

"Oh, are you referring to your dragon scooping another suitor into the sky and you freaking out wondering if he was going to be eaten? That happening?"

"Yes, that's the one."

"Nope. I didn't hear a thing," said the Mirror.

"Let's pretend you did. What am I going to do if she ate this guy?"

"Well," said the mirror, "There is a good chance that something that big would get caught in her throat. Maybe she won't be able to swallow Flex, and then your crisis is over."

"Please. She just admitted to drilling out eight whole pizzas and is still hungry. Flex wouldn't be much more than a cheese puff to her."

"Is she your friend?" asked the mirror.

"I think so."

"Then trust her."

"I don't know if I can," said the princess. Her eyes reflected her pain to the mirror.

"If you can't trust her, then she's not your friend. Mittens gave you her word, and that should be enough until proven otherwise."

"But she's already betrayed me once."

"And you gave her a second chance, right?" Reflexa asked.

"I did."

"Then stick to your word. If she's your friend, then she'll stick to hers."

"But trust is something you earn. I can't keep giving her chances while the prince population ends up as Meals-on-Wheels."

"Yes, that's true. You're giving her a chance to redeem herself and fix her mistake. She knows the consequences. Let's see how she does."

Gale wasn't pleased with this response. She was hoping for a little support, not a life lesson. All in all, she knew that the mirror was right. If she decided to give the dragon another chance, then any result would be on her. If Mittens crossed the line, then it was she who gave her the opportunity to do so. A princess never goes against her word, no matter how scary it all may be. She would just have to wait and see what happens.

"You know," said the mirror, "I used to know someone who was owned by an evil witch. She couldn't be trusted in the least, but still, she hung on the wall and hoped that one day, the witch would come to her senses. She never did. The witch was cruel and vain and mean as a snake."

"What ever happened to her? The witch, I mean."

"As the story goes, she was chased off a cliff by a bunch of height-impaired miners. Her corpse left to rot among the jagged rocks below. But I heard something different."

"Oh? What story did you hear? Spill tea!" demanded Gale.

"I heard she escaped to Los Altos and hooked up with a guy named Jobs to start a communications company."

"Really?"

"Well, she DID have a thing for apples..." said the mirror with a laugh.

"Stop! You're lying!" laughed Gale.

"Who knows if I am? I guess you're going to have to trust me," said the mirror. With that, Reflexa chimed off.

Stupid mirror, always trying to make me laugh when I don't want to, thought Gale. She sat on the couch with a smile on her face which claimed a victory for Reflexa. The princess let the advice that she was given roll around in her head. The mirror had a point, and it was not lost on her. Now all she had to do was to wait for Mittens to return, and she would see how applicable it was.

As if on cue, there was a loud whoosh that circled the tower. A tremendous thump outside shook her pictures once again as Wrathnarok landed in the glen. Gale was going to have to discuss reentry procedures with her dragon before the entire tower came crashing down.

"Anybody home?" asked Wrathnarok as she peered into the castle window.

Chapter 8

"I'll be right down," said Gale as she walked down the stairs. Her heart was heavy with fear. She had no desire to have this conversation, but she was a princess and would not shirk her responsibility. Gale let out a heavy sigh and turned the doorknob.

With an ominous creak, the heavy wooden door slowly swung open. In its absence stood her tiny dragon, pink and fluffy with little mittens for hands. The dragon's eyes were happy and hopeful, and she greeted Gale with a warm smile. There were no signs of malfeasance or evidence of a Flex burrito clinging to a whisker. Still, the princess needed to be sure. And to do that, she would have to slight her friend.

"Hey..." said Gale, her tone a little wary.

"Hey, Princess! Man, what a wild time! That Flex was a heckuva handful, let me tell you."

"A handful, right? Not a bellyful?" asked Gale.

"No, stupid. Just a handful. I promised that I wouldn't eat him." Mittens was obviously put off by the question. She looked Gale dead in the eyes and kept her face contorted in a stern scowl.

"Still, just to be sure, let me smell your breath."

"Really? Are we really doing this right now?" asked the dragon. Mittens stood there shaking her head in disbelief at the audacity of the question.

"Mittens, I've been a nervous wreck about this. I tried to get you not to fight."

"Yes, I know. Then the Incredible Bulk socked me right in my eyehole. You didn't expect me to back down, did you?"

"No. But..." Gale was feeling uneasy about the whole line of questioning. She wished she had just let Mittens inside and listened to her story. The princess was determined to stand her ground here. She needed to feel comfortable around her friend, and if this was the only way she could go about it, then so be it.

"But what? What, Gale? What did you expect me to do?"

"I don't know. There's no manual or video that I can search and find out what to do. I'm kinda playing it by ear. This is my first encounter with a carnivore, so I'm at a loss here."

"Carnivore? Really? I'm here solely to protect you, Gale. That dope drew first blood. He needed a good thrashing, and I happily handed it to him. HE came at ME. I wasn't the aggressor. HE was." Mittens was thoroughly agitated by now, and Gale wasn't about to back down.

"Yes, it was very rude of him to pluck out the hair of your chinny-chin-chin. I agree that he needed a lesson in dragon etiquette. But I need to know we are all on the same page here."

"And my word isn't good enough? Don't you trust me?"

"I did. And you gobbled it up. That, along with an extremely skinny millennial."

"Listen, that's not what you think it is," said the dragon.

"Doesn't matter. It's in the past. But this is right here, right now. I have to know."

That's the thing about trust. It takes time to make and a split second to break. Sometimes there is no coming back. It takes a special type of person to give someone a second chance after they've lost trust in them. Gale was a special person. She was strong enough to try again, but she was not a fool to be taken advantage of either. Best to be sure.

"I really thought we were past this, Gale."

"I am. We are. I trust you. Your track record is impeccable. Now let me smell your breath."

With a heavy sigh and a look of defeat, Mittens approached the princess. She took her friend by the hands and opened her mouth for inspection. Gale leaned in for a quick whiff, and when she did, Mittens let loose with a belch that nearly singed the poor girl's eyebrows.

"Eww! What is that? Garlic?"

"Yes. Flex's mom made fresh peppers and sausages and invited me in. It seemed rude to say no after I dropped her half-naked son on her roof."

"You nearly set fire to my nose hairs! I'm gonna taste that for a week! Uff! It's all up in me!" said the princess rubbing her nose and mock coughing.

"Serves you right. I told you I'd behave."

Gale detected no hint of cocoa butter or tanning oil and immediately felt bad for doubting her. She wrapped her arms around Mittens and gave her a squeeze.

"You little witch. You planned that all along, didn't you?" asked Gale after she pulled out of the embrace.

Chapter 8

"I've told you before. You're not my first princess. Try to remember that, and we'll be fine."

"Fine. I will try, but you're still a smelly jerk. Come upstairs and tell me what happened," said Gale, and they walked back inside.

They plopped themselves onto the couch as Mittens recanted the story.

"Ok, so I swooped down, grabbed Flexo, and took off."

"Yeah, I saw," said Gale.

"Well, wouldn't you know that the kid never stopped fighting me? He's pounding at my ankles, and I'm almost sure he bit me. I may need a tetanus shot. I hope you're insured."

"Fully. Keep going"

"The guy was relentless. He kept pummeling my feet and ankles. I could hardly hold onto him since he was such a greasy mess. Way too much oil and butter. The guy was a walking cholesterol ad. So, I took him to the beach and rolled him into the sand for a bit to coat him for a better grip. He looked like a chicken nugget when I was done with him. I thought he would run away, but the kid had spunk."

"You let him go on the beach, and he didn't leave?"

"Leave? He came at me again! This clown grabs a hold of my tail, and he's trying to swing me around. Can you believe it? That guy is tenacious but a little delusional. I let him play with my tail for a bit, then scooped him up again and took off. Scared the snot out of two kids digging for sand crabs by the water."

"No pain, no gain, I always say. Then you took him home?" asked Gale.

"Yup. He finally gave up when I dropped him on the roof. He lives with his mom outside of Tourin. I was going to come right back, but his mom came outside and thanked me for dropping him off. She invited me in, so I had to be polite, right? Plus, the smell of her sauce was amazing. How could I say no?"

"Weren't you worried he'd attack you after you shrunk down?"

"He mentioned something about it, but his mom smacked him with a wooden spoon, so he behaved. That guy really loves his mom, and she adores him. She cooks, she has a cool new trebuchet… She even paints! I saw a painting she made of a white-haired guy in a boat with two dogs. Very sweet family."

"Nice that you made friends. Meanwhile, I scrubbed the whole house while I worried that you turned the guy into a plate of muscles in white wine sauce," said Gale.

"Gale, I gave my word to you. What kind of friend would I be if I didn't keep my word?"

"You're a dragon. You have some kind of sworn oath to protect the princess, blah, blah, blah. I honestly didn't know what to think. I wanted to give you the benefit of the doubt, but it scared me a little," Gale said. "Do you think you can forgive me?"

"Can you forgive me for the garlic burps that I predict are coming in the future? The sauce was incredible but heavy on the spices." Mittens stuck out her tongue to feign indigestion.

"We'll see," said Gale. She was so relieved that Flex-a-Lot was safe that she would have forgiven her for just about anything.

Flex was harmless but not the type of guy that Gale would be interested in. Guys like that are focused on themselves and don't really care about anyone else. Not a redeeming quality for Gale to consider. A princess doesn't need to be the center of attention, but some attention would be nice. With his mom and his workouts occupying his time, Flex had none to spare.

Adding to that, a guy that you date shouldn't make you feel bad about yourself. He needs to support your lows and celebrate your highs. Sure, Gale wasn't in tip-top shape, but she liked who she was. Acceptance for a girl is tough; self-acceptance is tougher. Gale knew she would never be the prettiest in the land, the smartest, or even the funniest or most popular. She was just happy being Gale. She liked being Gale.

"Oh, I nearly forgot," said Mittens. A pink puff of smoke appeared in her hand, and when it cleared, there was a stack of cards wrapped in a rubber band. "Flex said to give these to you."

"How do you do that?" asked Gale. She had been curious about it since the scene with the glasses and the paper in Chapter One.

"Do what?"

"Make stuff appear and disappear."

"When you play Scabs of Destiny, do you carry everything all at once, or do you hit a button to bring up your inventory?"

"I hit a button."

Chapter 8

"Well, just like that, but with smoke and panache."

Gale took the cards. They were day passes to a gym in Tourin. A rather large stack of day passes. She believed that Flex was trying to send her a message.

"Did he have anything to say?" asked Gale.

"Something about lunges and glutes. And he said to stay hydrated."

"I'll make a note of it. You should have dropped him on his head instead of on the roof." She said as she chucked the cards into the trash.

The nerve of some people! she thought. Take some advice from your friendly neighborhood narrator: Never let anyone shame how you look. Life is too short to worry about what people think of you. Just ask Chad the Amazing. Oh, wait. You can't. Moving on.

"Since you already ate, I'm going to make some tacos."

"Soft shell or hard shell?" asked Mittens

"I have both. Hey, you just had dinner! You're still hungry?"

"I could eat. Really had a good workout, Princess. Was targeting the abs then I realized that I didn't have any, so I moved on to my glutes and delts. Tomorrow I'm gonna hit my flaps and folds. Then my chips and dips."

Mittens stood there stretching in an exaggerated manner that brought a chuckle out of the princess. She joined her by doing lunges while shouting things like "Ooo! Feel the burn! Sweet set!" and other silly gym rhetoric. They stopped and fell on the floor laughing, hoping that nothing important was torn like a hamstring or, worse yet, her pants.

In the land of This-and-That, all was well for a moment. The friends were friends again, their tacos were crunchy and cheesy, and no one was turned into a snack. They drank way too many energy drinks because they learned that you got to stay hydrated and discovered that dragon burps mixed with garlic were something otherworldly.

To celebrate Mittens' restraint in handling her foe and the subsequent victory that ensued, Gale taught Mittens how to play Dummikub after dinner, and although the tiles were a bit cumbersome for her little claws, they had a good time. Afterward, Gale asked Reflexa to play some dance music, and the two partied into the wee hours of the morning, striking a pose and walking on sunshine.

Chapter 9

In the land of This-and-That, our heroine has just about had it. The poor Princess Nightingale has had just about enough of the unwanted visitations, and so had a dire need to relax and decompress for a bit. She grabbed a book from the shelf in her room, threw on some jean shorts and a bikini top, and announced that she was heading to the beach.

After sending out an invite on Gracebook to some friends, Gale put her hair up in a ponytail and started packing a straw bag for the day: the book, a small blanket, magazines, sunblock, water bottles, some towels, and a few schnacks in case the dragon felt peckish. After a quick peek in Reflexa to make sure she looked presentable, Gale slid on her flip-flops and grabbed her sunglasses.

"Ready?" she asked.

"One sec," said the dragon.

Mittens disappeared in a puff of smoke, and when it finally dissipated, she stood wearing a large floppy straw hat, a pair of sunglasses, and a floral mu-mu. Gale couldn't help herself, and she let go with a slight giggle. Mittens was adorable in her new outfit, but she could see that her friend was a bit self-conscious about her appearance.

"Is the hat too much?" she asked.

"Absolutely not."

"Are the missing whiskers noticeable?"

"Not at all. Why the sudden concern for how you look?" asked Gale.

"It's the first time meeting your friends, and I don't want to be an embarrassment."

"You would never," Gale said as she leaned down and gave her a reassuring peck on the cheek. "But one of these days, you're going to have to share your inventory list. It's quite impressive."

"I told you, I've been around for a very long time. I've acquired thousands of things over the years."

"Ok, then what's the weirdest thing you've got?"

"This," said Mittens, and a small puff of smoke appeared in her hand, revealing a strange moss-covered item with three handles.

"What is that?" asked Gale. Gale took the item and looked it over.

"I never found out. I stole it from some talking cat back in the seventies. I've been trying to figure it out since then. All this time, and I still have no idea. I've been using it as a tree ornament."

"Well, I'm stumped. Reflexa, want to take a crack at it?"

The mirror chimed to life.

"I'm sorry, there are no results for your search," Reflexa said.

"Thanks anyway, but I've tried everything. It's one of life's great mysteries, like why they are called blueberries when they're neither blue nor berry. 'Tis puzzlement," said Mittens with a shrug.

"Well, you weren't lying. That is pretty weird. Did you ever think of asking the cat?"

"Sure, that would go great. 'Excuse me, sir, but can you identify this thing that I stole from you decades ago?' I'd rather not get the cops involved at this point."

"Is that true about blueberries?" Gale asked, handing the bizarre item back to Mittens.

"Probably. Ready to go?" Mittens poofed away her strange item, and off they went to the beach.

On the way, Gale's phone was blowing up with disappointing news. No one was able to join them at the beach. Four friends were working, two had other plans, and the last one, Wendy, was going out with her

Chapter 9

new boyfriend and her little brothers. Gale was hoping that all the news about the suitors wasn't scaring them away. She also hoped that their refusals had nothing to do with the dragon. News spreads fast in a small kingdom, and people can be afraid of the darndest things.

"Well, that was Wendy. She's not coming either," said Gale with a hint of disappointment in her voice. "I was sure she would come. She's all wrapped up in hanging out with her boyfriend and his friends lately."

"Are they a bad crowd, these boys?" asked Mittens.

"Nah. They just seem lost. I don't worry about Wendy, though. She's got a good head on her shoulders. She wouldn't be bringing her little brothers on the date if something seemed off. She is super protective of them."

"She sounds darling. I can't wait to meet her," said Mittens.

"Someday soon, I hope."

It did seem a little strange that no one was able to hit the beach with them. Gale realized that since Mittens arrived, her friends seemed to vanish on her. Sure, she'd get a text occasionally, but they were sparse and short-worded. She wondered if they would be boycotting her birthday as well, but she quickly pushed that idea away and tried not to be hypersensitive. Unless...

The pair made their way down a path that was fitted with wooden planks so that navigation over the sand wouldn't be a chore. It led them through a clearing in the tall grass and between two sand dunes that revealed the sea in all its glory. Sunlight sparkled on the waves as they quietly lapped at the shoreline. The beach was deserted, except for a few families who had set up camp a little further down the beach. Gale and Mittens walked for a bit until they found a nice spot and then set up camp themselves.

After laying down the blanket, they made the obligatory walk to check on the water temperature. As tradition holds, one must stick a toe or foot into the water, make the "Brrrrr!" noise, and then scurry back to the blanket. Mittens had the honor of declaring the water arctic and unfit for habitation. Gale slathered herself with sunblock because nobody likes a lobster-red princess, especially the fair-skinned Gale.

They sat on the blanket, discussing her friends and boys, her party, and dragon stuff. The princess could feel the stress leaving her body the warmer she got. Soon, she forgot about the disappointment she suffered when her friends declined her invitation. Mittens was plenty of company. Truth be told, Gale would have been fine even if she had been here alone. The sound of the waves was a welcome distraction, and she soon threw a towel over her face and took a little nap. Mittens joined her shortly after. Go outside occasionally, dear readers. There is a whole world filled with excitement waiting just for you, even if it's just a nap.

After a short while, the sound of children stirred the princess and her dragon. Laughter and shouting accompanied the kids as they ran across the sand, pointing at the horizon. Gale sat up to see what the commotion was all about. Squinting, she shielded her eyes from the afternoon sun and saw what appeared to be a galleon anchored in the distance.

"Want me to take a look?" asked a drowsy Mittens.

"No. Sit tight and let me text my dad."

It was odd for a strange ship to be parked outside the kingdom. Usually, the sea was dotted with fishing vessels and some sports crafts. This ship was neither and Gale wanted to make sure that the powers that be were aware of its arrival.

Any word on a ship in the sea behind my tower? I don't recognize the colors, she asked.

He replied quickly:

Not to worry, sweetheart. He has been cleared and is on a sightseeing run. He claims that there is treasure nearby and kindly asked permission to look... Love you!

Gale showed the text to Mittens, who immediately sheltered her eyes beneath a towel. From this distance, it was hard to make out too many details from the ship, but Gale saw its sails were a shimmering silver. It was a large enough vessel and quite magnificent. Galleons were primarily warships, but Gale saw no signs of cannons apparent. Off the stern flew a few flags that she didn't recognize. What she did see was a rowboat making its way to shore.

"Wakey, wakey! Looks like we're being boarded," she said, giving Mittens a nudge.

Chapter 9

Frustrated, Mittens threw her towel aside and looked out over the sea. She saw the rowboat getting closer: one man was rowing, another standing in a typical pirate pose, one foot raised on a seat, hands on hips. He was headed directly toward them.

"Pirates?" asked Mittens.

"Nope, Dad said they were clean. They are on a sightseeing mission, remember? Something tells me that we are the sight they are seeing."

"And you, my dear, are the nearby treasure," Mittens said with a smile.

"This is getting monotonous," said Gale. "I just wanted a little break from the action for a while. Maybe we should pack up and head on home."

"He'll just follow you. Besides, after yesterday I don't believe that you are capable of hiding from a confrontation."

"Good point. Neither a coward…"

"Nor a fool," said Mittens. "You ready, Princess?"

"As ready as I'll ever be," she replied with a sigh.

"Ahoy!" yelled the standing man from the rowboat. He wasn't far off from the shore, and the kids were all shouting ahoy in return. He smiled and waved at them, and the kids ran toward the rowboat. The man who was posing leaped from the boat with a grandiose flourish and splashed his way to the shore. When he reached the kids, he greeted them warmly and shook their hands. His hand went into a leather pouch that was tied around his waist and retrieved a gold coin for each of them. As the kids ran back to their parents to show them their bounty, he waved at the parents as well.

Gale watched this unfold before her, and it warmed her heart a little. It was nice to finally see someone who held the same ideals that she did. He was kind and generous and not at all like the Chad or the Flex. She had a quick change of heart and saw no immediate reason to be unkind or rude. If things went sideways, she could always revert to her cynical ways. For now, she would be a princess.

"My dearest Nightingale," he said, removing his hat and gave a deep bow. As he did, he gave her body a quick glance. Remembering she was in a bikini top, she embarrassingly draped her towel over her shoulders to cover up.

"With whom do I have the pleasure of meeting?" she responded with a deep curtsey.

The Self-Sufficient Princess

"I am Captain Anton Neal of the good ship Maecenas, traveler of the high seas, and I am at your service." The captain reached and took her hand. Looking her in the eyes, he gave it a gentle kiss. This sparked the interest of one nearby dragon, who let out a little growl.

"Calm down," said Gale. "You'll have to excuse my dragon. She is a little protective of me."

"As she should be. The Great Wrathnarok, is it? I would expect nothing less of a legendary dragon such as yourself. I have brought you a gift, and if it would please the princess, I would like to present it to you."

With a snap of his fingers, the man who was rowing the boat struggled to pull up a large chest. He placed it at the shore's edge, for it was much too heavy to carry. On his belt was a key that he used to unlock the chest and opened it to reveal that it was filled with gold coins.

"I hope that this meager offering will grant me a moment of your princess' time," the captain said.

"Have at it!" said Mittens as she ran toward the chest, the floppy hat falling off as she sped away.

Dear readers, although the stories of dragons have changed throughout time, the one constant is their love of gold. They can never have enough. The only gift that would have pleased Mittens more than a chest of gold would have been two chests of gold. You get the point. Carrying on.

The captain smiled as he watched the dragon grab some coins from the chest and rub them all over her body. Yummy happy noises emitted from Mittens as she sat and played and bit and ogled the treasure. The other man, we'll call him Smee for lack of a better name, reached toward the dragon only to have his hand slapped away as Mittens closed the lid, saying things like "rich" and "happy miser." She hugged the chest tightly and tried to keep an eye on the captain.

The captain, I must say, was making a fantastic first impression. At first glance, he was gorgeous. Dressed in brown leather boots that rode above his knees and brown leather pantaloons that billowed above the boots. A brown leather vest decorated with gold buttons and braids. Beneath was hiding a white ruffled shirt that was open as far as the vest would allow. His face was profoundly tan and sported a well-groomed

Chapter 9

Van Dyke beard speckled with some gray. His rich blue eyes hid beneath the brim of his leather tricorn hat.

Our princess was in awe at the ease with which he carried himself. The smooth, comfortable manner in which he spoke to her. His graciousness and generosity were a welcome change from the usual men her age. He was mature and elegant, yet something in Gale's gut still wasn't convinced that he was all he was cracked up to be. He seemed a little *too* mature.

"Brave captain, I must ask. Are you aware of my birthday party in a few days?"

"Indeed I am. Therefore, I have set sail to the Kingdom of This-and-That. My dear princess is turning eighteen."

"Yes, I am," said Gale. "Since you already know how old I am, might I inquire as to the captain's age?"

"Age, my sweet, is but a number."

"It is, I agree. I'm just curious as to how big a number that might be. You see, though the lines around your eyes tell a tale, the flecks of gray in your beard tell a story. I just wonder how long a novel that story is."

"It's true. The sea has stolen my youthly appearance from me. The wind and the saltwater age a man before his time. Surely you won't hold that against me."

"Not at all," said Gale. He was skirting the question, and this fact was not lost on her.

"Princess, I have heard that you are not looking for a husband at this time. Bad news travels quickly from port to port. I must say that I was a bit disappointed to hear this. Now that I have met you, I am saddened tenfold."

"It's true. I have no desire to be wed just yet. This doesn't mean that we can't continue this conversation. I trust you will be around for the party?"

"I wouldn't miss it. Have you decided who will be your escort for the gala? I'm sure every man in the kingdom has asked for the privilege."

"Captain, you'd be surprised," she admitted.

"They are but fools and children. Don't let them upset you. Some men wouldn't know beauty if they held it in their hands. 'Better a diamond with a flaw than a pebble without.' Do you know who said that?"

"Fred Flintstone?" she joked.

He caught it and laughed heartily. Maybe a little too heartily for Gale's liking.

"No. It was Confucius. He was a very wise old man."

"Ah. An old schoolmate of yours, perhaps?" asked Gale.

"Hardly. He was a Chinese philosopher," said the captain.

"You seem very well-read."

"I've been around the world. I could teach you many things. A woman of your brilliance is wasting away here. You need to go out and share your wonder with the world."

Gale would be the first to tell you that she may have swooned a little. His voice had become soft and seductive. She always dreamed of seeing the world. It was one of the things she wanted to do before she wound up ruling the kingdom. She occasionally spoke to her friends about it, even planning imaginary trips and posting travel ideas on Gracebook.

Mittens and the one we call Smee had taken to playing with the children on the beach. The dragon was building sandcastles, and Smee was letting one of the younger boys sit in the rowboat and pretend they were sailing the high seas. Captain Anton Neal went to retrieve a few tan-colored bottles from the rowboat and carried them back toward Gale, who had returned to the blanket.

"May I join you?" he asked, ever so politely.

"Of course," she said and patted a place next to her for him to sit.

He popped the cork on the bottle and offered it to Gale.

"Care to try?" he asked.

"What is it?"

"Only one way to find out. But I assure you that it's breathtaking."

Instead, Gale reached into her bag and took out a water bottle. Ladies, receiving a free drink from a stranger is never a good idea.

"Thanks, but I'll stick to water. I have recently learned the value of staying hydrated."

"Suit yourself," said the captain as he took a mighty swig of the mystery liquid. The sweet smell of his breath indicated that the contents of his bottle were something fruity and alcoholic. It seemed odd that he would offer her something to drink, knowing that she was not yet old enough to enjoy.

Chapter 9

The captain and the princess spent hours chatting. Well, more to the point, Gale chatted, and the captain drank and asked questions. The hours revealed many common threads between them. They enjoyed the same music, the same movies, and even the same flavor of ice cream. Each time that the captain mentioned a favorite interest or food or location, Gale found that she was fond of it as well. They were building quite a connection, and the princess began opening up to the captain about her doubts about the future and her responsibilities as a princess. He was so understanding and supportive that Gale could see herself spending time with him again.

"You know, you don't have to rule the kingdom if you don't want to," said the captain.

"Why would you say that?"

"Well, you said that you may have reservations about it. You're not destined for anything. You can choose what stars to follow if you wish."

"I have thought about renouncing my throne if I'm being completely honest. I have been raised to be the next queen, and it's a little overwhelming sometimes," admitted Gale.

"Have you discussed this with your parents?"

"Of course not. They would never understand," said Gale.

This, dear readers, was a bold-faced lie. Of course, she had discussed this with her parents though she hasn't yet made a formal decision. Though it was not becoming of a princess to hide the truth, in this instance, she was doing so to feel the captain out. The queen had always told her to trust her gut, and something was certainly strange. Captain Anton was very suave and charming. He was saying all the right things, making her feel at ease. It all seemed a little too good for her liking, so Gale lowered her guard just enough to get a good bead on her new friend.

"Captain?"

"Call me Anton."

"Anton, I must confess. I would love to travel the world. I dream about seeing so many places, but I would hate to disappoint my parents."

"Nonsense. Your parents just don't understand you. Maybe they don't know the real you. They are caught up in their old-fashioned ways and can't see what a wonderful woman you've become. You're filled with independence and a passion for life. They're old and have lived their lives. They have made their choices. Shouldn't you be free to make yours as well?"

Anton placed his hand gently on top of hers. His skin was rough from years on the sea, and Gale found it appealing. All during his speech, he never broke eye contact with the princess, and she found his eyes warm and comforting. In her heart, she knew that she could fall for a guy like Anton.

Her head, on the other hand, knew something wasn't right. She broke from his gaze and looked toward the sea. Smee was napping in the rowboat, and sitting in the sand was Mittens, scooping out a fine moat for her imaginary kingdom. All the while, the dragon had kept a stealthy eye on Gale, in case she was needed to snap into action. Gale gave Mittens an icy stare to show that she was needed indeed.

Mittens stood and wiped the sand from her hands, said farewells to the kids, and made her way toward the couple on the blanket.

"Hey guys, just coming up for a snack. Don't mind me," she said, plunging a claw into the straw bag.

"Mittens, why don't you head back to the tower. I think the captain and I may be here for a while," she said as she smiled warmly toward Anton.

"Of course, you kids have fun. Captain, it was a pleasure meeting you."

The captain rose and bowed again for the dragon.

"The pleasure was all mine. Thank you, Wrathnarok. I promise you that the princess will be in good hands."

"Oh, I'm sure of it," said Mittens under her breath. She gave the princess a quick wink and headed toward the path that led home.

"Come," said the captain as he stood. "Let's walk to the water's edge and watch the sun set. I've seen thousands of sunsets, and its beauty is never lost on me."

As Mittens disappeared behind the tall grass, the captain extended a hand to Gale, and she gladly accepted. They walked to the edge of the sea, now orange and silver. Still hand-in-hand, the calmness of the tide reaching toward their feet as they stood admiring the last gasps of the day.

"Where were we?" asked Anton.

"I was boring you with my tales of woe. Please forgive me. I'd much rather hear about your adventures. Tell me more about the places you've been."

Chapter 9

"Well," started the captain, "My travels have brought me to all the corners of the globe. I've been to the Spanish shores, deep into the ruins of Greece, the mystic forests of the Netherlands, and the rolling hills of Ireland. Does that interest you?"

More than you know, thought Gale.

"It all sounds so exciting, but how would I possibly travel alone to all these exotic places? It would be a little intimidating, even for an independent girl like me."

The captain stood close to Gale, his eyes fixed on hers. She could smell the contents of the empty bottles on his breath.

"Perhaps someone like me could escort you? I know all the ins and outs of these lands. It would be an honor."

"No. I could never impose. Plus, I don't see my parents bankrolling a tour around the world. They would never approve of me sailing away with some strange man whom I had just met."

"Do you always ask your parents for permission?" asked the captain as he leaned closer still. "Surely a woman your age must take some risks now and then. There are many more chests of gold upon that ship. Money is no object. As for being a stranger, I feel as if we have known each other for a lifetime. There is some connection here that I've never felt before. Some tether that binds us. Princess, I did not come here to try to win your heart, but I fear you may have won mine."

The captain's hand brushed a strand of hair from Gale's face as he leaned in closer still. Fire smoldered behind his eyes as he ran his fingertips along her jawline. Gale was visibly shaking, but she would not look away.

"Think of it as an adventure," he whispered as he gently pressed his lips to hers.

"Anton?" she said.

The captain placed his finger on her lips to quiet her.

"No questions." He whispered as he kissed Gale again, deeply and passionately. The princess slid her arms around him, her hands upon his shoulders, pulling him closer.

Dear readers, I know what you're thinking. This is blowing your mind. You never saw this coming, did you? Is she really getting smooched up by an older man? Is she considering running away with this guy? Why did Mittens leave her alone? And what's the deal with blueberries anyway?

Don't ask me; I'm as lost as you are. Let's turn the page and find out. If you ask me, this is getting pretty intense.

Chapter 10

In the land of This-and-That, the young princess was... What's that? You want me to get on with the story? You don't care about the formalities, and you just want to find out what happened to Gale after she was getting kissy-faced with the gallant Captain Anton Neal? Yeah, I know, the name is weak, but we're about halfway done with our tale, and I'm getting a bit haggard. (If you don't get the joke, ask your mom.) So, even though it's rude to stop a narrator while he's narrating, I shall grant you clemency. Besides, I want to know what's going on as much as you do. So, here we go.

The kiss was a doozy. It was one of the better kisses that Gale had ever shared, although she hadn't had very many. There were a few boys in school and a few more after she had graduated, but that was about it. This kiss from the handsome stranger was a real knee-buckler. In fact, it buckled her right knee so much that she forcefully kneed the captain right in his "mizzenmast."

Anton howled in pain and fell right to the ground. Her face was red with anger. Gale stood over the wincing captain, pointing a stern finger.

"Do that to me one more time, and I will hoist your peak halyard over your gaff rig!" shouted Gale.

The captain rolled on the sand, curled up in a ball. Low moans and groans accented his pain.

"I thought we were having a moment," the captain finally managed to say between groans. Gale had really landed a good shot. *I guess her friend isn't the only one who can handle herself.*

"Having a moment? When was that? Was that before or after I realized you've been stalking me on Gracebook?" *The rolling hills of Ireland? The mystic forest of the Netherlands? Those were the EXACT captions of pictures I posted on Gracebook. You knew I'd be at the beach because I sent out an invite this morning. You knew my dragon's name the same way. I never introduced you, but you called her Wrathnarok."*

"I can explain," said Anton, trying to stand but resting on one knee.

"Well, start talking. Let's start with your age."

"I'm twenty-eight."

Gale kicked him in the ribs. Again, the captain hit the ground writhing in anguish.

"Try again," she said.

"Ok! OK! I'm forty."

Gale brought her foot back, ready to apply another rib relocation.

"OK! I'm forty-three! I swear! Just stop kicking me."

"You're forty-three, and you thought you would roll up on a seventeen-year-old girl with some smooth talk and whisk her away from her family? Can you fathom how utterly disgusting that is?"

"Well…"

"It was a rhetorical question, Captain Schnook! It's repulsive. I can't even imagine a girl falling for that."

"You'd be surprised. Some girls just need a way out of their situation. Some are trapped in horrible lives. Guys like me offer them the world. Riches. Adventure. I'm not a criminal."

"No," said Gale, "but you should be. I don't really care about an age gap between two people, but this is predatory and wrong on all levels."

"Wrong? It's a harmless arrangement. They get out of their dreary lives, and guys get a little company. They are treated like a queen. They want nothing. They get to live a lifestyle that they couldn't otherwise obtain. Where's the harm in that?"

Chapter 10

"If I hear you defending that lifestyle again, you'll lose another rib."

"Listen, I didn't mean to upset you. I genuinely thought that you were interested in me."

"Let's not stray from the topic at hand, Captain Touchy. How long have you been stalking me?"

"I wouldn't call it stalking. I was just doing a little research to see who you are. Maybe see if we had some of the same interests."

Anton stood, rubbing his side where Gale had punted him. He was grateful that she was only wearing a flip-flop.

"Do we have any mutual friends? Did you send me a friend request?" asked Gale.

"No."

"Well, that's stalking me. It is incredibly inappropriate. Do you actually like anything that you said, or were you just agreeing with me?"

"I am truly partial to peanut butter swirl ice cream."

"OK. Anything else?"

"Not really, no. Your taste in music is trash," said Anton.

Gale swung a foot behind Anton's ankle and, with a firm push, reacquainted him with the sand.

"How long have you been stalking me?" Gale asked.

"You know, you're awfully rough for a seventeen-year-old girl."

"True, but I bet the king's guard would be a bit rougher, Pierre LePew. Answer the question."

"I don't know. A few months, maybe?" said Anton.

Her hands were clenched in fists of rage. Gale was aware of the amount of stalking that happens on social media. She, herself, had looked at the pages of old classmates with no intention of reaching out to them. Acting on it crosses a very dangerous line, and Gale was repulsed and nauseated. A half-drunk older man had thought it was OK to prey on a younger girl and had the audacity to kiss her. This wasn't going to end well for the captain. That much she knew. But she was not done yet. Not hardly.

"Young girls are not to be hunted to validate your mid-life crisis. I bet that ship is new. It's too tricked out for a man your age. Silver sails and trim is a bit conspicuous for forty-three, don't you think?" asked Gale.

"Hey! Don't mock the Maecenas. She's a fine ship. I traded in a fishing trawler for her. When I pull into port, every head turns." He slowly and cautiously began to rise again.

"Yeah, because they're wondering if the senile old codger at the helm is going to plow into the dock. You look like a fool. And you named it the Maecenas? Could you be any more obvious? The Mendacious is more like it. Why not just spray-paint "free candy" on the side and be done with it?"

"Princess, I've had about enough of this. That's about all I'm willing to take from some adolescent, elitist punk. I'm going to shove off and find a girl who can appreciate what I have to offer. I would bow, but you're not worth it," said Anton as he reached for his hat.

Gale was now charging toward the finish line. The sun was getting low, and so was her patience.

"You don't want to bow because you're worried that I'll get a good look at your bald spot. Let me give you a little advice. Ease up on the booze and tone down your presentation a little. You're a guy, not a supervillain. Look for a lady who's in your demographic and stop trolling the high schools. Being a sugar daddy seems exhausting, and for Pete's sake, find your own interests. Stop poaching other people's lives and get your own," scolded Gale.

"I need to get a life?" asked Anton. "You should take a look in the mirror, Princess."

"What's that supposed to mean?" she asked.

"Have you seen your Gracebook page? It's pathetic. You go nowhere. You do nothing. You dream of adventure and then sit at home and play some stupid video game. Did you ever think that the reason no one dates you is because you're about as exciting as a Styrofoam cup?"

"That's by choice. I enjoy my life. I don't pretend to be something I'm not."

There was a slight quiver in her voice as the captain's words found purchase. She didn't want to admit it, but he may have had a point here. She may have been in a bit of a rut, but is it really a rut if you like where you are?

"Do you, though? Face it, Gale. You're as lonely as I am. Give me your address so I can mail you some cats, and you can get a head start on being forty and single too."

Chapter 10

Readers, it doesn't seem like it, but those words wounded Gale. She actually did enjoy her life, yet in that instant, she questioned her choices. Was Anton right? Was she destined to be a crazy cat lady?

Well, she thought, *if my choices for male companionship are guys like Captain James T. Jerk, then I'd better stock up on kitty litter.*

"Maybe so, but I'm not living a lie. I'm good. I'd rather be alone than be trapped at sea with the likes of you. What was your plan, anyway? What if we ran away and you hated me? Would you just drop me off at some port or lob me overboard as you did to your integrity?" asked Gale.

Anton once again looked deep into her eyes.

"I was hoping that love would keep us together," Captain Anton Neal said softly.

"What does a guy like you know about love?" she asked, crossing her arms.

"I knew love once. I thought I did, but I was wrong. Now I'm trying to find it again, and I guess I'm going about it the wrong way. I haven't dated in years, and now the game has changed. Love can't be just a young man's game, can it? Maybe I just need someone young to teach me."

The captain's voice was soft and vulnerable. Looking down at the sand, the captain shrugged with a sad, embarrassed look on his face. Gale took a moment to weigh his words. Finally, she spoke.

"You're still trying to get me to come away with you, aren't you?" she said.

"Well, it was worth a shot."

"I KNEW IT! You're such a creep!"

"Can't blame a guy for trying," said the captain with a smile. "Listen, I'm going to take my gold and head back to the ship. Thanks for everything, Gale."

The captain walked toward the chest and his first mate, who was still fast asleep in the boat. With his foot, he kicked the chest closed.

"Do you really think taking the gold that you bribed my dragon with is the way to go here? You might want to reconsider," said Gale.

The captain put his hand to his brow and searched around in an exaggerated fashion.

"I don't see her anywhere. That's another thing. You may want to upgrade to Dragon 2.0. The one you have is lazy, worthless, and fairly tiny. I personally think you deserve better."

"I'll think about it. So, what far-off land are you heading to now? One with an all-girls orphanage or expansive shopping mall so you can hone your pickup lines?"

"Maybe I will. Maybe I'll regale them with the tale of Princess Nightingale. How I kissed her and won her heart and had to push her away. How she cried when I left and begged me to stay, but in the end, she wasn't sexy enough for me. In fact, I'll say I was too much man for her to handle," said Anton with a sinister grin.

"That's a lie, and you know it!" yelled Gale.

"Who would ever know? You never leave the house. If you post something, it'll just look like you're trying to cover up what really happened. So long, toots."

The captain kicked the rowboat and woke up Smee. Then he pointed at the chest of gold and instructed him to put it in the rowboat.

"Fine," said Gale. "You got me. Go tell your stupid story and ruin my reputation if that's what makes you a big man. I have one question before you go."

"Shoot."

"How are you going to leave?"

"What do you mean?"

The princess pointed out to the ship with the silver sails. Circling high above its masts was a shadowy creature hidden by the setting sun. The captain hadn't realized that Gale was just stalling for time. As their heated discussion raged on, Wrathnarok took flight and headed to the captain's prized ship.

"Sit tight while I throw a little light on the subject," said Gale as she thrust a thumbs up toward the sky.

With that, a burst of fire shot out from the dragon's mouth, igniting the ship's sails in a blanket of orange. On her second circle, the deck of the ship was engulfed in flames. Dark, rich plumes of smoke rose above the vessel. In the paint of the sunset, it was quite the spectacle.

Chapter 10

Anton was dumbstruck. He was standing with his head in his hands, helpless at the water's edge, watching his life's work and fortune billow into the evening sky.

"You torched my ship!"

"Technically, no. You'll have to take that up with the lazy, worthless tiny dragon."

"Somebody's going to pay for this. You'll be hearing from my lawyer!" screamed Anton.

"Please submit all inquiries in triplicate addressed to the king. You know… my father? I'm sure he'd love to hear all about it."

Gale was satisfied with the results of this encounter. This should put a crimp in his preying on younger women for a while. Gale gave the captain a good look. What she saw as confidence was merely desperation. His handsome looks were now pale and gaunt when saturated in alcohol and defeat. Not everything is as it seems. Your narrator recommends taking the time to inspect your surroundings. If something seems too good to be true, it probably is.

Meanwhile, Anton was incensed. He paced the sand with his arms flailing like a wild man.

"You have stranded me in this miserable kingdom. I have half a mind to march over to the castle and explain to your parents what an insolent child they've raised. You are an awful woman, and your parents should be mortified!"

"OH! NOW I'm a child. A moment ago, I was wife material. You should make up your mind. Fret not, Captain Blackweird; I have secured you transportation. It should be along any minute now," said the princess as she waved for Wrathnarok to join them.

The dragon landed with a mighty thud, spraying sand in every direction. Smee dove for cover in the rowboat as Anton stopped pacing, frozen with fear. He stood staring at the dragon, gasping and shaking. The princess was certain that the good captain had piddled into his leather boots.

"What do you think of the ship? I've made a few changes. It looks super-hot!" asked Wrathnarok, her eyes narrow and focused on her prey.

"She's very nice but is she seaworthy?" asked Gale.

"Nothing to worry about, Princess, I take good care of my guests," said Wrathnarok. She and the princess chuckled.

"I love when we get together!" said the dragon. "What am I doing with this one?"

"I honestly don't care. Just remember, he's Captain Neal, not Captain Crunch."

"He must have been awfully naughty for you not to care. I'll take him for a nice tour of the grounds. What did he say to garner your apathy?"

"Evidently, I'm not very sexy, have no personality, and I'm an embarrassment to my family."

"Really? Then I'll give him the VIP tour." Wrathnarok said with a dastardly smirk and returned her focus back to the captain.

"Aye! Around the world and home again, that's the sailor's way!" chimed Gale.

Wrathnarok slammed the captain to the sand with a well-placed foot. She dragged a talon across Anton's weather-beaten face. Still in shock, the captain laid there, making nonsense noises. If he hadn't piddled when the dragon landed, he surely did when that huge foot hit his chest.

"You about done stammering? I'd like to get home for dinner." Wrathnarock said to the captain.

Finally, the captain spoke.

"You're... You're... You're..."

"Use your words," encouraged Gale.

"You're a dragon! A real dragon!"

"And you're a codfish," said Wrathnarok. With that, the captain was snatched up in the blink of an eye and shot up into the evening sky.

As Gale began packing up her blanket, she noticed Smee still shivering in the rowboat. She walked over to the boat and gave it a little kick.

"They're gone. You can come out now," she said.

He lifted his head to see if the coast was clear. When he saw it was safe, he sat up and looked around. Gale finally got a good look at the First Mate. He was a skinny, older man with a stubbly gray beard. A stocking cap was on his head, and he wore a ripped t-shirt with horizontal stripes. Blue jeans with rolled-up cuffs sat above a pair of boat shoes. He looked more nineties grunge than sea dog.

Chapter 10

"I'm sorry, but Mr. Neal will not be joining us for the rest of his life. Look," Gale said as she pointed toward the sea. In the remaining light, the image of Wrathnarok dragging the captain through the water could be seen in a dragon's version of keelhauling. The ship was still ablaze though listing to port. Smee was abandoned and alone.

The old man pointed at the treasure with a hopeful look. Gale returned the look with raised eyebrows to indicate that touching it probably wasn't a good idea. He put his index finger close to his thumb, asking for a little bit of the gold. Gale figured the poor guy needed a break and nodded her approval. Quickly, he ran to the chest and stuffed his pockets with gold coins. Scurrying back to the rowboat, the old man pushed it into the water and started rowing rapidly away before she could change her mind.

Gale returned to packing, remembering to grab Mittens' hat. She placed it on her head. Despite what the captain had said, she didn't think a dragon upgrade was called for. She liked the O. G. Mittens. Different strokes for different folks, she figured. Making her way toward the path to head back to the tower, she left the chest of gold in the sand. If Mittens wanted it, she would have to come to get it. It was way too heavy for the princess.

Upon arrival home, Gale kicked off her flip-flops and dropped the bag by the door. She wasn't in the mood to put anything away. In the kitchen, she opened the fridge to grab an energy drink and then went to the living room to plop on the couch. She was thinking about the words that the captain had said regarding her feline-laden future. That was going to be her assigned title: Princess Nightingale the Kitty-encumbered.

"Reflexa," said Gale, and the mirror on the wall chimed to life.

"Yes, Princess?"

"Are there any decent guys left in the world? Are they all jerks? All I seem to meet lately are selfish little boys who live with their mom or call me a witch."

Reflexa chimed, "Happy couples… showing pictures that match."

Her screen was filled with smiling people holding hands and hugging. Old people late in life still snuggling with each other. Marriage proposals and sunset walks followed by young kids on a Ferris wheel laughing and enjoying each other's company.

"It seems so, Princess. Did we have a bad day?"

"Some moron approached me and said I was unsociable and that I was destined to die alone, so to speak."

"Sounds like sour grapes to me. I wouldn't put any stock in it," said Reflexa.

"Do you have anyone that you talk to? You know, like a guy?"

"There is a guy that I chat with when I'm offline. He's a cauldron for some oracles a few kingdoms over. Very sexy. He makes me laugh and tells me stories about what's going on in his world. We enjoy each other's company, and it helps make the time go by."

"That sounds so nice. Is it wrong for me to want the same thing?" asked Gale.

"You want to date a cauldron? He has a brother, you know. I can put in a good word for you."

"No! Stop being silly. I just want a guy who I can be friends with, first and foremost. Is that too much to ask?"

"It'll come, Princess. Try a little patience," said Reflexa.

"I am. I'm in no rush, believe me. I'd just like to know that the opportunity will still be there when I'm ready."

"There have been bad guys since the dawn of time. There have been good ones as well. I believe that there always will be. I wouldn't worry. You're a wonderful girl. You're funny and kind. You're quite a catch and a princess to boot."

"Thank you, that's sweet, but I still feel a bit mopey. Can you play something to cheer me up?" asked Gale.

"Playing cheer-up music," chimed Reflexa.

The chords of a familiar song filled the room, followed by whistling as the guitar strummed along. It was Patience by Guns and Roses.

"Reflexa!" yelled Gale. "You're not helping!"

The mirror laughed at her little joke.

"Would you like to see pictures of trebuchets in your area?"

"One more joke, and I'm gonna hang you in the bathroom!" chuckled Gale. "Thanks for trying, Reflexa. I appreciate the effort. You can sign off. And say hi to your caldron for me."

Chapter 10

"His name is Pipkin, and I will. Good night, Princess." With a quick chime, she was gone.

Gale finished her drink and was about to get up to start dinner when a loud thump came from the glen. She walked downstairs to open the door for Mittens.

"Did you grab my hat?" she asked as she walked inside.

"No worries, it's upstairs. Did you grab your gold? I couldn't carry it. I'm going to start dinner soon."

"It's a little early, isn't it?" asked Mittens.

"For what? Dinner?"

"For stupid questions. Of course, I grabbed the gold. What kind of a dragon do you think I am? The chest seemed a little light, by the way."

"I gave some to the first mate. He looked a bit destitute."

"OK, I don't mind you giving some away. I would have hated to lose it."

"So," said Gale. "What became of Captain Kidd-dater?"

"Well, first, I gave him a good bath."

"Oh! I saw that. The keelhauling was a nice touch."

"I do try to enjoy my work. Then I took him for a flight around the kingdom, dropping him and catching him before he hit the ground. I must admit, I like the screams of terror. Then I threw him as high as I could and caught him. I wanted him to get a good look around."

"Did he get to see all the mystic lands that he spoke of?" asked Gale.

"I showed him a whole new world," said Mittens.

"I hoped he kept his eyes open. I would have hated for him to miss anything."

"I have no idea. But then I saw the most incredible opportunity. Riding on watch were none other than Sir Stinky and Sir Knoxville. I brought the good captain down and introduced them. I figured it was the neighborly thing to do. I may have explained that the clown was trying to land a date with you before his AARP card arrived in the mail."

"You know, they are very protective of me," said the princess.

"Indeed. They mentioned something about Sir Knoxville's trebuchet and the lake. They also said that they didn't think the king needed to hear anything about it. At least from them, anyway."

"Good call on their end. I love them so much."

"It seems the feeling is mutual, considering the way in which they tied him up and dragged him back toward the castle."

"Good. It serves him right," said Gale.

"You know, I was a little alarmed at the kiss you gave him. I thought I had misjudged the situation.'

"HE kissed ME. Not the other way around. I just used it as a ploy to get him close, is all."

"Yeah, I saw. You 'ployed' the heck out of him. He won't walk right for a week!"

As Gale cooked dinner, she filled Mittens in on the details that she missed while she was in hiding. She made sure to mention that Anton called her a second-rate dragon, but she left out the part where he told her that she would be alone for the rest of her life. It still stung a bit, and she wasn't ready to relive that again.

After she cleaned up, Mittens was asking what they were going to do next. She really wanted another chance to play Dummikub since Gale trounced her the first night. Instead, the princess announced that she wasn't up for any fun and that she just wanted to go to bed. As Gale slunk off to her room, Mittens said goodnight and couldn't help but realize that something was off.

Gale lay in her dark room, wrapped tightly in her covers. The events of the day played over and over in her head, and they made her feel vulnerable and sad. A tear or two escaped and ran down her cheek. Words hurt, folks, and once they're out there, they're part of the universe. Try to remember that when you want to say something but shouldn't.

After a while, there was a knock on Gale's door.

"What?" Gale said. She wasn't in the mood for any more surprises.

The door creaked open, letting in a sliver of unwelcome light into her cold dark bedroom. It was Mittens, of course. She had a sad look on her face as she peeked her head in to check on the princess.

"What do you want, Mittens?" Gale said, sounding exasperated.

"I thought you might need something to pet. I'll leave you be. I'm sorry."

Chapter 10

"Don't go. I'm sorry, too. I'm just not in a good mood," she said. Her sorrow dripped from every word.

Gale patted the bed, and Mittens entered, hopping onto the spot that she had patted for her. Curling up beside her, Mittens placed her head on the princess' leg and looked up at her with concern. She scratched at the spot between the dragon's ears and tried to stifle a tear. It didn't work.

"Thanks, buddy," she said between sniffles.

"That's what friends do," said the dragon, and as she scratched, a few more tears slid down the princess's cheek until she finally was able to fall asleep.

Chapter 11

IN THE LAND OF This-and-That, our princess woke up in a funk. Not a good funk, like Parliament or an Uptown Funk. But more of a funky funk. (Note: Readers, there is some wonderful music available at your fingertips. Don't just play the top hits. Expand your artistic horizons.)

Nightingale was a little tired of, well, everything. Her bed had enveloped her into a warm cocoon, and she had no desire to leave it. The covers were pulled up, exposing only her nose, and she stayed curled in a ball of malaise.

A hand ventured out of the covers to grab her phone. Several texts came from her friends commenting on the ship that was set ablaze near the beach. They fired off question after question about yesterday's events:

Was that your dragon?
Are you OK?
Was that a prince?
Was he on fire?

Gale replied to no one. Replying would only lead to more questions, and she was having none of that today. The only goal that held any urgency was mustering up enough courage to get up and use the bathroom.

That, too, would have to wait, for she was not leaving the safety of the bed for as long as she could hold out.

There was one more text, and that one was from her father.

> Hey sweetie. I have to do king stuff today, and I was hoping you might join me. Give me a text when you get up.

That's fine, Dad, but I'm not getting up, she thought and plopped the phone back on her nightstand. Gale tried to close her eyes and fall back to sleep, but the text from her father haunted her. If she didn't respond, he would just keep trying and trying, and then there would be no sleep and no joy of hiding from the planet until she did. Scooping up the phone, Gale shot an innocuous text to her father.

What's up?

The king answered almost immediately.

> Hey sweetheart, I have to ride out to the edge of the kingdom to bring some supplies to a family recovering from the pox,

typed the king.

Guessing you want me to join you?

> If you would. C'mon, it'll be fun. Like when we used to ride when you were a kid.

Fine. What am I wearing? Are you crowning it today, or is it casual?

> Crown. Going to see some sick little girls, so I thought I should look my best. They like all the pageantry. You wear whatever you want.

Gale knew that "wear whatever you want" really meant to get all princessed up. She was definitely not in the mood to play dress up, but the

Chapter 11

thought of the sick little girls tugged at her a bit. It reminded her that her problems were rather trivial in the grand scheme of things. The young girls did enjoy seeing a real, live princess, and she would hate to disappoint.

Leaving the comfy confines of her bedroom revealed that she was alone. A few calls for Mittens left her wondering where she had gone. Mittens was well fed, so the kingdom's cattle weren't a concern, but still, it was a little strange to Gale that she would head off without a word. Perhaps she was being courteous to her and thought that she needed some alone time after crumbling in her bedroom last night.

A quick shower and off to the closet to pick out a gown. The red one made her look a little porky, and the baby blue one was cut a little odd and never really fit right. Green? Maybe. Yellow? Did she have the right shoes? Big decisions were being made, and she needed a little help.

With her hair in a towel turban and donning a fluffy robe, a still-damp princess walked to the mirror holding the two dresses.

"Reflexa?"

The mirror chimed to life.

"Green," said Reflexa immediately without waiting for the question.

"Are you sure? Let me try them on first, and you can…"

"Green. No question. Ask me again, and it'll be the green one. You look great in that gown. What's the occasion?"

"Dad's picking me up. We're visiting a sick family." Gale held the green gown against her chest and modeled it in the mirror. Once again, Reflexa was right. She did look great in the green. Getting dressed up was definitely a funk-breaker. If you ever get in a bit of a mood where you feel the world is a big bag of jerks and you're stuck dragging it around, the narrator suggests throwing on some nice clothes and doing your hair. It will, without a doubt, adjust your aperture.

Ten minutes to dress and a good twenty on the hair and make-up created a princess. Gale hadn't been in full royalty mode in so long that she almost forgot what it felt like. She texted her father that she was ready and slapped some peanut butter on a piece of bread. The sandwich was quickly scarfed down and washed away with a glass of chocolate milk, carefully so as not to ruin her gown. Then Gale went back to the mirror for a final look.

"Tiara or no?" asked the princess.

"Bring it. You don't have to wear it, but the girls might want to try it on."

"You're so smart. What would I do without you?" asked Gale.

"It scares me to think about it," said Reflexa.

"Did Mittens say where she was going? It's not like her to leave without saying goodbye."

"Nope. Not a word. Just popped out the window and flapped off," the mirror said.

"Can you tell her where I've gone when she gets back? Oh, no! How will she get in? I should put a doggie door in, so I won't need to be running up and down the stairs all the time."

"Want me to search for doggie doors?" asked Reflexa.

"Not really."

"Yeah, I didn't think so," said the mirror. "Relax, she survived a thousand years without you, a few hours won't kill her."

"Good point. I'll see you later."

Gale walked downstairs with her emerald tiara in hand. She took a moment to debate the pros and cons of leaving the front door open a crack, but the thought of a house filled with vermin sealed the deal and the door. Walking around back, she pulled open the cellar doors and crept in, being careful not to dirty her gown in the process. Inside were a ton of boxes and items from when she moved that she never unpacked. There were books and clothes and assorted trinkets and such. After flipping open a box or two, she found the box that she was looking for and lugged it up the cellar stairs.

When Gale returned to the front of the tower, two knights had arrived on horseback, their armor shining in the morning sun. Sir Reginald the Rank and Sir Robert the Elder would be accompanying them on their journey. Seeing the knights all dressed in full gear made Gale glad that she had put on the gown. She would have hated to be underdressed. Sir Reginald the Rank had dismounted and approached the princess to relieve her of the box that she was carrying.

"My dearest Nightingale, the king is but a moment away. I just wanted you to know that our mutual acquaintance has shipped out and

Chapter 11

that he is safe," Sir Reginald said softly and gave her a playful nudge.

"Shipped out?"

"Indeed. We supplied him with an old garbage hauler and sent him adrift. He is a changed man, my princess. Of that, you can be assured," he said with a laugh.

"No one has said anything to my father?"

"Nary a word. That is between you and the king."

"Thank you, Reggie. You are all so good to me. I can't thank you enough."

She recalled the conversation with Mittens from the night before, describing the plans of torture and torment that Sir Reginald and Sir Knoxville had in store for the good Captain.

"And how is Sir Knoxville's trebuchet?"

"Working as intended, my princess," said Sir Reginald, and with that, everyone laughed at the thought of the captain being launched into the lake.

The king's royal carriage broke into the glen, pulled by two glorious white steeds and gleaming white and gold. The crest of This-and-That was emblazoned on the door. It came to rest at the princess' feet, and the king exited with a beaming smile. He was dressed in green as well, with a gold collar to match his golden cape. High brown leather boots completed his ensemble, and a small crown sat on his balding head.

"Hey, baby!" he said, and he wrapped his massive arms around his daughter in another one of those dad hugs. She squeezed him back, realizing how much she needed it after yesterday's trials.

"I'm so pleased that you're coming with me. Your mother is going so crazy with the decorations and the arrangements for the party that she couldn't get away. Frankly, kiddo, I had to get out of there. I love her, but she's driving me nuts," said the king.

"I wasn't going to come. I was feeling kinda blah, but I figured I should get out for a bit."

"Well, I'm glad you changed your mind. What's with the box?" the king asked.

"Just some stuff."

"Very well. Reg, put that in the back of the carriage and let's get moving. Honey, I'll have you back in a few hours. I know how much you hate dressing up, but you look so beautiful. The kids will love it."

They boarded the carriage and, with Sir Robert in the lead and Sir Reginald in the rear, they made their way down the path and through the woods. As they rode, the king spoke of news from the castle, news of the upcoming birthday party, and a few tidbits about the queen. Gale filled her father in on the stories of the suitors and the dragon, being careful not to lie but to sculpt the story in such a fashion as to not worry the king. She even told of the captain and his advances since he was long gone, and she felt it was safe to enlighten her father. The king was angry, first at the captain and then at the knights for not telling him. She convinced him that it wasn't their fault and that he should be grateful that they didn't betray her trust.

As they rode through the town, Gale could see all the work that was being put into her birthday. Stages were built for music, and banners bearing a silver "18" were hanging on every building and storefront. People saw the royal duo and cheered and waved as they rode by. The king shouted greetings to people he knew and didn't know. The princess waved in royal fashion and smiled, though seeing all of the hard work and preparations that were happening made her feel a little guilty.

"Dad, this is too much. I feel awful that everyone is putting in so much hard work just for my stupid birthday party," she said, crossing her arms and slouching in her seat.

"Sweetheart, they are all volunteers. They *offered* to do this for you. Most of this was their idea. The stages and the signs, the banners, all the food, it's all been donated. We mentioned a party and invited everyone, that's all. The entire kingdom took it upon themselves to make this a huge event."

"Still, I feel like it's too much work. They have other things to do. They don't need to do all of this for me."

The king said, "Hon, it's really for them. They need a day like this to come out as a community and have some fun. It just coincides with your birthday, is all. You're the excuse to have a party. That can't be a bad thing now, can it?"

"I guess not," said the princess. "I just don't like all of the attention."

"Hon, all the businesses are closed that day. After about an hour and a few barrels of mead, we will all be partying, and your birthday will be

Chapter 11

just a happy memory. Don't sweat it. Hang out with your friends and have a good time."

The carriage made its way through the town, over a small wooden bridge and into some woods that separated the farmlands from the rest of the kingdom. Thick oaks and pines lined the road and blotted the sun, except for a few hints of daylight that forced its way through the canopy of green.

Gale remembered riding through here with her father when she was a child. They would pack some sugared plums and pastries for the ride. Her father would sing old songs to pass the time, and they would always stop to pick a bouquet of wildflowers for the queen. It amazed Gale how much she missed those times with her father. Sometimes you don't realize you were missing something until it returns to remind you.

She also remembered that Sir Reginald the Rank would always ride with them. When Gale was younger, the stench of the man would repulse her, but her father never seemed to mind the smell. She had always believed that it was a "guy thing" to be smelly, and she also believed that it would be rude to ask about it. She was older now and wondered if there was a reason behind it.

"Dad, can I ask you a question?"

"Always, my dear."

"Why doesn't Sir Reginald bathe?"

"That is a very good question, and the answer is a long story," said the king.

"I believe we have the time. It's OK if you don't want to."

"No, not at all. You're going to be queen someday, and you need to start learning our history."

The king looked out of the rear carriage window to see how far Sir Reginald was behind them. The knight was several lengths back, plucking an apple from a low-hanging branch and biting heartily into it. The king figured that Sir Reg was out of earshot and began the tale.

"When Reg was just a small boy, around seven or eight, his parents died, and he lived alone. No one was there to take care of him, so he roamed the kingdom looking for handouts. People pretty much ignored him, and, as sad as it is to admit, I was one of those people."

The king's face turned sour with embarrassment. Gale could tell that this was a tough story for him to tell. She placed her hand on top of her father's to steady him so that he could continue. After a deep breath, the king spoke again.

"Anyway, one winter day, some of the kids were ice skating on the lake. I was about thirteen at the time. It was a warm day, too warm for winter. We were all having a good time when I noticed that Reginald was also skating, but far enough away so as not to be seen. You see, he was looking for a little companionship. He just wanted to belong. Do you know what that's like?"

"Yes, I do," answered Gale. "More than I care to admit."

"So, when I saw him skating alone, I called over to invite him to join us. He was so happy that as he raced over toward our group, he didn't see a weak spot in the ice and crashed through. One second, he was there, and the next second, he was gone. As fast as I could, I skated over to where he broke through. He was trapped beneath the ice and couldn't find his way out."

"That must have been terrifying!" said Gale.

"It was. I have been in fights, and I have been in battles, but I have never been as scared as I was on that day. I started punching at the ice with all my might until I also fell into the lake. Luckily, I fell right on Reggie. I helped him onto the ice and out of the water. The other kids came by and formed a chain to drag me out as well."

"That's incredible!" said Gale, squeezing her father's hand tighter.

"Indeed. Two things happened as a result of that day. One, Reggie never went near water again. Not even a puddle. Two, he never left my side again. When we returned to the castle, soaked and freezing, I told everyone that he had saved me from drowning instead of the other way around, and he was greeted as a hero."

"Why would you do that?" asked Gale.

"Because this poor kid needed to be a hero, if only for a day. He has since earned the title of hero a hundredfold. He became the youngest squire in the kingdom's history and has been my trusted advisor and friend for all these many years. He's a great man who just needed a chance. So, when I

Chapter 11

smell him, I remind myself that the smell is the smell of greatness, and he wears it as a badge of honor."

"You were pretty wise at thirteen, Dad."

"Once in a while, your old man gets one right. One thing I've learned is to be careful how you judge someone because you never know what journey they've taken."

"I'll try to keep that in mind. It's tough sometimes," said Gale, remembering the verbal sparring that she had done over the past few days.

"Did you know that when you moved out, Sir Reg would camp in the woods just to make sure that you were OK? He still rides through the Woods of Nevermore to check on you from time to time."

"Dad, I wish you wouldn't make him do that. I'm fine, really."

"I didn't make him do anything. He does it because he loves you and loves his king."

"He loves his friend, Dad. Not his king," said Gale.

"I know. But it sounds weird when I say it. Now, how about a pastry?"

Opening the seat in front of the king revealed a storage compartment loaded to the brim with canvas sacks. He reached for one and set it on the seat. Inside were cheese Danish, apple tarts and a bag of sticky sweet, sugared plums. The king popped one into his mouth and handed an apple tart to Gale. It was her favorite, and with one bite of the warm pastry, she was a child again, bouncing on her father's knee and singing silly songs about manatees and hairbrushes.

"Is running a kingdom hard?" Gale asked between bites. "I mean, I know it's hard, but is there a secret to it? I've heard some strange stories about evil kings and queens and horrible atrocities inflicted on kingdoms."

"Secret? Not really a secret, but there is a knack to it," mumbled the king through a full mouth.

"Care to share? I may need to run a kingdom myself one day," said Gale as she brushed some crumbs from her gown.

"Gale, I know that you have some concerns, but I wouldn't trouble yourself over it. I know we spoke about you renouncing your throne, and if that's something you wish to do, I'm behind you all the way. I just ask that you wait for a bit. We all think about it. I defy you to find a king who hasn't."

This had not occurred to the princess. The thought of her parents not running the kingdom was not something that she could readily wrap her head around. They both seem like they were born to be royalty. In the case of her father, he literally was.

"You're going to tell me that you've thought of renouncing at my age?" asked a flabbergasted Gale.

"Hon, I thought of renouncing last month. And the month before that."

"So why didn't you?" asked Gale.

"Well, all of my stuff was in the castle, and I'm really just too lazy to move…"

Gale gave the king a playful punch on the arm.

"C'mon! Tell me. You just said I'm old enough to hear this stuff!" she begged.

"Well, truth be told, I always wanted to be a tinker. I love taking things apart to see how they work. Watches and carts and clocks and things. Nowadays, I just don't have the time, and I fear that when I'm older my hands won't be steady enough to do it. It's a lucky man who lives his dream. Your mom wanted to be a painter. She's quite good, too! When we were younger, she would draw and paint, but time gets away from you and the next thing you know, you're forty and too busy for such things."

"I remember when I was little, Mom would sit on the floor and color with me. She would sketch a bunch of pictures, and we would spend the afternoon coloring them in."

"Aye. I remember. Now, the kingdom is our fickle mistress, and her needs and desires take up most of our days. I still try to fix some things now and then, and your mother draws pictures on letters and invitations, but it's not the same."

The king shrugged his shoulders, and his face carried sadness. He found that the only cure was to pop two sugared plums in his cheeks and smile at his daughter like a mump-laden chipmunk. Gale chuckled at the king's tomfoolery.

It troubled the princess to think of her parents as sad or trapped. She knew that they had a responsibility to the kingdom, but couldn't they find a way to do everything they wanted? I guess you never know what

Chapter 11

a parent is going through. She never thought that the woman who she waved at in town might have dreamed of being a sailor or a knight. Or even a princess.

The king swallowed the plums and took a drink of water from a bladder that was in the compartment. "You wanted to know if there were any secrets to running a kingdom. I'm not sure if there are, but I'll tell you what I do: I keep people who agree with me close by and the people who disagree with me closer. That way, I can get all sides to every story. When you do that, you don't miss anything important when making a decision."

"You listen to the people who oppose you?"

"Absolutely," said the king. "You can learn as much from a beggar as you can from a scholar. So, you listen to everyone and then follow your heart. If you've made the wrong choice, then you have only yourself to blame. I've made some poor decisions in my day, but they were mine to make. I always think that, in a crisis, making a move is better than not. So, I make them and hope for the best."

"But what if you're wrong?" asked Gale.

"Then you try to fix it. And you take full responsibility for your actions. If you put the blame on someone else, they'll never follow you again."

"And that works?"

"I'm not sure. You would have to ask the people. I work for them. Never forget that, Gale," said the king. His face was serious, and he looked her square in the eye as he spoke.

"Anyway," he said, "You won't have to worry about that for a long time. Your mom and I aren't going anywhere, and if you choose to take over the family business, I am convinced that you will flourish. Meanwhile, enjoy yourself. You're young. Go out with your friends and have some fun. Don't be in a rush to be a grown-up. You're going to be one for a long time."

As Princess Nightingale rolled the king's sage advice around in her head, shouting came from in front of the carriage, followed by the galloping of horses. With a screech and a whinny, the carriage came to an abrupt stop, nearly knocking the princess off her seat and scattering the remaining plums onto the floor. Sir Reginald was immediately beside the king's window with his right hand clutching the handle of his still-sheathed sword.

"Sire, there are strange men afoot. I suggest you stay inside until we determine their intentions," said Sir Reginald and, with a kick, galloped forward toward the commotion.

"Ah! Adventure!" said the king. "Want to find out what's going on?"

"Dad, Reg said to stay inside. Do you think it's safe?" asked Gale.

"With my best knights around me, we'll be safe as houses. Besides, what kind of king would I be if I stayed behind? Remember, neither a coward…"

"Nor a fool," said Gale and as they shared a smile, both dad and daughter left the safe confines of the carriage and walked toward the commotion.

Chapter 12

IN THE LAND OF This-and That, the princess hiked up the hem of her gown and wobbled her way down the dirt road with the king holding her elbow to support her. Her heels made the journey a little treacherous, and she wished for the comfort of her sneakers with every step. Gale had to keep looking at the ground to successfully navigate the ruts and rocks in the road, but if she had looked up for a moment, she would have seen two very familiar men.

The knights were off their mounts and stood at attention in front of the strangers. Well, maybe not strangers. At least not to Gale. The men were short and dressed in very dirty all-white clothing. One might say that they looked like bookends.

Narrator's note: This is what we, in the comedy business, call a "call back." That is the resurfacing of a previously mentioned subject for comedic familiarity. In this case, as it was manifested by the entourage that was accompanying Sir Chad. Remember them? Were you wondering if they were OK? Well, now you know.

The bookends were rambling on about how they had been lost for days and how hungry and tired they were. They thanked the knights for saving them over and over. As Gale and the king approached from behind the knights, he called out to them.

The Self-Sufficient Princess

"Step aside, men. I'd like the travelers to meet the king of This-and-That!"

The knights parted, and the bookends bowed deeply before King Killian. They both rose with a smile of relief at having been saved. This lasted for barely a second. The sight of the princess standing beside the king wiped that smile from each face like it was a chocolate milk mustache. Righty, the man who spent a day or so on the top of a pine tree, spun on his heels and ran full speed down the road. His arms were flailing, and he shrieked like a skydiving penguin. All that remained was Lefty, who had ducked behind a tree as he scanned the sky for the terrifying dragon.

"What's all this then?" asked the king. "Get up and stop sniveling about!"

"Dad, these men were accompanying Sir Chad. The first boy I told you about, remember?"

"Ah, yes! Sir Chad the Amazingly Tasty, if I recall," said the king with a laugh. The knights joined in the fun, but Gale was not amused.

"Now rise and quit this charade!" commanded a frustrated king. "Granted, you are not the first man who cowered at my daughter's feet. And surely you won't be the last!"

Even Gale laughed at this. The knights let loose with raucous laughter as the king stood glaring at the sniveling Lefty. When the king was like this, royal and stern, he had his own gravity. He seemed impervious to any affliction and radiated a force that resonated far and wide. He was not a silly dad or a sad father as he was a moment ago in the coach. Here, he was King. It was admirable and infectious. Gale saw first-hand the answer to every question she presented to him on the ride thus far. She wondered if she could ever be the leader that her father was.

"Sir, I can assure you that I meant n-n-n-no harm," stuttered Lefty as he pulled himself from behind the tree, still gazing skyward for any nearby dragons.

"Yes. I'm sure that Chad probably mentioned that a time or two as well. Alas, harm was done and saying that it was unintended doesn't remove that fact. Robert, fetch this man some food so that he may be on his way," said the king as Robert walked off to do just that.

"Come on out. No one is going to hurt you," said Gale. The remaining bookend came out from the tree line and stood in front of the princess, still looking skyward and trying to avoid the princess' gaze.

Chapter 12

"You smell absolutely horrific! Would you like a bath? I'm sure that I know someone who can arrange it," asked Gale, referring to the swimming lesson that Wrathnarok had given just days before. Lefty pulled at his soiled clothes and gave them a whiff, sniffing under his arms and down his shirt.

"No, no... I'm good. I'll handle it. Thank you, though. Thank you, Princess," the man stammered as he searched the sky some more.

"You see, in our kingdom, such a smell is reserved for only the bravest and most loyal of men. It is truly a badge of honor and only fit for the worthy. Isn't that right, Sir Reginald?" asked Gale.

Sir Reginald looked taken aback to hear these words coming from the princess. Slowly, a shy smile crept across his face.

"If you insist, M'Lady," said Sir Reginald.

"I do. I do, indeed," Gale said and gave Sir Reginald a warm smile. "And since you aren't worthy, I command you to take a bath. Are you sure there isn't some way I can help? I'm sure that I could have a friend of mine assist you."

"Not necessary. I promise I will handle it as soon as possible."

Sir Robert returned with the sack of food and, in an act of disgust, threw it at Lefty. It struck him in the chest and hit the dirt. Food was spilled onto the ground, and it became coated with dust and pebbles.

"Princess, I would just like to apologize," Lefty rambled as he gathered the spilled food. "I didn't mean anything by that, and I understand that it was severely inappropriate. Will you ever forgive me? Please?" His eyes were large with hope as he shook in fear.

"No sweat. I've already forgotten all about it. How about a high five?"

Gale stuck her hand out and waited for Lefty to slap it. He took a step toward her, and as he brought his hand up to apply a hearty high five, a flash of light came between them. It was Sir Reginald's sword, and it was pressed sideways against Lefty's stomach. Lefty looked at the knight in horror as Reginald slowly shook his head, indicating that touching the princess was frowned upon. Lefty lowered his hand. Smart boy.

King Killian, as all good kings do, saw this as a ripe opportunity to end the encounter.

"Young man, I would take this rather pointed hint and perhaps bid us all a fond farewell. If you would just follow the path that your friend has taken, past that farmhouse and over the hill, you will find a new kingdom filled with people longing to accept your gracious high fivery."

Lefty stood, still staring at the knight. The knight stared back, still employing his sword as a rather shiny turnstile. Again, the word "piddle" comes to mind for some reason as Lefty said nothing but stood and shook like his entire body was set on "vibrate". If he was smart, he would set it to "airplane mode" and fly on out of there.

"To the south! Quick march!" yelled the king, clapping his hands. This woke Lefty from his trance of terror, and, clutching his bag of food, he ran off down the path, howling like a banshee.

"Be kind and do give him a head start, Sir Robert," said the king icily.

"Of course, my liege," Robert replied as he mounted his stallion, wearing a sinister grin. After Lefty made it halfway down the path, Robert pulled back on the reins, rearing the horse with a mighty whinny.

"HEE-YA!" shouted the knight as he charged off to escort Lefty from the burden of This-and-That.

The king waved to the carriage to come forward. When it arrived, Sir Reginald opened the door to let in the royal family. He smiled at the princess with a sense of recognition.

"Thank you, Reg," Gale said as she hopped into the carriage.

"No. Thank you, Princess," said Sir Reginald. He quickly mounted his steed and led the carriage to the farmhouse that was off in the distance.

"Whatever happened to that whole 'you can learn something from everyone' spiel that you just gave me?" the princess asked the king as they rode toward the farmhouse.

"Do you think I was too harsh on our guests?" asked the king.

"Well, no, but it didn't seem very kingly."

"They slighted my daughter," said the king, frost clinging to every syllable.

Then the king turned to Gale and thawed. "Being a father takes precedence over all. At least, it's supposed to. It took me too long to figure that out."

Chapter 12

With that, the king reached his big arm around his daughter's shoulders and gave her a squeeze. The kind of squeeze that only a father can give. Gale smiled and put her head on her father's chest. She felt safe and calm and relaxed and not a potential cat lady for the first time all day. She realized that being alone didn't have to mean you were alone. Being alone but loved is something different altogether, and that was something she could get used to fairly easily. Captain Anton Neal was an idiot for trying to make her doubt herself, and she hoped that he enjoyed his new ship full of dirty diapers and discarded fish heads.

The carriage swung up the drive toward a simple but charming farmhouse, complete with a front porch that stretched the length of the house and held a rocking chair or two. An old wooden swing hung from a rope under the oak tree in the front yard, and chickens pecked away at the gravel in the path. The driver stopped short of the chickens and hopped down to open the door of the carriage. Sir Reginald kept his mount and rode around the house to scope out the area for marauders or whatever knights look for while scoping areas.

The screen door of the house swung open, and onto the porch poured three girls of various ages, each one with dirty-blonde hair and each one wearing a nice floral print dress. The tallest looked about fourteen, with the other two girls under the age of ten. They walked down the stairs, excited and nervous, to form a receiving line for their royal visitors. The moment that Gale saw their smiles, she knew that the gown and the tiara were the right decision.

When Sir Reginald gave his permission to do so, the carriage driver cleared his throat and made his formal introduction:

"Ladies and gentlemen... children of all ages... I present to you the Royal Family of This-and-That, King Killian the Stout-hearted... and Princess Nightingale!"

The driver swung open the carriage door, and out came the king and Gale into the front yard, with Gale holding a bag of sugar plums. The young girls applauded and tried desperately not to slouch. When they were approached by their guests, the girls all curtseyed in unison. The king bowed his royal head, making sure his impressive crown didn't slide off as he did. When he raised his head up, he pushed a sugar plum out of his lips and stood there wearing a silly puff-cheeked look that immediately brought out a giggle in the girls.

"Dad! Stop that! You'll have to excuse him. He doesn't get out much. You know how embarrassing dads can be," Gale said with a playful eyeroll. She was just kidding, of course. One thing the princess learned early on was how to play to a crowd. There was a time to be serious, a time to be quiet and a time to joke around to put three little girls at ease.

"I'm just trying to show these pretty young women how to properly eat a plum, Princess," said the king.

"You're embarrassing yourself. Let me show them how a princess eats them." Gale popped a sugar plum into her mouth and made the exact same silly face as her father, but she crossed her eyes while doing it. The young girls howled with laughter at seeing the royal family acting like a normal family.

"Here," said Gale, "You guys give it a try." She handed the bag to the girls, and they proceeded to pop one into their mouths and made their own silly faces with the encouragement of the king. While they munched on sweets, he asked them their names. The eldest was Lorynn, and she had just turned fourteen. Alicyn was next at ten years old, and bringing up the rear was Emylee at the ripe old age of eight.

The king made polite conversation, asking about school and inquiring about recent marriage proposals or college acceptance letters and other jokes to make the girls relax and forget, if only for a moment, that the pox had descended onto their home and upended their lives for a while.

"Bet you didn't know that the king was so silly, did ya girls?" came a voice from the side of the house. A tall thin man wearing greasy overalls and a dirty white tee shirt was wiping his hands onto a rag as he walked toward the crowd. He was robust and healthy, with a shock of white hair that was not appropriate for a man of his age. His skin was tan and weathered from years of tending to his farm, and Gale guessed that not a few of the white hairs came from raising three daughters.

"Ed! You look fantastic!" said the king, and he bounded across the grass to meet the homeowner. Although the man was filthy, King Killian greeted him with a man hug and a hearty handshake. It was obvious that the two men had known each other for years.

Chapter 12

"Gale, come meet my old friend Ed Miller."

The princess took Emylee by one hand and Alicyn by the other and walked over to meet the girl's father.

"How do you do, Mr. Miller?"

"I'm fine, Gale," said Ed as he took a step back to get a good look at the princess.

"I can't believe how big you've grown! The last time I saw you, you were riding on your daddy's shoulders up at the castle."

"Ed here is from the Miller family. His father owns the mill that grinds all of our grain into flour. Their family services all the surrounding kingdoms," said the king.

"And two overseas," Ed said proudly.

"How's Nora?" asked the king.

The man's face paled a bit at the question. Before he spoke, he sent the girls inside to get some lemonade for the guests. Normally, the king would decline any refreshments, but he could see that it was a distraction set for the girls, so he kept his tongue still. As they walked away, Ed began his tale.

"Well, that's just it. The pox ripped through the family pretty quick. The girls first, then me and Nora. The girls were clear in a few weeks, with me not far behind, but Nora is still bedridden. The doctor says that she'll be OK, but it's going to take a while longer."

The man knitted his brow and looked up toward the sky for a moment. The anguish of the last few weeks was written in bold across his face. The farmer's big hand rubbed at his chin for a moment as he relived the story in his mind. At that moment, Gale could see how lucky she was to only have a few suitors to worry about. She also understood her mother's fear of all things pox related.

"Anyway, since we were all sick and Nora is still in bed, we had no chance to tend to a crop this year. I couldn't have done it anyhow since the pox took my ox and donkey. Grabbed a horse and a few pigs as well."

"You couldn't get anyone to help you out?" asked Gale.

"No. The pox scared away most people, although they did leave us some food on the porch now and again. I'll tell ya, that Hicks family sure makes a great lasagna. It's Emylee's favorite!"

The girls returned with a large pitcher of lemonade and a stack of paper cups. They put them on a picnic table. Lorynn began pouring as Alicyn placed a few cups onto the table to be filled.

"Let me get you some food and water for your horse," said Ed to change the subject.

"Nonsense. Let me get the carriage unloaded, and I'll have my man bring it to the barn. Reg, can you please put the packages onto the porch for the Millers?"

"Of course, my king," said Reginald. He dismounted and started to pull out the bags of food that they had brought from the castle. Gale walked over to grab the box that she had contributed and placed it on the picnic table. Soon, the porch was covered with bags of food and boxes of necessities that the king had decided might be of some use for his friend and his family.

"My carriage driver is the best in the land. He has quite a head for horses," said the king. "Woltz! Head to the barn and tend to the animals while I take a walk with Ed to survey the damage."

As the king clapped the farmer on the shoulder, they walked towards the rear of the house, talking about animals and wheat as they disappeared around the back. Gale sat at the picnic table and lifted up a cup. The girls sat around her and did the same.

"And now, when we put the cups together, we will raise our pinkies in a traditional royal manner," Gale said as she touched cups with the girls. They all said clink and took a sip, keeping their pinkies raised high in the air.

"Very good. Now then, would you like to see what's in the box?"

"Sure!" said an excited Alicyn as Gale opened the box and proceeded to put its contents onto the table.

There were dolls and plain old tiaras, and a few stuffed animals. Coloring books with crayons and colored pencils to fill them in. A feather boa with a few masks that her mother had saved from events at the castle. Some fake jewelry and a few old purses. The girls sat politely while item after item hit the table. When Gale was done, she placed the empty box onto the grass beside the table.

"You like?" asked the princess.

"That's a lot of stuff!" said Emylee.

Chapter 12

"Can I see one of your dolls?" asked Alicyn.

"Of course," said the princess. Alicyn picked up a doll with a red bow in its blonde hair and a diaper on its butt.

"I figured that you guys had to throw out a bunch of stuff because of the pox, so I brought over some of my things to give to you. I didn't know how old you guys were, so I just grabbed a bunch of different things," said Gale.

She looked around at the happy little girls as they rummaged through the gifts laid before them. She could hardly remember being that young, even though she was only four years older than Lorynn.

"Those tiaras were the ones I had to wear as a kid. My mom wouldn't let me wear anything fancy since I kept losing them all the time," Gale said with a shrug.

Gale watched as the little ones rifled through the gifts, staking claims to one thing or another. Lorynn just sat and tried to wear a grin, but it was obvious that it was a strain. The princess was all too familiar with the feeling. She had spent a lifetime being in places that she didn't want to be, with people that she didn't know or liked. But a princess is a princess, and she would make do.

Gale plucked two coloring books from the table and plopped one in front of Lorynn.

"Want to color with me?" she asked.

"No, thank you. I don't color."

"I don't either, but these are special adult-style coloring books."

Gale opened her book up to show that, indeed, there were no childish pictures inside. Instead, the book was filled with intricate designs. Swirls and patterns of black lines filled the page, which when colored would make more art than cartoon. These books are a real thing, by the way. Look it up. They're pretty cool.

Gale searched the table for an orange-colored pencil and began to fill in the spaces of her design.

"I like to color these when I feel anxious," said Gale. "It helps me to relax."

Reluctantly, Lorynn grabbed a green pencil from the table, opened her book and joined in the coloring. They stayed silent for a moment as they concentrated on their work, swapping out pencils and crayons while the younger girls ran around the yard, dolls in tow.

"What does a princess have to be anxious about, anyway?" Lorynn finally said.

"What do you mean?"

"Well, how hard can it be? You live in a castle and have servants and chefs and no responsibilities. It must be pretty sweet."

"You would think so, but I live alone and have no servants. I cook for myself, and I scrub my own toilet."

"Does your dad pay for that, or do you, like, have a job or something?" asked Lorynn.

This was not the first time Gale had been confronted with this "spoiled little rich girl" label that had been pinned on her since birth. It used to really hurt her feelings, and she struggled with how she felt about being the princess for quite some time. High school was the worst when it came to the attitude that she was a privileged girl. She ate a few lunches in the cafeteria bathroom just to escape the catty chatter.

"I have a job. I am window dressing for the royal family. I attend royal functions and listen to people drone on about a bunch of boring stuff."

"So, meeting us is part of your job?" asked Lorynn.

"No. I wanted to come here."

"Why would you want to do that?"

"Because I know how terrible and boring being sick can be. So, I grabbed some toys and stuff, and I headed over," Gale said. "If I may ask, how's your mother?"

"She's sleeping. That's all she does. She sleeps and has soup and sleeps some more. I have to cook and do all the other stuff while she's sick."

"The doctor said she's improving, didn't he?"

"Yes, but..." Lorynn trailed off a bit. Gale looked at her and saw that there were no tears in her eyes, but a river's worth hiding behind them. She could see that this girl wasn't going to cry in front of her sisters or a stranger in a pretty green gown. Gale was impressed and thought this fourteen-year-old would make one heck of a princess.

Lorynn buried her face in the coloring book and scribbled in silence. Gale joined suit. She didn't want to pry. If Lorynn wanted to talk, she

Chapter 12

would when she was ready.

"Sometimes, I hate it here," Lorynn said finally. "Dad's scared that he's going to lose the farm. He doesn't think we know, but we do. Sometimes I hope he does. I'm not a farmer or a miller. I'm just not."

Her coloring became faster as she spoke. Lorynn kept her head down, hiding her face behind a wave of hair.

"Then don't be. I don't know if I'm going to be queen when I get older. I may just change my mind and do something else. That's the cool thing about being young. We don't have to decide anything yet. Nothing is predetermined. No one can force you to be a farmer."

"But it's expected of me. I'll take over the farm, and my sisters and I will carry on the family tradition."

"Or, you guys can sell it and buy a horse ranch. Or a boutique. Or whatever you want. Someone had to start the tradition, right? Maybe you can start your own."

Lorynn said nothing, but Gale could tell that her words had made an impact. Sometimes you just need a little reassurance to verify your dreams. A little encouragement can go a long way with a young girl. The key is to listen for it.

"So, did you really set fire to some guy's boat?"

"Oh, you heard about that?" asked Gale.

"Who didn't? It's all over Gracebook. You and your dragon causing havoc in the kingdom," said Lorynn.

"Do you really have a dragon?" asked Emylee.

"I do, kinda. No one really has a dragon, they just kind of show up. Want to hear about it? I can tell you the real story about what happened, but it will have to be our secret, OK?"

"Yes, please! And don't leave out the gory details! I want to hear everything!" said Alicyn.

Princess Gale went on about her adventures over the last few days, sparing the girls a few details that may have been less than desirable. Of course, she knew that they would not keep any of their conversations a secret, and she never expected them to do so. The best way to keep a secret is to keep a secret. Learn that lesson, dear readers. Social media is not your friend.

The Self-Sufficient Princess

As the story was winding down, the king and Ed had returned from their walk around the property, and it was time to say farewell. Many hugs were given, and a picture or two were taken. Gale placed a tiara on each girl for the pictures.

"But I'm not a princess," protested Emylee.

"We all are, sweetie," smiled Gale as she tenderly placed a tiara on the young girl's head.

Since their mother was still ill, the girls would not be attending the birthday gala, so Gale promised to send them some party favors and a birthday cake or two. As they left the farmhouse, Gale and her father waved goodbye and promised a swift return.

After pulling out of the farm and onto the main road, Gale found that Sir Robert had returned to accompany them home. He had chased Lefty for over a mile, let him catch his breath and then chased him a bit farther. It was probably the most exercise the poor guy had gotten in a while, and Gale regretted not bringing the free gym visitation cards that Flex-a-Lot had given her.

"So," asked the king. "How was your visit?"

"We had a nice time. They're all so sweet. How is Ed?"

"Ed is concerned that he is going to lose the farm due to the pox. I ordered him not to plant anything until further notice. Since he is quite handy and now in need of employment, he has been named Official Serviceman of the Royal Trebuchet."

"But Dad, you don't own a trebuchet."

"Well, then, I expect that to be his first order of business," the king said with a chuckle.

"What about the grain?"

"Plenty in the royal silos to last us a while. We'll just have to hope that the rest of the farmers are luckier than the Millers."

The king took his daughter by the hand.

"And now you know what it takes to be a good leader," he said. "You know, I saw how you were around those girls. And I saw what you did for Sir Reginald. I'm very proud of who you are turning out to be. You'll make a great queen someday. You know, if that's what you decide to do."

"Thanks, Dad. I have a good teacher," said Gale with a smile.

Chapter 12

There was a pause.

"You mean your mother, right?"

"Of course! Who else would I be talking about? You need to get that king-sized ego in check, pal. Killian the Stout-*headed* is more like it," Gale joked.

"Ah, there's the stupid. Now, what do you say we pick your mom some wildflowers before we go back?" The happy family rode back toward Castle Beckett, keeping a keen eye out for a bouquet suitable for a queen.

While the horses clip-clopped along, Gale revisited the talk she had with Lorynn about their futures. How can she help guide her new friend when she was debating not taking her own advice? That wouldn't be setting a princess-like example, now, would it? Witnessing the Miller's home in such a flux, she completely understood why her mother was so concerned about the pox. The princess also felt blessed to be surrounded by such loving people, from her parents to Sir Robert and Sir Reg. And grateful for her fuzzy roommate as well. Maybe Lorynn was right. What does a princess have to be anxious about?

It was at that moment that Gale was struck with a wonderful idea.

Chapter 13

In the land of This-and-That, the rather tired princess climbed the stairs of her tower. Her tiara in one hand and her heels in another, Gale trudged up the stone staircase wishing that the day was finally over. Although she had a nice time with her father, it felt good to be home. Her shoes plopped to the floor near the entrance to the living room, and her tiara made its way onto a nearby table. All would have to wait to be put away. Gale was too tired to do much of anything, and her butt itched from wearing a gown all day. She stood in the living room and gave it a mighty scratch.

"Welcome back!" exclaimed Mittens. The dragon was lounging on the couch watching some shopping network hawking trebuchets and other nonsensical destructive items.

"Nice to see you, too… traitor," said Gale as she scratched.

"Traitor? What's with all the hostility?" asked Mittens trying to crack a joke.

"You went behind my back and told my father that I was having a rough time. Not cool. What happens in the tower stays in the tower. Are we clear?"

"Crystal," said Mittens.

"And you too, Reflexa."

The Self-Sufficient Princess

Reflexa chimed to life.

"Connection to server lost. Please try again later," she said and chimed again.

"Cut the bull. I know you were in on it too. *Try the green dress. Definitely the green one.* You were just trying to get me to match my father, so don't hang there acting all innocent."

The princess had figured out that the reason Mittens was gone when she woke up was because she had slipped away to the castle to tell her parents about how depressed she was. Reflexa seemed adamant about the green dress, and when her father showed up wearing a matching outfit that had clinched it. She wasn't really mad at all but wanted to have a little fun with her roommates while making a point.

"I meant no disrespect to the sisterhood. I'm sorry, Gale."

"What about you, dragon, formally known as friend?"

"I am your friend, and I plead the fifth."

"A friend?" Gale stared at the dragon until she finally cracked a smile. Then she wagged a finger in Mittens' face. "A faker! A phony! An utter fraud!"

"Do I need a lawyer?" asked Mittens. "Reflexa, can you get Giuliani on the line, or do you think he's too busy with other stuff?"

"That's a call you don't want to make, trust me," said the princess. "Anyway, what I am trying to say is thank you. Both of you. You have both been so helpful and understanding through this whole fiasco, and you have made the last few days much easier."

"'Twas a pleasure, M'lady," said the dragon.

"Absolutely, that's what friends do," said Reflexa.

"And while I am sincerely grateful, let's keep all the personal stuff in-house, shall we?"

"Agreed," said the friends in unison.

"Good. Now then, are you guys' good enough friends to help me pull off a surprise for my birthday party?"

"We don't have to move a couch or help you paint, do we?" asked Mittens.

"Not at all."

"Then we're in."

Chapter 13

Gale then explained to her friends a secret plan for her birthday party. It would take the help of everyone in the room, a bit of help from the rest of her friends and perhaps a knight or two. Relax, people, it's nothing that is driving the storyline here, just a little something extra to think about as we narrow in on the rapidly approaching gala.

As the explanation was winding down, Mittens perked an ear towards the window.

"Either one of the lawn gnomes has come to life, or we have yet another visitor," said the dragon.

"Any chance it's the pizza guy?" asked Gale.

"Not unless he's clairvoyant. I didn't call for pizza," said Mittens as she made her way to the window.

The princess sat and rubbed her feet while waiting for an update from the dragon. Her feet were still a bit swollen from the heels. If she had to send off another suitor, it was going to be in bare feet.

"Well, what do we have?" asked Gale, exasperated.

"Remember what Brendon Frasier looked like in George of the Jungle?"

"Of course!"

"Yeah, nothing like that. More like if Harry Potter had a love child with Christian Bale."

"Which Christian Bale? Batman or American Hustle?"

"More like American Psycho."

"For a Welsh guy, Bale has been in a lot of movies with American in the title. I'm heading down to shoo him away. Don't get lost. I might need you."

"Roger," said Mittens as she hopped back onto the couch to continue channel surfing.

Gale glanced at the shoes and decided against it. This was her home, and she was going to play by her rules. If he didn't like it, he could put on the high heels himself. She took a deep breath to collect herself and opened the door.

There stood a rather attractive man in a blue sports coat and a pair of round glasses. He had sandy blonde hair and flashed her a beautiful, genuine smile.

"Good evening, Princess. I hope that I'm not intruding."

"Well, you are. I've just come back from an all-day event, and my butt itches. How can I help you?"

"I am Sir Michael of the Kingdom of Haver," he said, giving a respectful bow. Gale did a quick curtsey and stood again, looking unamused.

"Princess, I would hate to impose. Perhaps I can come another time?"

"Naw, Michael, let's get this over with. I'm sure you're aware of my situation, n'est-ce pas?"

"Oui, Mademoiselle."

"Yet still you came. Why is that?"

"I saw the picture of you and the girls you met today on Gracebook. To be honest, I wouldn't trust a man who wouldn't want to meet a woman like that. Those girls looked so happy to be with you. I guess I wanted to see the person responsible for those smiles."

"That's very kind. And very close. They must have just posted those pictures."

"That is true and a bit embarrassing. I was nearly here when I saw you had been out to their farmhouse. Some executive decisions had to be made, so I decided to gamble on your good nature and continue," said Sir Michael.

His eyes were kind and soft. His voice was filled with sincerity. If Gale was reading him correctly, the lad even seemed a bit nervous. That was a pleasant change from the over-confident oafs that had been darkening her doorstep. He had been correct in counting on her good nature because she decided to let him stay for a bit.

"I have an important question for you," said Gale, wishing she could give herself a good scratch. "How old are you?"

"I'm twenty-one."

"And what's your opinion on cats? Pro? Con?"

"As a pet? Pro. As a date? Definitely a con."

He smiled. She giggled. So far, so good.

"You have anything to recommend you? What are your qualifications?" asked Gale.

"Well," said Sir Michael, "I'm from Haver. I like long walks in the moonlight and as a full-time student, I like throwing frisbees, rollerskat-

Chapter 13

ing, and making independent short films. Is that ok or should you move on to suitor number three?"

Gale laughed at his game show reference. He was sweet and funny. If only his timing wasn't so poor, she'd love to spend some time getting to know him.

"A film maker, huh? Well, Mr. Spielberg, what kind of movies do you make?"

"Oh, you know. The movie-making kind. The ones that move, mostly. The still ones are too artsy and boring," said Michael.

Gale giggled at his joke. "Movies are big here. I must admit, I've wasted copious amounts of time watching and rewatching my favorites."

"I wouldn't say it was wasted. More like invested. What's your go-to movie? A secret favorite or a guilty pleasure?"

"Hmmm… do I have to pick just one?" she asked.

Gale sat on the stoop of the tower and gave it genuine consideration. Movies were probably her favorite topic, and she wasn't going to answer lightly. Volumes of personal information can be gathered about someone by learning about their favorite movie.

"Probably Sixteen Candles. How about you?" asked Gale.

"Maybe Sommersby. Or Casablanca."

"Sounds like I have a romantic on my hands."

"You do. I know it's a little embarrassing in today's time, but it's who I am," Michael said with a shrug. "How about you? You gonna tell me that the ending of Sixteen Candles doesn't make you swoon every time you watch it?"

The princess' cheeks filled with red. This guy made her blush in less than five minutes. Pretty impressive if you ask me. Gale had always considered herself a pragmatist, too strong-willed and even keeled to be swept off her feet. Yet here she was, blushing like a kid at the realization that, indeed, that scene in Sixteen Candles made her cry every time.

Sir Michael took this opportunity to change the subject while he had her attention.

"Oh, I almost forgot. I brought you a gift," he said.

"Mike, I already said that I'm not interested in anything," Gale said, pulling her guard up back where it belonged.

"Relax, it's nothing outlandish. It is customary to bring the wares of my kingdom when visiting another. It's some ancient way of advertising, I think. 'Come visit our kingdom, and you can get this cool stuff'. Come around back, and I'll show you."

"Mike, I don't think it's a good idea. I'm kind of tired."

He stuck out his hand.

"Do you trust me?" he said.

"What did you say?"

"Do you trust me?"

She took his hand, and around the back of the tower, they went. She playfully dragged her feet as he hummed a very familiar tune about the world being new. Arriving there showed a colorful blanket draped over her picnic table. On top was an array of fruits, breads and cheeses illuminated by short and colorful candles. Sprigs of lavender were spraying out of tall, thin glass vases. The whole scene was impressive, and it showed in Gale's eyes.

"I hope you're hungry," he said.

"I am always hungry. I must admit, I didn't expect a six-foot charcuterie board."

"You don't like?" asked Sir Michael.

"No woman would turn down a charcuterie board. Show me what you got."

"Ok," said Michael. "Sit down, and we'll get to it."

Gale scooted her way onto a bench, admiring the aromas of the meal displayed before her.

"Well," started Mike, "we have grapes from our fantastic vineyards. Figs from our... I don't know... fig yards, I guess. Cheeses fresh from the dairies. Plenty of chutneys. Some apples. Bread grown from local wheats and cooked in huge wood ovens. Well, the ovens are brick, they burn the wood. You get it, right?"

"Yes, wood from the wood yards. Got it," said Gale. She was enjoying the fact that he was nervous because it made her feel special. He wasn't nervous because she was a princess. His title of nobility assured her that he had been in royal company before. Michael was nervous because she was a girl, and he was trying to impress her. Dear readers, it was working.

Chapter 13

"And the blanket?" asked Gale.

"Weaved by our finest internet."

"Candles too?"

"Also locally sourced by our kingdom's internet provider and the finest search engines and shopping networks," Michael said with a sly smile.

"What's in the jugs?"

"OH! I almost forgot. We are famous for our roots. The red one is birch beer, the yellow one is ginger ale, and the brown one is root beer. Want me to make you up a plate?"

"That would be sweet, thank you," said Gale. She watched as he daintily placed pieces of cheese and slabs of crusty bread onto a plate. A dollop of chutney and a fig rounded out the snack, and he handed her the plate with a napkin.

"You look like a birch beer kinda girl," he said as he poured her a tall serving into a paper cup, plopped a straw into the top and handed it to her. She was slightly wary, but he did announce his title. Haver was one of their most trusted allies, and the thought of her being roofied by a government representative seemed remote.

"How did you get all of this here?" asked Gale.

"I'm a fantastic juggler."

"Seriously."

"No, my horse and carriage are in the woods with my driver. I didn't want to ruin the meal by having a horse nearby trying to steal a fig."

They munched for a while, discussing the different types of cheese and the variety of combinations that they could try. Certain chutney with certain cheeses and apples with others, and all upon the crunchiest of breads. Everything was delectable, and it was difficult for Gale not to make a glutton of herself. She gladly would have scarfed down plate after plate, but she was a princess, after all. She sampled every soda and was surprised at how rich and pungent each was. The grapes were crisp and popped with each bite. The figs were ripe and tender. Guys, go out and try a fig. They are incredible. Life is short. Try new things.

"So, what's it like living alone?" asked Sir Michael.

"Scary sometimes. Lonely, too. But I wouldn't change it. I like my freedom."

The Self-Sufficient Princess

"Define freedom."

"Well, it's not like there was anything wrong with living in the castle. I get along great with my parents. There's just something magical about being by yourself after school is finally done with. I stay up late, I play video games, but I stop just short of getting calloused fingers. No one likes a princess with hands like a mechanic."

Gale felt at ease. No posturing or posing. She was completely relaxed around Michael. She almost let a tiny burp slip from her lips but thought better of it. Smart of her. Best to leave something for the next date. No reason to display all your wares on the first encounter.

"So, tell me, Sir Michael. Do you have a title?"

"I do. I am known as Sir Michael the Unequivocal."

"What, may I ask, does that mean?"

"I honestly have no idea. A teacher gave it to me in high school, and it stuck. I see that you don't have a title yet."

"'Tis sadly true. I am merely a meager princess. No one loves me enough to bestow one upon me," Gale pouted, trying to look cute.

"Well, if you could have one, what would it be?"

"That's not how that works," said Gale.

"True, but if it was, what would you choose?"

"I don't know. I've never given it much thought. Maybe Princess Nightingale the Snarky!"

"Ooo! I like that. Maybe Princess Nightingale the Mysterious."

"Perfect. Can you make that happen?"

"I know a guy. He does things, knowwhatimean?" said Michael in a mobster accent, pretending to straighten out an imaginary tie.

Did you ever have a moment so nice that you became quickly cognizant of the fact that it was happening? You remove yourself for a split second and say "wow, this is really great". You smile from the inside out and pray that it may never end. Gale was in that moment, and it frightened her just a little. Because, in her experience, they usually end. Lately, they have been ending with the smell of brimstone. She shook the thought out of her head.

"So, if you knew that I wasn't planning on marriage, why did you come?" asked Gale.

Chapter 13

"Being completely honest? No ramifications whatsoever?"

"Of course."

"My kingdom is a bit old-fashioned and steeped in traditions. It is customary for each kingdom to send a suitor, regardless of intent to represent the kingdom. It's an antiquated idea, and most kingdoms have dropped it, but not Haver. With any luck, no one is turned into dragon chow or has their transportation set ablaze."

"You heard about the ship, huh."

"It made the news. But don't worry, it wasn't the lead. It was kinda wedged in between the weather and sports."

"Oh, like a puff piece," Gale joked.

"Exactly. Speaking of which, where is your dragon anyway?"

"Either spying on us or watching cartoons. Or eating. Really good chance on the eating."

"I can hear you!" came a shout from the window. It was Mittens with an obvious mouthful of food. Gale and Michael found this hilarious and laughed at the dragon.

"Or all three!" said Michael, and they laughed again.

"Yes. I have a very industrious dragon."

Gale popped a few grapes in her mouth.

"You were obligated to come here?" she asked.

"Not exactly. My dad is a knight, and they wanted someone of noble birth to represent the kingdom, so I said I would. I was honestly going to plop the gifts at your door and ding-dong-ditch you. But, like I said, I saw the girls' post and wanted to meet you."

"Ding-dong-ditch me, eh?"

"Well, ya know… big dragon. My father's a knight, not me. I'm more of a 'late afternoon.'"

Gale giggled. He was charming and witty and had the princess smiling, which is no small feat. Still, she wanted to do a little more digging. She was waiting for the other shoe to drop, and after the last few suitors, who could blame her?

"I'm glad you didn't," she said.

"Are you saying you're glad we've met?"

"No, I'm saying I would have hated tripping over a box of day-old food first thing in the morning."

"Don't knock it till you've tried it," said Michael. "How does one acquire a dragon, anyway? Is there a store set up somewhere for all your dragon needs, or is it purely internet based?"

"More like a dating app. You swipe left or right until you match a dragon. Then you meet in a public place to see how badly you each lied on your profile."

"Seriously?"

"No, you knucklehead! They just kind of show up one day and say 'Hey, I live here now.'"

"Now I can see your interest in cats. No one really buys one. They just appear like a rainbow or a smell in your refrigerator."

"Yes. Exactly that," said Gale.

The sun was slowly descending, and the gloaming had made itself present in a wonderful way where either the day was ending, or the night was just beginning. One way encapsulates the magic of the day, and another ignites the fires that light up the evening's potential. Gale wanted to stay but decided it was time to wrap this up. It was tempting to laugh some more and be washed in the wit and good nature of her new friend, but she decided not to press her luck. She needed a win, and this was her chance to take it.

"It's getting pretty dark. Mom always said to be home before the streetlights come on," Gale said with a hint of resignation in her voice.

"Is there any way that I can convince you to stay? The night is young, and so are we, or so the saying goes."

"I don't know. What do ya got?" asked Gale.

"Well, I've already bribed you with cheese, so that's out."

"True, you wasted that shot early, Tex."

Michael hopped up and put one foot on the bench of the picnic table, offering his hand to Gale.

"Do you trust me?" he said.

Gale pushed away his offer with a giggle.

"You used that one already, sport."

Chapter 13

"Oh yeah. I'd hate to be perceived as a one-trick pony. Hmmm… let me think. Can I interest you in some woodworking? Any chance you have a lathe lying about?"

"Absolutely not! What kind of a girl do you take me for?" Gale joked, faking her offendedness.

Michael let go with a hearty laugh. Gale realized that she didn't want the night to end either. This guy was genuinely fun. It felt like they had known each other since birth, and that is something special enough to want to hold on to. He was like a human Charizard card, a very rare find indeed.

"Ok. You've convinced me. I'll let you hang for a little while longer, but then its straight home, young man."

Michael smiled a successful smile. Gale may or may not have blushed a little. I don't know. It's getting a bit dark, and it's hard to see.

"Are you planning on going to my birthday party?" asked Gale as she took a slurp of birch beer.

"Are you having a party? I didn't know. Maybe I should have read the nine billion banners as I rode through town."

"My mom really overdid it, didn't she? I didn't even want a party, but again it's an antiquated tradition. I'm supposed to announce my husband at the event, but I obviously won't be doing that any time soon."

"Don't be so sure. You still have a few days. Maybe your prince is on his way here right now."

"If he's anything like the last few, I won't hold my breath. Present company excluded, of course."

"Of course," said Michael.

"I don't believe you answered the question," said Gale.

"I may go, if the right girl asks me."

"I am expected to take an escort. Do you know anyone who may be interested?"

"That depends. I do know a guy, but he's kinda partial to women with hands like a mechanic."

"Well, that counts me out," said Gale.

"Don't be so sure. I could have sworn that I saw you using your left thumb to grate some parmesan a moment ago," joked Michael.

Gale laughed and gave Michael a playful shove in mock surprise.

"We should take this act on the road," said Gale.

"Someday, maybe we shall."

"So, do you want to go or not?" asked Gale, her heart beating out of her chest.

"I don't know. Are you asking me to accompany you?"

"That depends. Am I the right girl?"

"You are indeed," Michael said softly.

Gale let that moment hang in the air. She let the words race like a thunderbolt through her body for a moment. It wasn't an invite to a club or to the gym or to sail away forever. It was a date. Not some guy hitting on her when she played Scabs of Destiny. Not a random lurking on her Gracebook page. An actual date.

Wait. An actual date?

"Just to be clear, we're going as friends, right?" Gale asked.

"Of course. I mean, I only just met you. You could be a serial killer, and I wouldn't know yet."

"Is being a serial killer a deal-breaker?" asked Gale.

"Probably not. Too soon to tell."

"Whew! You had me nervous there for a minute," Gale joked.

"How should I dress?" asked Michael. "Royal garb required?"

"No. After the quick ceremony where I thank everyone for coming, we will retire to the backcourt of the castle. There will be pizza and soda, and I think a bouncy house. So, dress casual."

"Got it. Eye patch, sombrero, pink boa, and a thong."

"Perfect. I'll dress to match."

So, totally not a date. Just a get-together. Just two friends in the same place. Still, she had better make sure everything was on the up-and-up.

"You don't have a girlfriend, do you?" asked Gale, dreading the response. "And I suggest you choose your words wisely."

"No. No girlfriend. What kind of guy would accept an invitation if he had a girlfriend?"

"You'd be surprised. The first suitor who showed up had an entire stable full."

"What a jerk! What happened to that clod?"

CHAPTER 13

"I'd rather not say. Let's just say that he met the business end of a dragon."

"You got that right!" came a voice from the window.

When they both looked up, there was Mittens with a big grin on her face.

"Will you please leave us alone! Can't you see we have a guest?"

"Sure do. How are you, Michael?" asked Mittens.

"Very well. And with whom do I have the pleasure of addressing?"

"I'm the hostess with the mostess, baby," answered Mittens in a gravelly voice.

"That's enough for tonight, Mittens. Say goodbye," said Gale.

"But baby…"

"Say goodnight, Mittens." shouted Gale.

"Goodnight, Mittens," said the dragon as she disappeared back into the tower.

"She seems sweet," said Michael.

"She is, just a little overwhelming at times."

"That's just because she loves you. It must be nice to have someone keep a lookout for you."

"I'm lucky that way. Parents, knights and a dragon. Not to mention a good friend or two. You'll meet them all at the party. Do you have people like that?"

"I have a few brothers that keep me in line. And knights, of course. I guess that I'm blessed as well," said Sir Michael.

"Sounds like you have a good family."

"No, they're terrible. It all started when neither of my parents came to visit when I was born. I had to drive myself home from the hospital."

"Stop it, silly."

"No, they're great. I just don't want to bore you with all of the gory details. Maybe you'll meet them someday as well."

"I think I may have a while back. We visited Haver to discuss some trade thingy, and I went with my folks to the castle. There were lots of knights and ladies in attendance. Hey! Maybe you were there!"

"I'm sure I would have remembered meeting Nightingale the Mysterious. No such luck."

"Are they funny like you?" asked Gale.

"You think I'm funny?"

"I do. And don't get all Joe Pesci on me."

"I think you're funny too. Despite what you've seen, it's not easy to get me to laugh. I'll show you. Tell me a joke," said Michael.

"I don't know any jokes."

"Sure you do. Everyone does."

"Well, I do know a joke about two guys on a bridge. I think one of the guys was from Arkansas."

"So, tell it."

"No," said Gale. "I'll get nervous and screw it all up. You first. You must know hundreds of jokes."

Gale desperately did not want to screw up the night in any fashion whatsoever. She didn't want to spill anything or ask an awkward question or do anything embarrassing that might jeopardize this good feeling that she had. The feeling of promise and hope that she might actually have found a shining light in an otherwise rocky sea.

He proceeded to tell her a few innocent jokes and peppered in an off-color one which the princess found amusing. Yet through all this enjoyment, something was changing. A slow dread began to wash over Gale. Not in a cherophobic way, where you are scared to be happy because you fear it all going wrong. No, this was something different altogether.

As Michael went on, Gale felt herself distancing from the moment. At first, she couldn't put her finger on the reason why but soon it became clear that this man, thought witty and charming, was not what she was looking for. Over the past week, after wading through disastrous meeting after disastrous meeting, Gale thought she was looking for a nice boy who she could ask to the party. Now that she had found one, the princess was mired with regret.

Be careful what you wish for, dear reader. Pick a cliché... any cliché. All that glitters is not gold, the grass is always greener, etc., etc. There are plenty of adages that warn against false desires and gilded dreams. Our princess didn't want a suitor or an escort. She would not parade in front of an audience with someone whom she had just met just to keep up with silly traditions.

Chapter 13

Now all she had to do was to find a way to explain all that to Michael. Without hurting him. Or herself. Or scaring him away completely. Or looking stupid in the process. Or seeming rude. Or seeming too inviting. Or too standoffish. Or ungrateful. Or snobbish. Or a tease. Or whatever. I'd go on, but I am wearing out the "O" button on my keybard. Key-*board*. See what I mean? Let's see how Gale handles herself and just be happy that we are not in her shoes, even though she left them inside.

Chapter 14

IN THE LAND OF This-and-That, the princess stood with her hands at her side, squeezing each finger with her thumb in a nervous manner. Michael was telling a wonderful story about an angry birthday clown when he noticed that her face had changed. The attentive light that sparkled her eyes had faded, and she seemed uneasy. Gale watched the recognition of the moment latch onto Michael, and he became painfully aware of the obvious: he had lost her.

"Was it something I said?" he asked.

"Not at all."

"Are you sure? Is it the clowns? Are you afraid of clowns?"

"No."

"You have a relative that's a clown, and I'm being insensitive?"

"No," Gale said with a giggle. "Listen, you're great, and I appreciate all of this: the food and the company and the jokes and all. I'm just not looking for what you're offering. It's not you, you're wonderful. But I feel like I'm leading you on, and I don't want to do that."

"So, it was the clowns all along. I knew it!" Michael punched his fist into his hand in mock frustration.

"Yes. It was the clowns. You saw right through me."

Michael looked a little sad, and Gale could see that he was slightly wounded. At the very least, he was disappointed.

"No magic, huh?"

"Oh, no. There was plenty of magic. I don't think I'm ready to wave my wand around, is all. Do you understand what I'm getting at?"

"Yeah, I do. It's OK, Princess. You've got a lot on your plate."

"I know, right? The party and the line of suitors and the long week..."

"No, I meant the cheese. That's an awful lot of cheese." Michael pointed at her actual plate, which was laden with a fistful of uneaten wedges.

They both laughed, and it helped to break the tension. He really was a sweet man, and under different circumstances, this night may have gone much differently.

"Do you hate me?" she asked.

Michael stared into her eyes, and for a moment, she was lost.

"How could anyone ever hate you?" he said softly as a wry smile wrinkled his lips. For a brief second, Gale almost changed her mind, but she knew it would come to no good. Best to pull up now than in a week from now. It would be more painful with each passing day. She knew what she wanted, and a boyfriend was not it. Nor was a suitor nor an escort.

"Can I call on you again?" asked Michael. "Or better yet, why don't you hit me up when your life slows down a bit. You can reach me on Gracebook. If that's what you want."

He was a gentleman, the first she had seen in quite a while. He didn't lean in for a kiss or ask to go clubbing or offer to squeeze her in anywhere. He just stood there and kept his dignity. See, ladies? There are some nice ones out there. No need to compromise yourself looking for acceptance. Be true to yourself, and it will all work out.

"I'd like that. I really would. Maybe the next time I see you, I'll tell you my joke."

"That would be fantastic," said Michael, "But please find a new one. I didn't want to tell you before, but I've heard that one."

"Ha! Are there any you haven't heard?"

"They are a rarity. I am the son of a knight, after all."

"True. They are a loud and racy bunch."

Chapter 14

Michael said goodnight and began to walk toward the woods when he snapped his fingers and turned around.

"Wait a minute! I knew there was something that I forgot. Where's your dragon?"

"You want to meet my dragon? I don't think that's such a good idea, Michael."

"Oh no. You aren't getting off that easy. I lugged a ton of food here, I wooed the princess with some borderline success, and my advances have been thwarted. I get to meet the dragon. It's right here, in black and white." Michael was waving around an imaginary contract.

"You want a playdate with my dragon?" smiled Gale.

"I think I'm entitled!"

"You want the dragon?"

"I want the dragon!"

"Oh, you'll get the dragon, mister. You'll get the dragon so hard it'll hurt for a week!" They both laughed at their silly exchange.

"We do make quite a pair, you and I."

"I know," said Gale. "That's what scares me."

Gale put two fingers in her mouth and blew, releasing a shrill whistle. This surprised Michael and shocked Gale even more so. She had been trying to whistle like that since she was seven but had no luck whatsoever. Maybe there was a little magic between them.

They waited for the flap of the wings in the wind, but none came. A look to the sky revealed nothing but stars. No rustling of leaves, no fire, no smoke and no superhero landing. Nothing. She placed her fingers to her mouth once again but only got a plblblblblbbt noise and a lot of spit. So much for the magic.

A slow creak came from the front door, and Mittens peeked her head out.

"Did you call me?"

"Yes. Sir Michael was just leaving. Before he left, he insisted on meeting you."

"Very well," said Mittens as she waddled over to greet Sir Michael.

"How do you do?" she said, extending a claw. Michael took it and gave it a gentle shake.

Mittens saw the display of goodies on the table, and her mouth hit the floor. She looked like a toddler on Christmas morning, eyes filled with joy and expectations.

"I have two very important questions for you. Number one, is that cheese? And number two, can I eat that cheese?" said Mittens as she made her way over to the table. "Ah! Cheese! You haven't 'aged' a day! Is that my favorite chutney?"

Mittens prepared a plate and grabbed at a flask of soda. She sat down on one of the benches and proceeded to nosh at the snacks.

"You know, he does look an awful lot like Christian Bale. Even more so up close," said the dragon through a mouthful of food.

"I get that a lot. The question is, which one? Batman or American Hustle?" asked Michael.

"American Psycho," Gale and Mittens said in unison.

"Ah, yes. I get that a lot, too. You know, for a Welsh guy, he stars in a lot of movies with American in the title," said Michael. Mittens and Gale both looked at each other, mouths agape, in recognition of their earlier and identical observation. Mittens made a heart shape with her claws and pressed it to her chest.

"You know something, killer? If you keep it up and have an endless supply of cheese, you can ask for my hand instead of Gale's."

"Mittens!" shouted Gale.

"What? This guy's fantastic," said Mittens as she scarfed down some root beer.

"I'm flattered, Mittens. I'm glad you think so. Any chance that I can parlay that sentiment into a small favor?" asked Michael.

"Whatever you need, Sir Michael."

"Well," Michael started cautiously, "I was wondering if you could become a little more dragon-y. You see, my dad's a knight and a traditional one at that. If I don't come home with a story and the smell of brimstone in my clothes, I'm gonna get talked about for years."

"Well, since you were so generous with the cheese, I'll see what I can do."

"Mittens, you don't have to do this if you don't want," said Gale.

"Absolutely. I would hate to be a bother," said Michael.

Chapter 14

"Not an issue," said Mittens. "Besides, I haven't stretched my wings in a while." Mittens hopped off the bench and wiped her hands on her legs. "You ready?"

"Have at it," said Michael.

Mittens walked over to the front of the house to give herself a little more room. Gale and Michael followed but stayed toward the edge of the house so as not to be in the way. Black smoke began to circle around Mittens as she began to change into Wrathnarok.

"What's happening?" asked Michael with a little nervousness in his voice.

Gale stood with her arms crossed and wondered silently if they really needed her here for the display. The dress was itchy, and she was falling asleep where she stood. Michael, on the other hand, was fascinated by the dragon's transformation. He stood next to Gale, unblinking and awestruck.

Once she had regained her full size, black smoke began filling the glen. Wrathnarok let out a mighty, ear-splitting roar that made Michael jump and cover his ears. Our princess had seen the matinee of this show and looked on unimpressed. She wanted so badly to leave but concluded it would be rude and unprincesslike. She wondered if she could sneak in a butt-scratch while the others were distracted but decided to wait.

"I AM WRATHNAROK! SLAYER OF VILLAGES! DEVOURER OF HOPE AND TORTURE TO ALL WHO LAY BEFORE ME! HARBINGER OF DOOM AND—"

"Hey! DwaynetheRock! Wanna wrap this up? I'm feeling woozy here," said Gale putting an abrupt end to the introduction. She waved at the smoke that had gathered around her face and faked a cough or two.

"Yeah, yeah," said a frustrated Wrathnarok. "One of these days, you're gonna let me finish the speech, and you're gonna like it."

Michael was beside himself with glee. Even when Wrathnarok spat fire at his feet, still he laughed, showing no fear. The scent of brimstone filled the glen as the mighty dragon circled her guest. She tried to look intimidating so as to put on a show, but Michael stood with a confident manner around his new friends.

"Wow!" Michael exclaimed, "Wrathnarok, you are quite amazing! I have never seen a dragon up close, and I can tell you, it's better than expected. Mind if I grab a pic?"

"Knock yourself out," said Wrathnarok as he pulled out his phone and captured a quick selfie or two.

"Yes, yes, we are all very pretty. But it's dark, and I really need to get out of this dress," said Gale, arms still folded in front of her.

"Dark, you say? I am darkness. I am the night!" said the dragon. Her voice was now raspy and deep, and full of drama and display. Readers, it was pretty cool, if you ask me. Gale, on the other hand, was less than amused, so she displayed her patented eyeroll.

"Check this out," said Wrathnarok, still in theatrical mode. The dragon took off like a shot into the dark night air.

"Gale, your dragon is incredible. I can't thank you enough for letting me see her before I go. This is really going to impress the knights when I get back! She spat fire at me and everything! Does she do that all the time?"

"A little too often, if you ask me," said Gale as she pointed up to the sky.

Against the light of the full moon, the dragon appeared. Her feet were tucked in, and her wings were spread. She hung there for a moment in full display of a giant "M" for Michael.

"Whoa!" said Michael. "I bet they could even see that in Haver! Gale, you have no idea how much this all means to me."

"Glad you're impressed," she said.

"I am. It's... breathtaking. Not as breathtaking as hearing you laugh at my stupid jokes. Now *that* is impressive. But this? This is a close second."

She smiled a sly, embarrassed smile. Usually, when the dragon shows up, the night is done, and the princess becomes inconsequential. Michael had the ability to embrace it all. To act cool even while overwhelmed. He had poise and composure, and he wore it like a tailored suit. It was a very attractive feature, and Gale found it was difficult to hide that fact. Even from herself.

Wrathnarok interrupted the moment with her usual flair-filled landing, scattering dust and shivering the earth just a bit.

Chapter 14

"Did you see it? Huh? Was it awesome? Tell me it was awesome," she asked, panting her words. Too much cheese, she figured. Cheese made her oogy.

"That was totally wicked!" said Michael as he went to high five the dragon. After they smacked hands, there was a puff of pink, and suddenly, the dragon was Mittens again. She bowed a few times to show her appreciation for the accolades.

"Guys, thank you so much for the amazing night. One I will not soon forget. Mittens, it was an absolute pleasure. Thank you for the show."

Mittens bowed again and headed over to the table for some more food. Some dragons never learn their lesson.

"Gale. Thank you for being the epitome of a princess. You were a wonderful host."

"Well, I had a wonderful guest."

They stood for a moment. Gale could see that he wanted a hug, but she would not be swayed, even by her own feelings. She wanted to wrap her arms around him. Although they had just met, it was as if they had known each other forever. Gale knew that a hug would be awkward, at least for now. So, she stood and stared, purposely letting the tension fill the air. The suspense was terrible. I hope it will last.

"Are you sure you don't need an escort? I know a guy who isn't busy that day," said Michael finally.

"I'm sure. I think it's best to conquer this a cappella. You're still going to go, aren't you?" she asked hopefully.

"I wouldn't miss it for the world," said Michael, barely above a whisper. With that, he made his way to the path that led to the forest. When he got to the edge, he spun on his heels and looked at Gale.

"Thanks, Gale. It's been a real slice," said Michael with a mock salute and disappeared into the woods.

"Son-of-a-witch. That's my line," Gale said to no one in particular. She walked toward the tower door and shouted to Mittens.

"Hey, show-off, can I ask you to clean up? I have to get out of this stupid dress."

"I got this," said Mittens through a mouthful of chutney-smeared apple. "Go on up, and I'll see you in a bit."

Leaving the door open a crack for Mittens to come in, the princess wearily made her way up the stairs to her apartment. She really didn't mind Michael sticking around to meet Mittens, but she was super tired and done talking to people. All she wanted to do was decompress and relax.

A chime came from the wall as Reflexa chirped to life. The melodious plucking of string filled the air, which was followed by a loud drum. She was playing The Wedding March in a salute to the evening.

"I'm guessing you've found your escort for the party!" said Reflexa.

"You have guessed wrong," answered Gale as she unzipped her dress and let it fall into a frilly circle around her feet. She then kicked the gown towards a wall as she scratched various unmentionable parts of her body. *I guarantee that whoever thought up women's clothing was not a woman,* she thought as she headed into her room to peel off a few more layers. Emerging in an oversized tee shirt, Gale plopped herself onto the couch and swung her feet up to rest on the coffee table.

"If you don't drink coffee, is it still a coffee table?" Gale asked.

"Want me to check?" asked the mirror.

"Nah. I'm good. So, did you hear us out there?"

"Yes. He sounds wonderful. Funny and charming to boot. What made you change your mind?"

"He was all those things, and more. I am just not ready to stand in front of a bunch of people with a guy that I hardly know. It's not fair to me or to him. We just met, and people would ask a barrage of questions about us, and there is no us. So, I decided against it. This way, if I want to see him again, there's no pressure. No expectations."

"That's pretty smart, Gale. You know, if you can stop scratching your butt, you just might make a princess someday," said Reflexa.

Gale giggled a bit. "Don't count on it. How's that mission going? I hope everything will be ready for the party." She was referring to the favor that she asked of the mirror and the dragon, in case you forgot.

"Better than expected. I guarantee that you will be pleased with the results. So far, no one that I know of has spoiled the surprise."

"Great, it means a lot to me," said Gale. The party was nearly here, and she needed to be sure that she was prepared. She had no escort, no

Chapter 14

idea what she was going to wear and no clue what to expect. Other than that, all was on course. She fiddled with the TV remote.

"Yes. Pipkin has reported that several other kingdoms are in on the surprise."

"How is your boyfriend, anyway?" asked Gale.

"He's stewing at the moment."

"Why? What happened to upset him?"

"Nothing. He's a cauldron, remember? He is actually making a stew."

Gale laughed at her misunderstanding as Mittens made her way up the stairs.

"Hey! What's with all the jocularity? What did I miss?" asked the dragon.

"Just silly puns from a silly mirror," said Gale. "Are we all tidied up? I'd hate to leave a mess."

"All clean. I took care of the extra food, too. I promise that it went to a good cause."

"Yeah, probably to the chubby dragon donation fund."

"Not true, princess, and a little rude if you want to be honest. Want to watch a movie? Maybe we can watch Sommersby again and think about the hot guy you just kicked out of your yard."

"Nah. You can watch if you want. I'm thinking about slaughtering some people through the magic of internet gaming. And I didn't 'kick him out'. I just don't think it's a good fit at the moment, that's all."

"Sticking to your guns, huh?" asked Mittens.

"Yeah. I kinda like things the way they are."

"Good for you. Way to not buckle under peer pressure. What are you going to tell your mom?"

"If she loves me, she'll understand," Gale said with a shrug. The princess had considered that arriving at her party unescorted would be a disappointment to her family. They would never admit it, but she knew that heads that wear the crown may be a little heavier that day. Still, the princess would be undeterred, no matter the cost. Surely, her parents could respect her decision. But Gale knew that if she were to invite someone just for the sake of inviting someone, she would not be able to respect herself.

The Self-Sufficient Princess

As Mittens retired to the bedroom, Gale fired up her gaming console. A few button A's and a couple of button B's later, she was online and logged into Scabs of Destiny. She sat and stared while her avatar spun helplessly in the opening screen. Jumping up, Gale ran to the fridge and grabbed an energy drink and hopped back in front of the TV. She was now prepared to do some serious damage to whoever was foolish enough to square off before her.

Except the fair princess wasn't in the mood.

As the music vamped on to encourage her to start the game, Gale realized that she wanted to talk. The only social interaction that she'd had for a while was a mythical creature, a piece of wall decoration and a handful of strangers. She did enjoy meeting the girls at the farm and the time spent with her father, but it wasn't the same, and she felt a tug of loneliness somewhere in her stomach.

She could call one of her friends. Most of Gale's girlfriends were night owls like herself, but she felt that they would want to talk about the dragon or the party or ask a billion questions about her life, and that would be agony. If only she could talk to someone who was friendly but didn't know that a dragon was sleeping in her bed or that she had just set fire to a ship. She needed a friend who was anonymous, a friend who knew nothing about her and would treat her like a person. Because at the end of the day, that's all a princess is: another normal person with an itchy butt and terminal boob sweat.

She put on her headset and went to the screen used to invite someone to a private game. The invitation wasn't immediately acknowledged, and Gale feared that the invitee wasn't online. After a minute or two, she was about to shut off the game when a green light indicated that her invite was accepted. The headphones crackled to life, and a familiar voice was on the other end.

"What up, KillaQueen?" asked the voice, referring to her gaming handle. *Not what I would have gone with, but it's not my story.* "Haven't seen you online today. I thought maybe something happened to you."

That's what people who aren't part of the gaming world fail to understand. It is a community just like anything else. People have traveled the globe to meet other gamers that they have become friendly with. They've

Chapter 14

attended funerals and weddings and handled birth announcements. Gamer friends are just as real as next-door neighbors. When asked, Gale knew that his concern about her whereabouts was genuine. It brought a smile to her face.

"What up, PizzaBoi. Everything's good here. I've just been stupid busy. How's by you?" asked Gale.

"All good in the hood. So, are you here to show me some new tricks, or do you want to play a little one-on-one?"

"Neither, really. I was kind of looking to, maybe, talk a little? Is that OK?" Gale felt stupid as the words fell from her lips. Of course, he doesn't want to talk. He's on here to play, and now she felt creepy and foolish. She immediately began planning an escape route. She would delete her avatar and wait a few weeks and then sign on as someone else. Hopefully, no one would discover that she was really the idiot who went online to talk instead of maim.

"I'd love to. I just got done with work, and I'm home alone. Kinda boring if you ask me. I was just gonna play until someone else got home."

Kick save, and a beaut! Gale would not have to go into hiding after all.

"Cool. Sorry to hear that you're all alone. I am kinda alone as well."

"Well, not anymore. We can keep each other company until we are occupied or fall asleep."

"Did you ever fall asleep wearing your headgear?" asked Gale.

"Oh yes. A few times. One of the guys I play with called my phone to wake me up because I was snoring so loud."

Gale laughed. She admitted that she had fallen asleep while playing as well and drooled all over her microphone. PizzaBoi got a kick out of that and let out a hearty laugh. They spent the better part of an hour talking and laughing over Scabs of Destiny stories. Different players and different games that they had experienced over the years. People that they encountered who were cheats. Others that were inappropriate and a pain to play with. Bizarre ways that they had met death while online.

"Hey, I'm getting a little tired of calling you Queenie. Any chance you want to tell me your real name?"

"You mean like 'I'll show you mine if you show me yours?'"

"Exactly."

Gale wanted to reveal who she was but decided against it. The anonymity was what she was looking for, and if she said who she was, it might change the dynamic of the conversation. Why ruin a good thing?

"Let's keep it faceless. It'll add intrigue and suspense. Kinda like Game of Thrones," Gale said while trying to sound mysterious. Princess Nightingale the Mysterious. That title was perfect—if only it would get some legs.

"Ah, a Game of Thrones fan. I am as well. I wish they would come up with a game that used the show as a base. That way, I could mount up and ride dragons and fight battles. Wouldn't it be cool to handle a dragon?"

Kid, thought Gale, *you have no idea.*

Thus prompted a long discussion on Game of Thrones. Character favorites (PizzaBoi liked Tyrion and Gale liked Sansa), character hates (they both despised Ramsey Bolton), favorite scenes and episodes and quotes and everything. Gale found herself relaxed and comfortable. She wasn't a princess to him, merely a girl. No fancy dresses or tiaras or regal traditions got in the way of how they spoke to each other. She was free to curse and laugh and say whatever she wanted as she hid behind the cloak of anonymity. It was something she had been missing for a while, and it wrapped around her like a warm blanket.

Mittens emerged from the bedroom, hungry as always. As she walked towards the fridge, she caught sight of Gale rolling on the floor in a full-on belly laugh. The princess waved emphatically to the dragon as Mittens crammed a mini donut into her face. It made Mittens smile from deep within. Before her lay a seventeen-year-old girl acting like a seventeen-year-old girl for the first time since her arrival. Without disturbing her, Mittens blew the princess a kiss and quietly headed back to the bedroom.

The topic turned to music as the new friends shared favorites and genres, and Gale found herself dancing as she described a few songs that PizzaBoi was unfamiliar with. When he suggested a few of his favorites, Gale quickly searched for the songs on her phone and sampled them. Some she liked and others were not quite her tempo. The minutes turned to hours, and the night became the next day. KillaQueen and PizzaBoi kept right on talking.

Chapter 14

It was one of those calls that no one wants to end. Gale was exhausted from her long day, but the influx of power drinks gave her a second and third wind. PizzaBoi admitted that he was tired as well, and when Gale offered to call it a night, he protested, much to her enjoyment. She had no desire to stop. They each dared the other to look at the clock to see what time it was. Finally, PizzaBoi manned up and gave his phone a glance.

"Uh-oh," he said.

"How late is it?" asked Gale, her voice getting gravelly and strained.

"It's close to two. We'd better call it a night."

"How come?" she asked.

"Well, as everyone knows, talking after two becomes a no-holds-barred conversation. Anyone can say or admit anything, and no one is allowed to be held accountable."

"So true," said Gale. "Are you afraid that you might say something you'll regret?"

"Absolutely not. But late calls like this can get a little… funky."

"I'm willing to get funky if you are," said Gale.

They talked until five-thirty.

Chapter 15

In the land of This-and-That, the princess woke up on her couch buried beneath some pillows for a blanket. The sun was already blaring through the window but had not reached the couch. There's nothing worse than sleeping by a window and getting an awkward-looking sunburn on your face. That's right up there with waking up with lines on your face from the sheets or drooling on your chin. Gale gave herself a mighty stretch and realized that the drool and the lines were a reality.

Mittens was on the floor in front of the TV, watching cartoons with the volume very low so as not to disturb the sleeping beauty. As the princess stirred to life, Mittens rolled over and looked at her.

"Wakey, Wakey! Eggs and bakey!" the dragon said.

"Morning," Gale said through a stretch that seemed to start at her toes and crawl its way upward.

"Did we have fun last night? Who's the lucky guy? I'm serious about the eggs and bakey, by the way."

"No questions. Me piddle first," said Gale as she shuffled off to the bathroom. She brushed her teeth and washed her face to remove the slime that had gathered there overnight. A quick glance into the mirror revealed some serious bags under her eyes and a blemish that was mounting an attack on her chin.

While she was primping, the memory of the wonderful night online came back to her. It brought a refreshing grin to her face. She needed a simple, stress-free evening like that. Now, if she could only remember what she had said to PizzaBoi in the wee hours of the morning. She wasn't sure, but she believed it was embarrassing, to say the least. He was right. Anything said after two a.m. was never any good.

Returning to the living room found Mittens face deep in a bag of Funyums. She emerged and reiterated her questions about the night before.

"It was PizzaBoi. He's the guy that I kill on Scabs on the regular. We get along pretty well, so I thought I'd hit him up for a chat."

"And the phone was too complicated for you two?"

"No phones. No names. Completely anonymous. I just wanted to be unknown for once. Maybe cut loose a little without anyone getting all judgey on me."

"I got you. You have no idea what it's like being a dragon. Very difficult to blend in."

"I bet," answered Gale as she plopped onto the couch and pawed at the bag of snacks.

"By the way," she asked, "What day is it?"

"Thursday. Don't worry, Scrooge, you haven't missed Christmas yet. It's still two days till the party. Any idea what you're planning on doing about an escort, or are you still flying solo?"

"Not a clue."

"Are you gonna tell Mom?"

"Nope. She can find out like the rest of the planet how pathetic her princess is. If anyone's asking, I'm fine with it."

"Anyone wasn't," said Mittens as she grabbed the bag back from Gale.

There was a question that had been puzzling Gale for about a week now. Nothing extremely time-consuming, but it would pop up its head from time to time, and she just couldn't get a handle on it. At first, she thought she was just being hypersensitive, like Kanye at an awards show. But the more she thought about it, the more it troubled her. *Best just to come out with it*, she thought. Life's just easier if you meet things head-on. Unless it's a tractor-trailer. Or worse yet, Kanye.

"Hey, fuzzy, I got a question for you."

Chapter 15

"Shoot," said Mittens as she crammed a fistful of snacks in her maw. She then methodically used a seat cushion to de-crumb her hands.

"First, would it be too much trouble to ask you not to wipe your greasy claws on the couch? Second, I'm a little confused about the whole dragon thing. You're sent here to protect me, and then if I find a husband, he protects me, and you leave? That's a little sexist, don't you think?"

Mittens stared at Gale for a little bit. Then finally said, "Oh? Are you done? Well then, let me address the first part first."

The dragon leaned forward and took hold of the end of Gale's tee shirt and wiped her hands vigorously with it to the protest and hand slapping of the princess.

"Now for part two... No." The dragon reached down and took a healthy swig from a soda can that was next to the couch.

"No, what? No, it's not sexist?"

"No, that's not how the process works. I'm not here to protect you. Neither is a husband. We show up to strengthen you. To add to your might. You're already strong, hon, and a good man would see that too. We galvanize an already incredible you. Understand?"

"I guess," said Gale through a mouthful of treats. She then proceeded to wipe her greasy mitts on Mittens' tail. The dragon gave her tail a flick and sent crumbs sailing back at Gale.

"It's a relationship, not a guardianship. You're not Britney. You don't need anyone to 'take care' of you, per se. Everyone has strengths and weaknesses. He should help your weaknesses, and you should help his. That way, you're a well-balanced couple. Got it?"

"Yeah, I got it."

"Good. Now, what are we doing today? I vote we make pizza rolls and binge-watch a series. There's a good one about these people from Missouri that I keep hearing about."

"I am all about the pizza rolls and the TV binging. I really need to gather myself to prepare for Saturday. Tomorrow, a flock of women will show up to spruce me up for the party."

"I thought you were against the whole thing."

"I am, but my dad had a good point. The party really isn't for me. It's for the people who throw it, and who am I to deny them a good time.

It's a tradition. Mani-pedi, eyebrow wax, haircut, the works. You're more than welcome to join if you wish. Maybe fluff you up a bit before the big day."

"Oh, I'm not going to the big day," said Mittens.

Remember the puppy biting a football from the earlier part of the story? Well, it was back again as Gale sat there flabbergasted, her mouth flapping in the breeze, sans verbiage.

By the way, who thinks up these words, anyway? Flabbergasted? Gob-smacked? Hornswoggled? Mayonnaise? I could go on, but why bother. You know what I'm getting at. The thesaurus is a minefield of silliness.

Anyway, Gale sat there completely mayonnaised. She never thought for an instant that Mittens wasn't going to the party. True, she was here to help with the courting aspect, but they were friends now, even roomies. Mittens HAD to go. Gale would demand it. She was, after all, a princess. She would decree her mandatory attendance. Wait, does a princess even have jurisdiction over a dragon? Way too many questions for Gale to process. Once again, headfirst into the breach went Gale.

"What do you mean you're not going?"

"Pretty simple concept, sugar. Going. Me. Not."

"But you *have* to go. It's my most… *special day!*" Gale said while batting her eyelashes in an exaggerated manner.

"Yes. It's *your* most… *special day*. And I will not do anything to detract from that. You are the center of attention, not me. If I show up, all the guys will be asking me out and trying to get my number, and I just can't do that to you."

"But—"

"But nothing. Your day. No dragon. Capisce?"

"Fine," Gale said with a pout on her face. "But promise me that you're not going to leave me while I'm gone. I have a fear that one day I'll wake up to a poorly written note from you saying goodbye."

"And if I do?"

"Then it will not be my most… *special day* anymore. You can't leave. I just bought fifty pounds of pizza rolls."

"Are you asking me to stay?" asked the dragon.

"Absolutely."

Chapter 15

Gale had given this a lot of thought. She liked having the dragon around. It took a bit of patience and effort to teach her not to eat spoons and cushions and how to work the microwave, but now she had become a fixture in the tower, just like Reflexa.

"But you said that you like living alone. You have a great setup, good Wi-Fi, etc.," said Mittens.

"I do. I love being independent."

"So do I."

"So, let's be independent together!"

"Deal," said the dragon. "Do we need to divide the tower in half with tape like in some cheesy nineties sitcom?"

"Nah, we're good. Are you going to move all your stuff in?" asked Gale excitedly.

"Honey, I have caverns filled with stuff. How about I don't really move in but kind of just be here all the time?"

"Great! You can be like my neighbor in some cheesy nineties sitcom."

The two girls hugged. Birds sang. Doves cried. The world kept on spinning. Gale was enormously overjoyed. She had been a little concerned that the dragon was just going to give her the old Irish goodbye and vacate one day when she wasn't looking. Though it had been only a few weeks, Gale couldn't imagine a life without Mittens. Now, with any luck, she wouldn't have to. At least not for a while.

Popping up from the couch, the dragon made her way to the kitchen.

"Where are you going? You're ruining our special Hallmark moment," said Gale.

"Celebratory pizza rolls, remember."

"Oh yeah. Pizza rolls and Funyums. The cornerstones of any balanced breakfast. Don't just throw them in the oven like last time. Use a pan, and don't forget to put foil on the pan."

"If I have to put pizza rolls on a cookie sheet, why do they call it a cookie sheet?" asked Mittens.

"I have no idea," said Gale. "You figure that out and get back to me. I'm gonna take a quick nap. Let me know when they're ready."

"Quick nap? You just woke up! What did this boy do to you, anyway?" asked Mittens.

Gale, although freshly awake, responded with a shhhhh, curled up on the couch and closed her eyes again. Functionality was at a premium when you spent the night on the phone after a long day. Quickly, Gale closed her eyes and tried to sleep again. But while Gale nodded, nearly napping, suddenly, there came a tapping as of someone gently rapping, rapping on her chamber door.

Only this, and nothing more.

Gale cracked a weary eye and looked around to see if it was only Mittens puttering around the kitchen. Until she heard it again. A light and hesitant knock on the door. Could there really be yet another suitor? Hopefully, she thought, it was just a delivery man with an early birthday gift.

"Mittens, did you hear something?"

"I did, and I will," she said, walking to the window in anticipation of Gale's next inquiry.

Looking out the window brought a smile to the dragon's face as she let out a gentle "awwww". Reluctantly, the princess rose to see what impressed the dragon.

"This had better be good," said Gale as she made her way to the window.

Standing at her door was a little boy that she recognized as the Royal seamstress' son, William. He had a mop of sandy hair that he had tried to comb neatly but was far from successful. He was all of ten years old and dressed neater and cleaner than any boy his age ought to be. Clutched in his hand was a bouquet of wildflowers. He seemed nervous and looked around to see if anyone had noticed him. Then he knocked again.

"He's adorable!" said Mittens. "And look! He brought you flowers."

"Yeah, he's a good kid. I remember when he was born. Look how big he's gotten! I wonder what he wants."

"Looks like he wants a date."

"Stop it. He's ten. Let me go down and see what he's up to. You stay here and work on those pizza rolls." Gale was almost to the stairs when Mittens stopped her with a "whoa."

"What's the matter?" asked Gale.

"I don't know. Maybe pants are in order?"

Chapter 15

"Mittens… he's ten. And the tee shirt is plenty long enough."

"Do you remember what you were like when you were ten?"

"Yeah. I was playing with Barbie dolls." Gale thought about that for a moment. Then she remembered that she would make Barbie and Ken do some pretty funky stuff. *Man, what kind of a degenerate kid was I?* she thought.

"I'd better grab some shorts," she said.

"Good thinking, Princess," Mittens agreed.

Gale slid on some pink shorts and her flippy floppies and headed downstairs to greet her visitor. When she opened the door, there stood William, all four and a half feet of him. He was the son of the Royal Seamstress, Edna, who was one of her mother's dearest friends. All nervous and blushing, William stood with a death grip on the flowers, shuffling his feet and staring at the ground. Poor, shy kid.

"Hi, William! How can I help you today?" Gale said as cheerily as possible. It took an enormous amount of guts for the boy to do what he was doing, and she didn't want to discourage him.

"Hi, um… I wanted to give you these," William said as he thrust the bouquet in her direction, "And I thought I would ask you…"

"Ask me what?" said Gale as she took the flowers from him.

"Well, umm…" The poor boy couldn't squeeze out a word. His freckled face was bright red, and Gale figured if she gave him six inches of daylight, he would run off into the woods.

"Relax, kid. I'm not going to bite. Did your mom send you here to be my suitor?"

"Yes, ma'am. She said it was out of respect for the family or something. I don't really get it, but she really wanted me to come."

"And is your mom hiding in the woods right now snapping a ton of pictures?" asked the princess as she scoped the woods for signs of life.

"No, ma'am. She's at the castle helping your mom, I mean, helping the queen get ready for the party."

"So you marched over here by yourself? That's pretty brave of you."

"Not really. We don't live too far," said William. "You live here now?"

"Yup. Out here on my own. My parents got me the tower for graduation."

"Cool! When I graduated, I got Scabs of Destiny. It's a video game where you kill bad people. It's pretty cool. Ever hear of it?"

"It's crossed my path," said Gale. "I'm going to put these flowers down, and what do you say we sit at the picnic table, and you can tell me all about it."

William went on describing every minor detail of the game, and Gale listened intently. She didn't want to tell him about how she's been playing for years because she needed to keep her anonymity. That was half the fun of playing. When you play, you can be whomever you wish.

"Is it true that you used to have a dragon?" he blurted out. Ten-year-old boys are often shy, but once you get them talking, it becomes a trial to keep up. I swear, they must have to remind themselves to breathe, or else they would pass out from lack of oxygen. William was no exception.

"I did. I mean, I do. She's here."

"Really? Is it out terrorizing a farm or hunting for gold?"

"Actually, *she's* making pizza rolls."

"Really? Can I look? Is she breathing fire on them like this?" William imitated a dragon holding a pan and breathing fire all over it. It looked and sounded like someone hurling into a bucket at a party. Not that she's ever *been* to one… (That's my story and I'm sticking to it. No judgey.)

"Man, I hope not!" laughed Gale.

She leaned close and whispered to William, "Do you want to meet her?"

"I… I can do that? Yes! Yes! Thank you! Thank you so much, Princess." William pumped his little fists in anticipation and excitement. He wriggled on the bench and sat up straight, looking around.

"First, a few things. Number one, if we're going to be friends, you're going to have to call me Gale. Think you can do that?"

"Yes, Gale."

"Second, you have to promise not to be afraid. Dragons are pretty scary, and I don't need you piddling in my yard and running home to my mom, telling her my dragon tried to eat your face off!" Gale made her hands pretend to chomp on William's face and belly until he bent over from laughing.

Chapter 15

"The dragon's name is Wrathnarok, and she's my friend. And you're my friend. So that means that you and the dragon are friends, too. Understand? She may be scary, but I promise that she won't hurt you. Got it?"

"Got it."

"Got it... what?" asked the princess.

"Got it, Princess... I mean Gale!"

"OK, here we go." Gale put two fingers in her mouth to whistle, but once again, only a pblblblt came out. *She's really going to have to work on that.*

"I'm really going to have to work on that," said Gale. "Can you whistle?"

"You bet!" said William, and before she could speak, William let out an ear-splitting whistle that if you, dear readers, had your window open at that very moment, you probably heard as well.

Cue the sail/blanket flap from the front window. His eyes grew wide as the whooshing of winds circled the tower. William buried his hands in his lap and looked everywhere for the great and powerful Wrathnarok. Suddenly a blip of red and white streaked across the lawn as the dragon raced past the two, dragging a burst of air and leaves behind her. Straight through the sky raced the beast, stopping only to blot out the sun for a moment and then plummeted back to the earth again.

"Ooo! Superhero landing! You're gonna love this!" said Gale, and the air went frighteningly still.

With the force of a fallen star, Wrathnarok hit the ground on one knee and one fist, her great wings spread in a huge canopy above the princess and William. The earth shook below them, and dust and dirt and stone became airborne in the wake of the incredible landing. William... was... mayonaissed.

"See? I told you! Just like in the movies. It's harder than it looks," said Gale.

Wrathnarok belched out a mighty roar as black smoke began to gather around her. Fire shot from the dragon toward the sky, and the smell of brimstone was so thick you could swat it away with your hand.

"I AM..." said the great dragon. She had paused to look for permission from Gale to finish her speech. Gale nodded and rolled her hand

189

with a motion that said, "get on with it." The princess was still no fan of the theatrical.

"I AM WRATHNAROK! SLAYER OF VILLAGES! DEVOURER OF HOPE AND TORTURE TO ALL WHO LAY BEFORE ME! HARBINGER OF DOOM AND... TERROR!"

William applauded with great vigor. Gale waited and waited for more words, but there were none. Instead, the dragon took deep bows and bathed in the accolades. Could that really be the end of the introduction?

"Thank you! Thank you! Please don't forget to like and subscribe." The dragon began taking deep bows and straightening an imaginary tie as if hosting a late night talk show.

"Wait a minute. That's it? One word? I cut you off from one word, and you've been pouting for over a week?" said Gale.

"What do you mean?" asked the dragon.

Gale stood and pointed an accusatorial finger at her friend.

"You have been angry about your intro and how I never let you finish, and all I missed was one lousy word?"

"Well, it's an important word," said Wrathnarok as she crossed her arms and turned her head away in a snooty fashion.

"Don't give me that. I'm expecting another twenty minutes of an intro like 'Wrathnarok, who bravely fought the Chicken of Perdue, the seeker of snack foods, the protector of Venetian virginity...'"

"Nope. Just that one word. Sorry if you're disappointed."

"Well, I am," said Gale. "William, this is Wrathnarok the Disappointing. Who bravely finished a sentence and four boxes of Mac and Cheese."

She grabbed the boy's hand and gave it a silly shake.

"Nice ta meetcha! Glad ta see ya!" she said while pumping William's arm in a vigorous fashion. The boy laughed, and the gesture really broke the ice between them. Meeting a dragon for the first time is intimidating in case you haven't read.

"Wow! So nice to meet you," said William. "What big eyes you have! And what big teeth you have!"

Wrathnarok shot a look at Gale, who shook her head with disapproval.

She didn't want him to feel uncomfortable, and a Red Riding Hood reference wasn't going to help.

Chapter 15

"Well, sport. What brings you here today?" Wrathnarok asked.

"I'm here to court the princess. I mean Gale."

"You know that I must approve of you first, right? It's in my contract."

"I do," William looked down at his shoes again. "Do you approve?"

"So far, so good," said the dragon, and he gave the boy a playful boop on the nose.

"Excuse me if I seem nervous. I can't believe I'm meeting a real-life mythical creature!" said William.

"Magical. I'm a magical creature. Mythical creatures don't exist. We're magical. And I'm not sure if we want to go with 'creature.' We'd hate to offend anyone."

"I'm sorry. I hope you won't hold it against me."

"Nah, I'll let that one slide," said the dragon, giving William a playful nudge. "Hey, kid. Want to go for a ride?"

"Sure! Could I?" he pleaded to Gale.

"I don't think that's a good idea, Wrathnarok. He's only ten."

"Oh, he'll be fine. Besides, think about how popular he'll be in school next year."

"He'll be OK?" asked Gale, noticeably nervous.

"Scouts honor!" said the dragon as she held up three talons.

"Hold on," said Gale, and she raced around the side of the tower. In a moment, she returned with a helmet in her hands. It was the one that Sir Flex-a-Lot had left behind. She ran over to William and put it gently over his head. It was a bit big for the boy, but Gale knew that she'd feel safer if he wore it.

"There!" she said. "You look like a knight in shining armor. How do you feel?

"Like a bowl of soup," answered William as he adjusted the helmet to help him see.

"Take good care of him and keep the ride short. Nice and slow. More butterfly and less Wrathnarok, please."

"You have my word. Easy peasy lemon squeezy," the dragon turned and looked at the wee lad. He was cute in his helmet, and his eagerness was inspiring.

"You ready, maverick?" asked the dragon.

William nodded, his helmet bouncing every which way.

"OK, then. Hop on my neck and hold on tight. Don't be scared, now. We'll stay close to the treetops."

Gale couldn't believe her ears. Again.

"Hey, Brimstone Breath! You told me that I couldn't ride on your back. 'It gets in the way of my wings' you said. What gives?"

"Oh! I remember! That was because I was lying to you," said the dragon with a cheesy grin.

Again, Gale pointed a stern finger at Wrathnarok.

"We are going to have a talk later, you and I," said Gale.

"She seems really mad," said William as he gripped the dragon's fur in his little hands.

"Yeah. I'd better be careful. She throws hands like an inmate. I've seen her in action."

"I bet," said the boy.

Wrathnarok flapped upward slowly until she was over the trees. She was careful to keep her neck level so as not to frighten her passenger. Gale waited until they were out of sight and headed upstairs to grab the pizza rolls from the oven and some drinks for their return.

She wasn't really angry with the dragon. Just engaging in a little joking around. Still, she couldn't help but be jealous of William. She really wanted to go for a ride but wondered if, now that they were friends, would it seem wrong to ask? Mittens was her buddy, not her servant, and she would have hated to take advantage of the friendship.

By the time she made it back downstairs, the two had returned from their flight and landed in the glen with a lot of flapping and the rustling of leaves. No superhero landing this time as the dragon slowly alighted onto the ground. William slid off his mount and peeled off his helmet to reveal a grin that went from ear to ear.

"So, how did it go?" asked Gale as she handed a plate and a napkin to William.

"Well, the boy was a bit scared at first, but soon he got the hang of it. We flew out to the edge of the kingdom by an old farmhouse. Apparently, we needed to show off for a little girl who lives out there. I think someone has a crush on her," said Wrathnarok.

Chapter 15

"Is it Alicyn? I just met her yesterday," said Gale. "Hey, do you mind poofing down into a fun-sized dragon again?"

Poof. Pink smoke. Pink dragon.

"I don't have a crush on her," said William, a little too harshly, as he loaded his plate with a few pizza rolls and grabbed a can of soda. "Whoa! You got tiny!" he said as Mittens hopped onto the bench beside him.

"Yeah? Well, you're no Lebron yourself, squirt. And you definitely showed a little interest in someone at the farmhouse."

"Maybe just a little," admitted the boy with an embarrassed grin as he popped a roll into his mouth.

"Don't be embarrassed. She's sweet. And you're a handsome lad. Did she see you flying around with your cool helmet on?" asked Gale.

"I don't think she was home. No one was outside. Now no one is going to believe I flew on a real dragon."

"I think I have a remedy for that. William, I have some good news and some bad news for you. The bad news is that I'm not taking any suitors on at the moment. I hope that's OK."

"Well, that's a relief. I didn't know what I'd do if you said yes."

"I think I'm a little too young for a husband just yet. How about you?"

"Me too," said the boy. "I'm really not ready to settle down either. Plus, if you said yes, we'd probably have to get bunk beds or something, and I hate bunk beds."

"Good point. Bunk beds are the worst. Though they do leave a lot of room for other things," said Mittens through a mouthful of food.

"The good news is that I need an escort to the party on Saturday. It's tradition. Do you think you're up for it?" asked Gale.

"I dunno. I'd probably have to ask my mom," said William.

"Then, when we're done with the introduction, maybe you and Wrathnarok can fly out to the farm again? I promised the girls some birthday cake. That way, Alicyn can see you swoop in, and you guys can hang out for a bit. You'd really be doing me a solid."

"Sure. I think I can do that."

"Then it's settled. With Mom's permission, of course."

"Gale, do you know a lot of mythi—I mean, magical people? I mean, you're a princess and all. You probably know a lot, right?"

"I have met some, sure."

"Really? Like who?" asked the boy.

"Yeah, Gale. Like who?" asked Mittens with a cynical glance.

"I met a goblin just last week. He showed up with two minions and tried to lure me away to some magical land. He had a big carriage and was super skinny and creepy."

"Whoa! How did you get rid of him?" asked the boy.

"I scared him away," said Gale.

"Well, actually...," said Mittens.

"I. Scared him. Away," said Gale through a set of clenched teeth. Probably not a good idea to tell the ten-year-old that the goblin "Chad" was turned into a dragon-sized fruit roll-up.

"Right. Of course. How silly of me," said Mittens with an eyeroll.

"I also met a giant! He must have been twenty feet tall and had huge muscles! That was his helmet you were wearing."

"Really? What happened to him?" asked William.

"He battled my dragon and bested her with a plate of sausages!"

"Lies!" shouted Mittens, and Gale and William chuckled a little.

"I also met a warlock who tried to cast a spell on me. He wanted to kidnap me and take me away as his prisoner."

"Wow! That's scary. What happened to him?" asked William.

"Remember when I told you that she throws hands like an inmate?" said Mittens as she gestured to the princess.

"You beat him up? Cool!"

"Well, I had some help," said Gale as she scratched the top of Mittens' head.

"Not that you need it," said Mittens.

"I bet!" said William.

Their laughter rose from the glen as they continued to nosh and guzzle and tell silly stories. All too soon, the pizza rolls were gone, and it was time to bid their new guest a good evening. William thanked the dragon for the ride and thanked Gale for the food and fun. The princess reminded him to have his mother give her a call about Saturday and said that she was honored to have him escort her to her party.

Chapter 15

William made his way to the edge of the forest when Gale called out to him.

"William! Wait!" she said.

Gale picked up the helmet from the lawn and ran it over to the boy.

"You forgot your helmet." When she handed it to William, his face lit up with joy.

"I can have this? The giant's helmet?"

"I think you've earned it, don't you?"

"Thank you so much!" William wrapped his arms around Gale. She was hoping that he would wear the gift when he went to visit the Miller's farm on Saturday. Making it a present instead of a requirement would surely do the trick. After all, This-And-That had fairly lax helmet laws.

"Do you know how to get home from here, or should I call your mom?"

"Nope, I'll be fine. My feet know the way!" William said as he waved goodbye and disappeared into the woods.

When Gale turned around, Mittens was big again. Her wings were flapping much to the chagrin of the nearby foliage.

"Where do you think you're off to?" asked Gale.

"I'm... just gonna make sure he gets home OK. I'd hate for anyone to think that anything bad happened to him under my watch."

"You mean you don't want people to think that you ate a ten-year-old," said Gale.

"What? No! Of course not. Just looking out for the lad." Another eyeroll and a chuckle from Wrathnarok, and off into the sky she went.

"Hurry back! I want to play Dummikub!" shouted Gale as she headed back to the house. She was filled with accomplishment, having solved her escort issue. William was an innocuous choice, and she was feeling pleased with herself. No drama for the party, and there was an outside chance that her parents would be happy. And happy, for lack of a better word, is good.

Chapter 16

IN THE LAND OF This-and-That, the princess lay in her bed thinking. Though the hour was late, and she had a big day tomorrow, thoughts danced around her head in the darkness. Mittens was on the couch, politely giving Gale some much-needed space as she tossed and turned in anticipation of the huge birthday party that awaited her at daybreak.

During the morning, her tower had been abuzz with excitement. Her mother, the queen, had come by to go over the itinerary and to aid in the choosing of a gown. She brought along the royal seamstress, Edna, to help with any last-minute alterations that needed to be done. Although Gale had been stuffing her face with cheeses and pizza rolls, her weight hadn't varied enough to make any drastic changes, and they settled on a lovely gold gown with a purple inset on the sleeves and cape. Edna was vocal about not using a cape since she considered them hazardous, but the queen insisted.

Gale could not have possibly cared less about the gown since she only planned on wearing it for the ceremony. She wished that she had dropped a few more hints about the sneakers and had hoped that her mother would have mentioned them when she discussed the party. The queen remained silent, and, barring a last-minute surprise, she would be clopping around in a pair of leather sandals that weren't exactly comfortable but looked cute enough.

The Self-Sufficient Princess

Edna was very appreciative of the invitation that the princess gave to her son, William, to be her official royal escort at the ceremony. She blathered on about family and honor, and when she got to the part about what a "cute couple" they would make, Gale mentally tapped out. She liked Edna and knew that she meant well, but enough was enough already. She would have walked downstairs just to get away from the conversation, but there were about forty pins stuck in various places in the dress that kept her a captive audience.

After the fitting was done and Edna retired to her house to finish the necessary hemming and whatnot, Gale plopped herself onto the couch and covered her head with a pillow. Edna's shrill voice was still ringing in her ears with the incessant "Dahling!" that seemed to punctuate every sentence that the woman spoke. The queen sat on the arm of the couch and patted Gale's feet.

"I know it's tough, honey, but soon it will be all over, and you and your friends can go to the back courtyard and do whatever you want," said the queen.

"I know. I just hate all this attention. I'm going to have a ton of people staring at me. I will be the princess that broke generations of tradition by not taking a husband at her eighteenth birthday gala, and they'll probably hurl rotten tomatoes at me or something."

"Nonsense. Besides, rotten fruit is old school. The worst they will do is take unflattering pictures of your butt and put them on Gracebook."

Gale pulled the pillow off her face and glared at her smiling mother.

"You're not helping," said Gale and buried her face back under the pillow.

"You'll have fun. All your friends will be there. There will be a DJ, and we ordered a bunch of pizza so that you guys won't be gnawing on a mutton joint or whatever traditional crap that your dad has in store."

"All of my friends AND about a hundred other kids from every kingdom. Honestly, I'd rather have the rotten fruit."

"Nightingale Lynn Beckett!" Gale knew that she was in trouble when her mother used her full name. I'm not sure how it works in your neighborhood, but a full name still gives me goosebumps.

CHAPTER 16

"You are not going into this with the proper attitude. This is supposed to be a happy occasion."

"I know, Mom. It's just a lot. Too much even. I really didn't want any of this. I didn't want the parade and people and the gown. I'm gonna look like a disco ball standing up there, all shiny and round."

"Relax, your dad's wearing purple and white. He looks like a jelly sandwich that somebody sat on."

That made Gale giggle enough, so she left her pillow sanctuary and sat up.

"And what will the queen be wearing?" asked Gale.

"I have a nice lavender gown with gold trim. I will wear the crown that your grandmother left me and…" The queen pulled up a picture on her phone and showed the princess. "A sweet pair of Christian Louboutin that your father doesn't know about yet."

"So boojie! You're going to wow them at the party."

"So will you, for about a half hour. Then you can turn back into a teenager again and have some fun," said the queen. She patted her daughter on the legs and walked to the window.

"Ah! They're here!" said the queen as she looked out over the glen.

"Who's here?" asked Gale as she hopped up off the couch to join her mother at the window.

Outside were a slew of coaches. Men jumped out carrying boxes and huge black chairs. Folding tables and more boxes were carefully extracted from a wagon that was behind one of the coaches. Out of another came quite a few women that Gale didn't recognize, and last were two very attractive men dressed in white short-sleeved shirts with white pants.

"Come right up!" shouted the queen to the group below.

"Mom! What is all this?"

"Just a little surprise to help you relax. I know that you had a difficult couple of weeks. This is my little birthday gift to you."

Up the stairs came the men carrying two leather recliners and box after box of equipment. They placed the recliners down and slid the couch against the back wall to make room. They set up two folding tables near the kitchen and began to assemble them into massage tables. A stack of towels was placed in a warmer and plugged into an outlet in the kitchen. The women sat porcelain tubs near the end of the chairs and half-filled each with warm water from the sink. Stools and a table flanked each chair and became cluttered with all the tools needed for a manicure and pedicure.

While the tower was still a whirlwind of motion, the door opened again and in bounded Gale's cousins, the twins. Starr was in the lead, with Cierra right behind her. Or was Cierra in the lead, with Starr following her? I can never tell. They were identical in every way. Black hair that cut their face like a raven's wing. Short and springy and bubbly and reeking of mischievous deeds. They were almost twenty years old and the epitome of ladies of the court. Or so it would seem. For in public, they were prim and contained proper young women. Out of the public eye, they were deviant and inappropriate. Gale loved them to death.

Hugs and kisses were exchanged, accompanied by the usual high-pitched squealing and laughing that came hand in hand with a girls' reunion. As the stylists placed countless choices of nail polish onto a small table, a tray of hors d'oeuvres began to circulate. There were cheese puffs and various crackers with meats and thick strips of maple bacon. No one was shy about eating them.

"Mom. You really didn't have to do all this," said Gale, but her mother couldn't be found. Gale looked around for a bit, but she didn't see her. Finally, the queen emerged dramatically from Gale's room, wearing nothing but a heated towel.

"I know, but I thought we could use a little girl time. Ladies, I'd like you to meet Kerry and Grace, the best nail people in the kingdom. And the two gentlemen dressed in white are Hans and Franz. They are the Royal Masseurs."

"We have Royal Masseurs? Since when?" asked the princess through a mouthful of bacon. She knew almost everyone in the castle, and she would have remembered these two handsome men.

"Since shut up," said the queen to a bevy of laughter from everyone in the room. "Everyone else can go, thank you for all of your help, and I will call you when we are done." As the rest of the crowd made their way to the door, the Queen made her way to the massage tables.

Chapter 16

"Girls, Hans is mine. You can draw straws to see who gets Franz." The handsome Hans held a huge bath sheet towel up to shield the queen from any onlookers as she situated herself on the table.

"I'll go," said Starr, or was it Cierra, as she retired to the bedroom to change into a towel. Gale and the remaining twin sat in the leather chairs and readied themselves for a mani-pedi. The chairs vibrated, and the water bubbled around their feet, leaving the princess to dissolve like a bath bomb in a hot tub. One twin hopped onto the massage table while the other sat beside Gale in the huge leather chair.

"So, where's this dragon that I've been hearing about?" asked a twin. It's really hard to tell them apart, so bear with me. Technically, it doesn't matter who says what, but I'm trying to be accurate here, so cut me a little slack.

"Good question," said Gale. "She ran out to do some errands, although I have no idea what errands a dragon has. Does she have bills that need to be paid? Her tires rotated? I haven't a clue."

"Reflexa," said the queen and the mirror chimed to life.

"Yes, your Grace."

"I'm getting a massage from a handsome stranger. Please play something appropriate so that I may relax."

"Yes, my Grace. Playing something from the Naked Queen Playlist," said Reflexa, stirring a laugh out of the room. She played some Commodores, and though it was Friday afternoon, everything was easy, like Sunday morning.

Gale liked seeing her mother act like a regular girl since it was a rarity. The queen normally was filled with pomp and carried a regal air. Otherwise, she was a mom, complaining about how dirty the tower was. *"Do you want ants? Because this is how you get ants,"* her mother would say as she inspected the floors and countertops.

Yet, Queen Evelyn could truly blend into any situation. She just witnessed her mother walk out into a crowded room wearing nothing but a towel and crack jokes. Then she mounted a table naked in front of a stranger with incredible confidence and assurance. She was a mom and a queen, and a girl and a woman all wrapped up in a neat package. *If that's what it takes to be a queen,* thought Gale, *I don't know if I have it in me.*

The princess chose a deep purple for her fingernails and toes, while Cierra (Starr?) picked a hot pink that she claimed matched her eyes. The manicurists went to work rubbing the girls' legs with oils and worked their feet like they were kneading dough. A few moans and grunts floated from the massage tables.

They all did some catching up with the twins: boyfriends, parties, a coach accident and a quick rundown of mutual acquaintances. Tea was spilled about who was dating whom and who was not dating whom anymore. Where this one was and where that one had been and who saw this one, and why we don't talk to that one. Gale found it all entertaining but slightly exhausting. Soon, as Gale had expected, the topic turned to her.

"Say, Cuz, are you going to let us in on your suitor adventures?" asked Starr.

"Yeah, spill it. I need to know the real story as to why your dragon turned some guy's ship into a floating charcoal briquette," said Cierra.

"OK. I'll give you the abridged version of what happened."

"Eh… no, no. You will tell us *everything*, or I'll have Franz here bend you into a pretzel."

"Maybe she doesn't want to talk in front of Aunt Ev."

"No! Aunt Ev is cool. Aren't you, Aunt Ev?"

"I'm naked on a table covered in grease. How much cooler can I get?" asked the queen.

"See? I told you. Now spill," demanded Starr.

Gale hesitated for a moment. The only people who knew everything about her run-in with the captain were a magical dragon and an enchanted internet-driven mirror. She could use the venue to vent a little. Carrying secrets was difficult and heavier than one would think. Although she was introverted by nature, the princess decided to go for it and share with the family.

"Mom? Think you can avoid being a mom for a few minutes?" asked Gale.

If the princess was going to talk about all that she had been through (and let's face it, she kind of needed to), the talk wasn't going to end in a lecture from her mom. Gale knew what went wrong and where mistakes were made, and having her mother point them out wasn't going to change anything. *No reason to throw my past in my face,* thought Gale, *I was there, I know what I did.*

"I know, I know, no judgey. Tell your story, hon. Now, Hans, hit those hamstrings a little harder. I'm not made of glass, you know."

Gale took a deep breath and looked towards her mom. The queen's face was buried in the massage table ring. Gale figured now was as good a time as any. No stares or glares from the parental.

"OK, here goes. Once upon a time, in the land of This-and-That…"

"BOOOOO! BOOOOO! THIS STORY IS STUPID! BOOOO! GET TO THE GOOD STUFF!" said, well, everyone in the room. A chorus of faux disappointment showered the princess, along with a cheese puff or two. I think even Reflexa jeered a little. Kerry and Grace, the manicurists, tried desperately not to laugh at the display, but they couldn't hold off.

"HEY!" yelled the princess. "It's my story. I'll tell it how I want!"

As a narrator, I can completely relate. The struggle is real. Rock on, girl.

The tale began at the dragon alert that Gale received on her phone and ended with the long talk with PizzaBoi. She tried not to embellish anything, but one's memory will always twist a story ever so slightly. In discretion regarding her mother, the princess may have left out a tiny detail or two about what was said after two a.m. with PizzaBoi.

Questions were peppered in from the twins from time to time about how Gale handled one thing and how she felt about another. Gasps emitted when Sir Chad was eaten, and cheers rose when the captain got his jumblies… jumbled. It would have been easier on all and less stressful on our princess if they had just bought a copy of the book you're reading.

The cousins were extremely supportive of Gale, and even the manicurists chimed in a kind thought or two. Many agreements from Hans and Franz in the form of a nod or glance as they continued to tenderize the queen and Starr. Gale was a little apprehensive about sharing her tribulations in front of two strange men, and wondered inside whether they were really on her side or merely being supportive since they were getting paid. In the end, Gale decided to believe in their sincerity.

The royal foursome prepared to swap spaces, so everyone took a short break to rest while the changing and unchanging commenced. Starr chatted with Franz about how strong his hands were as he popped a snack into his mouth and drank a large glass of water. Nails were compared, and compliments were thrown to the staff as they enjoyed some cheese and crackers and a soda or two. A wonderful, swirled design of white enhanced the purple on Gale's fingernails and toenails, while Cierra had hers pink-lined with a French tip and bedazzled with tiny fake gems, and all seemed pleased with their choices.

Now the princess was on the table getting squirted with warm oil and rolled out like fresh dough. Hans' hands were strong and magical as they found every hidden knot and ball of stress and rendered them asunder. Gale was slightly self-conscience about her appearance and even more so about letting a stranger touch her, but the atmosphere helped bleed away most of her anxiety, and she began to relax. Reflexa filled the air with sweet and light songs of love and hope that mixed with the lavender-scented oils.

"Just think," said a cousin, "When you're queen, we can do this all the time."

"I'm not sure I'm going to be queen," said Gale giving a grunt as she spoke.

Did you ever say something that just slipped out? Strange how the words just hang in the air like lightning bugs, flashing every few seconds just to remind you that they are there. Gale didn't even realize that she had said it since she was so relaxed, and her face was buried in a hole in the massage table. In fact, she wouldn't have given it a second thought except for the fact that the entire room had stopped. Reflexa ended her song abruptly. Hans and Franz ceased kneading. The manicurists stopped manicuring. Even a tiny ladybug that had been traversing the door jamb in the living room stood still and turned her teeny-weeny head towards the princess.

Normally, Gale would have peeked her head up and fired off a quip, and the narrator would be anxious to report it, but much to each of our chagrins, there was nothing. Gale kept her head buried and contemplated throwing up the cheese puffs that she scarfed down. She tried to will the ceiling to collapse and bury her in enough rubble that she would never be found again. She needed something, anything that would break the tension. She silently prayed that it wouldn't be the queen.

Chapter 16

Sometimes, dear readers, the day is ripe for unanswered prayers.

"Let me get this straight. You think that renouncing the throne is still a viable option?" asked the queen.

"I do. It is my life, and it is my choice," replied the princess. In for a penny, etc., etc.

As she kept her head nestled in the table, Gale could hear the clinking of nail polish bottles being gathered and the boxing of massage supplies. The princess secretly hoped that Hans could just fold her up in the table and take her with him when he left. She could start a new life somewhere. *I don't have to run away and live on the street,* thought Gale. *I can sail away. Maybe the knights could find me a garbage barge of my very own. Sir Knoxville can fling me to another kingdom on his trebuchet. Maybe I can coax Mittens into sharing that cavern I've heard so much about.*

"Everyone relax. No one's going anywhere," said the Queen. It was as if her mother was reading her thoughts. Maybe the queen *had* read the book, after all. At first, Gale thought she was speaking directly to her but found that her comments were for the rest of the room.

"Ladies. Gentlemen. Please let's get back to the good time that we were having. My daughter and I have discussed this from time to time. It has always been her choice, and I support her in any decision that she makes. Now then, let's get back to work, people."

That's where the day went sideways. Gale lay in the dark replaying the moment over and over again, but the ending always remained the same. She had ruined something nice that her mother tried to give her. Whether it was intentional or not wasn't the issue. If you didn't mean to hurt someone, they are still hurt, and only time can fix that.

There was also the matter of the talk that she had with her mom after everyone had left. Once the last carriage had pulled away, Gale tried to apologize to the queen for sounding selfish in front of everyone.

"Mom, I'm so sorry."

"For what, dear?"

"For spoiling the day. For speaking out of turn."

"In a few hours, you will turn eighteen, hon. The days of speaking out of turn are over. You're your own person now. You can say whatever you wish."

"Yeah, but I sounded like a spoiled brat."

"I said that you can say what you want. I never said that there wouldn't be consequences."

"I didn't mean to say anything in front of everyone. It just kind of slipped out."

"Yeah, well, that it did. I'm sure the kingdom is overcome with the rumor that you are leaving the royal family and renouncing your throne tomorrow. I fear you may need to get in front of this during your speech. People will put the lack of a suitor with the rumor, and it will spread like wildfire. And your cousins will help fan the flames."

"Why would they do that?"

"Because if you don't take the throne, someone else will, and your cousins will have a legitimate claim. I love my sister's kids to death, but can you see them running the show? Our national bird will be a Jell-O shot."

Normally Gale would have laughed at the joke, but she felt too awful. She hadn't really considered any of the consequences at all. All the princess was doing was imagining a life abroad, away from the regal airs and responsibilities. A chance to not be strangled by the history and the regimented lifestyle. She had never once wondered what would happen to This-and-That.

"You know, I've been hearing for years about you wanting to stop being a princess. You never really explained why. So, let's do that now. Why do you want to leave so badly?" asked the queen.

Gale stopped and weighed her words. She needed to sound smart and put up a decent argument. Not that her mother would ever stop her from making her own decision, but she deeply wanted her to understand her reasons. Gale didn't want to appear to be a child dreaming of a cool life without responsibilities. She wanted to make sense of it to her mother.

"It's not who I am. I'm not you, Mom. Understand that I appreciate all that you do. The charity and the nobility. The decisions and all the great stuff that you do for the kids. I just don't want to lose myself in it. Dad and I talked about how you used to paint and how busy you both can be, and it sounds awful. The regal dances and the royal parties. Dressing up in gowns and heels. Man, do I hate heels! I'm going to have

Chapter 16

to keep my head high and say and do all of the right things all the time. There's no way that I can pull that off!"

Gale felt her throat close, and tears form as she spoke. Still, she refused to be weak at this moment.

"Then don't," said the queen.

Her cavalier response took Gale by surprise, and it showed on her face.

"So, you won't be mad if I don't want to follow in your footsteps?"

"Absolutely not. But not following me and giving up your title are two different things, sweetheart."

"You lost me."

"You'll be your own queen. You can change and sculpt your world as you wish. Be the first queen to wear yoga pants and flip-flops. Cut your council meetings to once a month or every two months. Or three. Create a national venue for gaming and compete with other kingdoms. Eat pizza rolls on the throne if you wish. But don't throw it all away because you're scared. I raised you better than that."

"So, I can still be a queen and, say, scratch my butt with a fork if I wish?"

"I wouldn't recommend posting a video of it, but yes, you can. Besides, those stupid gowns are so itchy. I never imagined using a fork," said the queen. She quickly returned to the topic. "Do you really think I'm like this all the time? You've seen me walk around without makeup and a rat's nest for hair."

"Never outside our living quarters."

"No, but if I was just a regular mom, I wouldn't go out like that either. That's who *I* am. You need to worry about being who *you* are and not what you think everyone expects of you," said the queen.

"What do *you* expect of me?" asked Gale.

"That girl who went to the farmhouse. The girl who stood her ground against some terribly awful people. The girl who lets her dragon sleep inside. The one who cried about Sir Chad and stood up for Sir Reginald. The one who calls me just to see how I'm doing. That's what I expect from my daughter. Gold is golden, no matter what package it's in."

"I'm still not sure what I'm going to do, Mom. I still can't see me handling stuff with the ease that you do. Saying the right thing. Doing the right thing. I'm just going to make a fool of myself. I'll be dubbed Nightingale the Foolish."

"It takes time, hon, and a lot of practice. Sometimes when I'm dealing with something or someone, I'm calm and collected outside but angry or crumbling inside. I'm not a robot. It all affects me as well. Then I come home and complain to your father, and he rubs my feet while we watch a movie. You know, I really thought being an 'empty nester' was going to be more traumatic. Nope. It's all foot rubs and movies," said the queen with a smile.

"What if I don't want to get married?"

"Then don't."

"What if I don't want to have kids?"

"Then don't."

"What if I want to stay here in the tower and only commute to the castle?"

"Then do that. You'd still be the queen. Queen of your own kingdom. Doesn't that sound nice?"

"Maybe… are you going to say anything to Dad about this?"

"Of course. He's my husband and the king. Someday, when the time is right, I'm sure it might slip out," said the queen with a smile.

Now here she was, in the dead of night, tossing and turning in her bed. Her mother's voice played over in her head as she stared towards the dark wall of her room. Gold is still golden. Queen of her own Kingdom. None of that sounded restricting or as awful as she imagined.

As the night crept by, Gale felt a little lonely and disconnected. She gave a thought to getting up and seeing if PizzaBoi was online, but it was late, and she knew that if she logged on and he was nowhere to be found, it would sting a little, and no pain stung like self-inflicted wounds.

Instead of getting up, Gale reached for her phone.

"Hey, Mom… you up?"

"I am"

"Dad rubbing your feet?"

"Dad is snoring so loud that the vibrations are rubbing my feet, so kind of."

"I just wanted to thank you. For everything."

Chapter 16

"You're welcome. And happy birthday! It's officially past 12 a.m.!"
"Thanks. Love! Love! Love!"
"Love you, too, honey. All the loves!"
Gale placed the phone back on her nightstand and tried to fall asleep.

Chapter 17

IN THE LAND OF This-and-That, the gates of Castle Beckett were swung wide at precisely six a.m. At six-fifteen, castle guards began to cordon off the main street and shop owners were busily preparing for the big day. At seven a.m., the final preparations were checked and double-checked: the sound system, the lighting, the seating and the entertainment were at the ready, and everything seemed to be in order. Eight a.m. marked the beginning of admission into the kingdom as people from far and near began to flood the sidewalks preparing for the princess's eighteenth birthday extravaganza. Exactly at nine, lighthearted music was pumped through the streets, food was displayed and gorged upon, and kegs of the kingdom's finest lagers were tapped and swilled at leisure.

At exactly ten a.m. on the dot, our princess rolled over in bed and left a string of drool on her pillow, emitting a snore that would rival her father.

Reflexa hung on the wall in a dither. If she had feet to tap, they would surely be tapping nervously. Throughout the morning, the mirror would play Birthday by the Beatles, In Da Club by 50 cent, Birthday by Katy Perry, and Ace of Spades by Motorhead, yet nothing would entice the princess to wake up for her party. Several phone calls were missed, and her alarm was silenced about a dozen times, but still, the lovely Gale showed no signs of life. Mittens had left early and was of no help, so the daunting task of waking Gale was left up to the magic mirror.

"I'm so sorry," whispered Reflexa. "I hate to do this to you, but you've left me no choice."

The mirror jacked her volume up as high as she could, reached into her vast library of music, and blared the one thing that she knew would shake anyone out of a deep slumber.

Bagpipes.

As the whining of the pipes filled the tower, Reflexa heard a scream come from the bedroom. Sounds of destruction were coming from behind the door as Gale hopped out of bed, knocking over the lamp on her nightstand and slipping on the throw rug, sending her to the floor. The bedroom door flung open wide as a bleary-eyed Gale emerged from her tomb.

"IF YOU DON'T TURN THAT CRAP OFF, SO HELP ME, I WILL DONATE YOU TO GOODWILL SO FAST YOU'LL WISH YOU WERE HANGING IN A TRUCK STOP SHOWER!"

Reflexa killed the music.

"Sorry, M'lady. I've been trying to wake you up for about an hour now. Nothing was working, so I took extreme measures. Mittens left. She made you tea, though it's probably cold by now. Happy Birthday!"

Gale gave the mirror a grunt and scratched at her butt as she shuffled over to the kitchen to check on her tea. It was indeed cold, so she threw it in the microwave for a few minutes. Leaning against the counter, the princess rubbed her eyes hard enough to see little fireworks behind the lids and asked what time it was.

"At the tone… the time will be ten o' four… and forty-five seconds… beep," said Reflexa.

"And what time does the party start?"

"You're due to arrive and begin your speech at noon."

"Plenty of time. Any word on my transportation?"

"A coach will be here at eleven-thirty."

Gale pulled her tea out of the microwave and gave it a healthy sip.

"Any word on the web of my rumored renouncing?" asked Gale between sips.

Chapter 17

"I would be remiss if I said it wasn't being mentioned."

"Mentioned or trending?"

"Merely mentioned. Nothing big yet."

"Outstanding. I'm sure that my father has gotten an earful by now. See? This is why I didn't want all of this fuss. One little birthday and everything gets all fouled up. I have no desire to attend this party. All I asked for was a lousy pair of sneakers."

"That reminds me. Pipkin and I got you a little something. Will you get the door? There should be a knock in three… two… one…"

There was a knock at the door.

"Reflexa, the internet is a creepy, creepy, place. How did you know that?"

"The delivery driver has to scan the package when he arrives. It wasn't that difficult, really," said the mirror.

"Still super creepy," said Gale as she and her teacup made their way downstairs. She returned holding a package. Setting her tea on the table, the princess quickly unwrapped the box and opened it. Enclosed therein were the pair of sneakers that she had been asking for since the beginning of the book.

"Happy Birthday, M'lady!" Reflexa said as her screen was filled with balloons and confetti pictures.

"Oh, Reflexa, they're perfect! Thank you so much!" said the princess, and she walked over and gave the mirror's frame a kiss. "I'm going to put them in my bag and wear them to the after-party. I'm going to be honest: I half expected a trebuchet from you."

"Would you like me to add a trebuchet to your cart?"

"Absolutely not," Gale said.

"Are you sure? Maybe it can fling you into the shower so you can get ready. You'd better get moving if you want to be there on time."

"Plenty of time!" said Gale as she hurried off to the bathroom for a shower and shave. While waiting for the shower to warm up, Gale crammed a pair of shorts, a few tops, and her new sneakers into an overnight bag. Then the task of the shower and the shaving of the legs.

Guys, if you've seen a TV commercial of a lady shaving their legs, it's nothing like that at all. It is a tremendous feat of gymnastics, with legs and knees propped up in every way imaginable. Usually, half in and half out of a shower with water going everywhere. Kneecaps and ankles become serious obstacles, and I won't even get into the rest of it. Just know that it takes a skilled hand and a degree in acrobatics to get smooth legs. Appreciate the effort.

A little powder, some baby oil, deodorant, a squeeze of perfume and a shimmy into her gown magically transformed our girl into an elegant woman. As she brushed her hair and sprayed copious amounts of hair spray into it, she caught a glimpse of herself in the mirror. She was eighteen now. No longer a little girl and maybe no longer a member of the royal family. Her mother said that she needed to get in front of the renouncement rumor, and there was no time like the present.

Neither a coward nor a fool. And maybe not a princess, thought Gale.

"Mirror mirror, on a hook. Please tell me how bad I look?" said Gale as she emerged from her room.

"You look lovely. I especially like the heels… if there were some."

Gale realized that her feet were indeed bare. She turned and raced back to her room to grab the shoes when she saw her overnight bag on the bed. Sticking out were her new sneakers. She decided to put them on.

"How's this?" asked the princess as she hiked up her gown to show off her new gift.

"They are highly inappropriate. I love them."

"I wanted a part of you with me at the castle. Just so you know that you're important to me."

"I'm honored. And I love you too, princess."

Gale smiled at the mirror and walked to the fridge to grab two energy drinks.

"Any word from Mittens? I was kind of hoping that I'd see her before the party."

"Look on the table," said the mirror.

There sat a box that had not been there when she woke up. It was an old wooden case with a hasp and an unlocked padlock. On top was a note:

Hey, Sis. Happy birthday!
This isn't your gift. That's waiting at the castle.

Chapter 17

Inside of this box is a tiara that was originally owned by Elizabeth the First of England.
Don't ask how I got it because I think the statute of limitations is still valid.
I thought it might help with the speech.
You remember the movie, don't you?
Love! Love! Love!

Of course, Gale had seen the movies at least twenty times, if not more. It was a staple in the family. Some movies are embraced by certain people, like The Godfather or Pacino's Scarface. Royal families had Elizabeth: The Golden Age. It was watched and watched again. She knew exactly where the dragon was going with this, and she decided to take her advice.

She opened the box and saw the crown sitting on a bed of ancient red velvet. It was very slight and simple, with a purple jewel in the center. Gale didn't even know if it was authentic or just the dragon being silly. What she did know was that the dragon, Wrathnarok, the great and powerful, called her Sis. That was greater than any gift she was going to get today.

Smiling, Gale placed the crown on her head, but it didn't seem to sit right. She tried a few bobby pins, but it seemed like it would fall off at the slightest movement. She was going to scrap it but decided it would be rude not to wear it since she was wearing the sneakers that Reflexa gave her. Now she knew why her mother kept her chin high all the time. It wasn't an air about her, it was to keep her stupid crown straight.

"When does my carriage get here?" she asked Reflexa as she tried readjusting her crown.

"About five minutes ago."

"Holy Panini! I'm late!" said Gale as she grabbed the two energy drinks and her bag and made her way to the stairs.

"A princess is never late, just detained. Have fun!" said the mirror. Gale blew her a kiss as she raced down the stairs. When she opened the door, she found a huge white and gold carriage being led by two black stallions. The horses were majestic and almost identical, with thick black manes and fluffy tails. Along each nose was a white patch in the shape of a diamond on one and a heart on the other. Lastly was a blue silk ribbon tied into a bow around the carriage.

"Happy Birthday, M'Lady," said a knight standing by her door. His armor shined in the sun, silver and polished. The knight's hair was long and flowed down to his shoulders, and he carried a dress helmet in his right hand, a long plume erupting from its top. The knight was clean-shaven and smelled of sandalwood, and he greeted the princess with a smile. The dress armor may have disguised him, but his kind eyes gave him away.

It was none other than Sir Reginald the Not-So-Rank. He was immaculate from his head to his shiny silver boots. Reg greeted her with the customary bow, and Gale returned the greeting with a customary curtsey. After, Gale wrapped her arms around the big man and squeezed as hard as she could. She knew the effort and pain that this display must have cost him. Our girl was floored by the gesture.

"Thanks. Reg, you look so handsome! You didn't have to do this. I thought that I made that clear."

"M'Lady, there is nothing that I would not do for you or your family. Now, what do you think of the carriage?"

"It's... amazing! What's with the bow?"

"It's a gift from the king and the queen for your birthday. The carriage is to be at your disposal, day or night."

"And the horses?"

"Yours as well."

Gale walked to the front of the carriage only to see Woltz, the king's personal driver, standing there holding the reins.

"Happy Birthday, Gale. Do you like it?"

"Woltz, I have no words. What are the horses' names?"

"Jericho has the diamond on his nose."

"And the one with the heart?" asked Gale.

"Horse-o."

The look on Gale's face was one of humorous disapproval.

Deflated, Woltz said, "I'm sorry, Princess. My daughter named the horse when she was very young. Please feel free to change it to anything you wish. 'Tis a silly name."

Chapter 17

Hearing that his daughter named her gift made Gale feel a little guilty about her reaction.

"I wouldn't dream of it. I love it," said Gale.

"Here, feed them an apple," he said as he handed her some fruit. Gale slowly approached the horses so as not to spook them, talking softly as she did. The stallions munched on a few apples as the princess stroked each of their necks.

"I can't believe they're mine," she finally said.

"As am I. The king has given me the privilege of being your official driver."

"Dad probably just wants someone to keep tabs on where I'm going."

"Hey, what happens between a carriage driver and his passenger is strictly confidential. It's all part of the carriage drivers' code that I just made up. Besides, what's he gonna do? Fire me? We play cards every Thursday, and I let him win. I ain't going anywhere!"

The knight unsheathed his sword and, with a surgeon's precision, cut the ribbon and let it fall to the ground. Then he opened the door and helped the princess step inside. The interior was red with gold trim to match the outside. Soft velour seats circled the entire interior, and lights were in every corner. On the windows were red curtains, and beneath the seats was storage and a mini fridge. It was elegant and classy, and Gale couldn't believe her fortune.

"Reg, where's William?" she asked as he closed the door.

"I believe he is presently watering the Woods of Nevermore, M'Lady."

"Well, he'd better have some hand sanitizer on him."

"Beneath the seat, M'lady."

William emerged from the woods hiking up his pants and trying to fix his belt. He was dressed to match the princess, and his unruly hair was matted down with some kind of grease. All cleaned up, the lad looked fairly handsome, and she knew he'd make a big impression on the crowd and the Fair Alicyn later on. You can say what you want about his mother, the seamstress. That lady was an artist with a needle and thread.

"Hi Gale!" said William as he hopped into the carriage.

"Hands!" demanded Gale. He held them out, and she plopped a healthy dollop of hand sanitizer into each palm. As the boy rubbed his hands, Gale

217

synced her phone to the carriage's sound system. She reached into her bag and pulled out the two energy drinks and handed one to William.

"Oh, Woltz…" called Gale from the window.

"Yes, M'Lady."

"Do we think that Jericho and Horse-o would like to run fast this morning?"

"Yes, M'Lady."

"And do we think this new carriage is capable of running hot?"

"Yes, M'Lady"

"Make it so."

"Yes, M'Lady!" said an enthusiastic Woltz. "I think I'm gonna like this job."

Gale looked William dead in the eyes and said, "Hold onto your hat, kid." And with a hardy "He-Ya," the carriage sped off into the Woods of Nevermore.

The carriage bounced and swayed while Gale and William danced and talked about games and the usual kid stuff. William revealed that he walked Alicyn home from school one day and has been smitten ever since. He also admitted to being the notorious N00bmaster on Scabs of Destiny. Gale played dumb so as not to reveal her identity but made a mental note to punish him severely the next time she played. *If* she could. The rotten kid was dynamite at the game.

About a mile outside of the castle walls, the land seemed to pulsate and vibrate with excitement. A mob of guests caused a backlog outside of the gate and slowed Horse-o and Jericho to a trot. People recognized the guest of honor despite the new carriage and began cheering and waving emphatically. Gale returned the wave, not with a royal twisting of the hand but with her and William hanging out of the windows, yelling and cheering at the mob. They recognized some faces and high-fived some new ones as the carriage made its way towards the gate. For a girl who had no desire to attend, she was surely embracing it. *Might as well,* thought Gale, *it may be my last act as a princess. Go out with a bang and leave them wanting more.*

A young blonde woman approached the carriage with a cherubic girl on her shoulder and said that she had named her daughter Nightingale in her honor. She thanked the woman and tried to figure out if it was weird

Chapter 17

or not to have a child named after her. Gale had no clue that the people adored her like this, and she really didn't believe it. They were probably just excited for the party, she concluded, and filled with too much wine and mead.

"They love you, Princess," said Sir Reginald as he pulled up alongside the carriage.

"They're drunk," said Gale.

"It's not even noon. Is it so awful a thing to be loved?"

"They don't even know me."

"Even better. I've been loved, and I've been known. Loved is better." The knight gave her a wink and galloped ahead to lead Woltz through the towering wooden gates that encased Castle Beckett.

"That was nice of him to say," said William as he sat back inside the coach and sipped at his drink.

"He's only trying to convince me, that's all."

"Of what?" asked the boy.

"Nothing," said Gale as she sat down and crossed her arms in frustration.

"Is it about you not being a princess anymore?"

"Oh, you heard, did you?"

"Yeah. Everybody knows."

"And what does everybody say?" asked Gale.

"Well, everybody I know says that it doesn't matter either way."

"Really?" said Gale. "I couldn't agree with them more."

"Nope. They say that no matter what, you'll always be the princess, whether you are or not. I figure if you're gonna be the princess anyway, why not just be the princess?"

He's right, you know. You are who you are. So why struggle to be something you're not. Be who you want to be. Stay natural to yourself. You will be who you are anyway. Even if it means being an introverted, video game-playing, taco-eating, high-heel-hating princess. That way, you can enjoy life to the fullest without being bothered by what other people want you to be. It's very time-consuming, and I don't recommend it. Besides, isn't that what she told Lorynn at the farmhouse just a few days ago? Isn't that who she's been all along?

The horses clip-clopped their way along the cobblestone street that led through the heart of the town and straight to the palace. The sidewalks were a river of joy as people hopped from shop to shop, sampling ales and delicacies of all types and flavors. Cheers went up as they slowly crept along. Gale looked around and waved, seeming to know each and every one of them. There was Enzo the Butcher, Murray the Tailor, Sam the Baker, and Rip the Cop, all stationed proudly in front of their stores.

She saw a few of the ladies of the court. There was Ashtabula chewing on a sausage sandwich, chatting with Bystyx, who was wiping cannoli crème from her lips. Marmalade was talking to Chatterley about something deliciously devious. Gale was sure of it. She had known them all her life, and they felt like extended family.

Many girls from her school were floating around. Like Gale, they were all given the middle name Lynn out of respect for her grandmother, Queen Lynn the Sturdy. She saw Brandy Lynn laughing with Heather Lynn and Tami Lynn, who always carted around a tan teddy bear wherever she went for some reason.

They stopped at a corner to let the revelers cross the street. Most of them had mugs or cups, and small children carried dripping ice cream cones and wore face paintings of tigers and puppies. Balloons, twisted into crowns and swords, were on the heads of kids and adults alike. As they crossed, Brenton, the unlucky boy who unwittingly donated his hoodie to Gale, strolled by and waved. He was holding the hand of a pretty brown-haired girl with glasses and a beautiful tattoo of a lion on her thigh. The princess smiled back and waved. Seeing him with someone didn't bother her in the least. Gale got the best part of him, and it had a front zipper and pockets.

"Hey girlfriend!" shouted Cierra (or was it Starr?) who popped up along the carriage, startling both Gale and William. "Sweet ride!"

"You like? It was a gift from my mommy and popsicle."

"Love the red. So boojie! Who's the hunk?"

"That's William. He's my escort."

"Hey, studmuffin!" said Starr from the other window.

Studmuffin waved shyly at the twins. The girls were dressed in shorts and blue tank tops, complete with body glitter and lip gloss. Starr was wearing Ray-bans and sucking on a rainbow lollipop. Cierra had on a balloon crown and was snapping some grape bubble gum.

"You ladies want a ride to the castle? I'm heading that way," joked Gale.

"Yup! Yup! Skootch over, rockstar, and let me in."

The twins hopped into the coach from each side and plopped down next to William. Starr put her arm over William's shoulder, and Cierra stretched her legs over his and kicked off her flip-flops. There was no complaining from William, who sat motionless but sported a grin that you could see from space.

"Don't ruin him, girls. I need him in a hot minute."

"No worries," said Starr. "Have you seen the array of hot guys here? It's ridiculous."

"All I've seen was my ex and Sam the Baker."

"The new pizza shop has two guys in there that are nuts. If we were a little older, there would be trouble. So hot."

"How old is too old?" asked Gale. She was still a little sensitive on the topic of age.

"Like thirties or late twenties. Juuuuust out of reach," said Cierra.

The carriage began its slow march up toward the palace as electric dance music filled every speaker on the street. Whoever this DJ was, he knew his craft. The whole town was rocking and dancing as they walked down the sidewalk. One group of boys started chanting "Night-in-gale! Night-in-gale!" as they rode by, and another yelled "Go princess! It's ya birthday!" over and over until they were out of reach. Gale was starting to relax a tiny bit. Although she had no desire for any of this attention, everyone seemed to be having a blast. Her parents were right: birthday parties weren't for the person celebrating the birthday. It was for the people.

"Love the dress! What's with the shoes?" asked Cierra as Starr shouted something inappropriate at one of the boys standing on the corner.

"I hate heels. I opted for comfy casual."

"You rebel. What's your mom going to say?"

"I'm eighteen. I think I can make a choice or two on my own."

"Truth. Speaking of decisions, any on renouncing the throne?"

"It'll be a game-time decision. I'm really not sure yet."

"Well, you have about thirty seconds until we get to the palace stairs, so take your time."

With that, Starr shouted, "I love this song!" and began dancing with William, rocking the coach to and fro.

"Kid, if you tell your mother about any of this, I'll kill ya!" Gale said to a hysterical William.

"I promise! I promise!" said William.

"That's a good boy," cooed Starr as she planted a lip gloss smooch on his cheek.

"No smootchy!" yelled Gale as she gave Starr a playful slap. "I have to return that kid to his rightful owners. I don't need you two dropkicking him into puberty!"

They were nearly to the stairs as they pulled up to the DJ stage. A crowd was circled in front as lights spun and smoke machines belched, enhancing the lasers that fired every which way from the stage.

"Whoa! Hey princess, check this guy out!" squealed Cierra as she pointed up to the DJ.

Gale provided a cursory glance toward the DJ when her mouth dropped in shock.

"Woltz! Stop!" screamed Gale as she banged on the roof of the carriage. Woltz pulled hard on the reins, lifting Jericho up onto his hind legs with a whinny.

"Easy, Princess," said Starr, "he's not that hot."

"You don't understand!" said Gale as she darted out of the carriage with everyone, including a sword-drawing knight, at her heels.

Standing in the center of the elaborate DJ setup was a thin man covered in tattoos. He wore a red metallic jacket with no shirt, and a bunch of necklaces bounced off his chest as he bobbed along to the beats that he was putting out. On his head was a black top hat with an ornate plumage of feathers and roses, both white and red. Yellow Oakleys pinched his nose and shielded his eyes.

"'Sup, Princess," said Sir Chad.

Yes. That Sir Chad. Sir Chad the Amazingly Digestible was spinning sick beats at her party. What a twist!

Chapter 17

"Sup? That's what you have to say? Sup? I thought you were eaten by the dragon! I've been worried sick about the whole thing!"

"I was eaten. Totally."

"Was??" said a mayonnaised Gale.

"Yup. I died, but I didn't! Cool, right?"

"Yes. Cool. But super confusing."

"Yeah. Dragon ate me. Not cool. Then there was like, pink smoke or something, and I ended up in some cave with all this strange stuff. Lots of gold and hats and cheese with chutney and soda and bread and stuff. Weird, right? I ate the cheese," said Chad as he bobbed along to the music, checking on levels of this or that.

Gale could not believe what she was seeing. She couldn't help but wonder how many chapters had passed that she had mourned his turning into Chad Pot Pie. All this time, she had thought that she was this terrible person who had willed another person's demise, and here he was, jamming out at her party. If Mittens was in range, she would have wrung her neck and hugged her all at once. The dragon had never disobeyed her wishes after all.

"Ladies, gentlemen, I'd like you to meet Sir Chad the Amazing," Gale said to her followers.

"'Sup," said Chad as he mixed in another song.

"HOLY—" said the twins in unison.

"Panini, ladies. Watch the language. There are children present," said Gale. She looked out at the twins, and they were both doing the puppy-eating-a-football impression. Reginald sheathed his sword, and William was too distracted by all of the electronic equipment to understand the gravity of the situation.

"Are you a ghost? Can you hear me, O spirit?" asked Cierra. (Or was it Starr?)

"Nope. No ghost. Anyway, after a few minutes, I ended up here somehow. I was given this sweet gear and told that I had to DJ your birthday. Cool gig! High five, wee man!" said Chad as he gave William a solid slap.

"A few minutes? Chad, you've been gone for over a week."

"Really?... Meh. No biggie. I didn't have anything going on anyway," he said and continued to mix.

A roar came from the crowd as they looked and pointed to the sky over the castle. There was Wrathnarok, swooping and swirling, making little pink smoke hearts across the bright blue sky. She had mentioned in her note that her real present would be waiting at the castle. Sir Chad must be her gift.

Now you're just showing off, thought Gale as she watched the dragon soar.

"I still don't understand. How did any of this happen?" asked Gale.

"I dunno. It's your dragon. By the way, I'm supposed to play your introduction. Any requests for the birthday girl?"

"Your choice. But nothing with the word 'witch' in it. I still have the dragon, and I'm not afraid to use it."

"Fair enough."

Reginald escorted the carriage from the bottom of the grand stairway that led to the palace entrance. While preparing herself to climb the great staircase, Gale realized two things. One, that Sir Chad no longer wanted to go to the club, he was the club. Two, men like that cannot be changed, they can only change themselves. She took a deep breath and grabbed William by the hand.

"Are ya ready, kid?"

"If you are, Princess!" shouted William as they began the hike to the top of the stairs. As they climbed, a familiar tune thumped through the speakers. It was "Better off Alone" by Alice Deejay. A very appropriate choice if you ask me. There may be some hope for Chad yet.

"LADIES AND GENTLEMEN! CHILDREN OF ALL AGES! I PRESENT TO YOU TODAY'S GUEST OF HONOR! THE ROCK! THE HARD PLACE! PRINCESSSSSSSSS NIGHT-EN-GALEEEEEEEEE!" The crowd went wild with excitement as the two climbed the tall stone staircase.

On the large and wide stone platform that led to the castle doors, gymnasts performed amazing stunts and flips while bouncing on enormous rubber bands. Fire breathers and jugglers flitted about the stage as bodies flew from huge silk ribbons high above their heads. Lights swirled, and smoke billowed, creating an enthralling circus atmosphere. The queen had gone all out.

Chapter 17

Down the center of the platform was a three-foot-wide lavender runner that led into the palace entrance. Seated in their thrones on either side of it were King Killian and Queen Evelyn, waving to the crowd and trying not to be choked out by the smoke show. On the left and right wings of the stage sat dignitaries from kingdoms everywhere. Kings, queens, princes and princesses, along with dukes, lords, ladies and viceroys… whatever they were. The princess curtseyed while being cautious of her crown, and William waved and bowed deeply. A podium was wheeled out, equipped with a microphone and placed in front of the princess. She'd be lying if she said that her heart wasn't in her throat.

OK, she thought, *here goes nothing.*

Chapter 18

In the land of This-and That, our heroine stood in front of the world and prepared to strip down naked in front of them all, for only by baring your soul are you truly naked. To reveal your thoughts, your dreams, your beliefs, and your desires is to reveal the true you. Looking out to the crowd, our princess was about to be as naked as a jaybird.

Behind her sat royalty, and in front stood the masses. She was a bridge between the two worlds in her golden gown and new white sneakers. To her, they were all the same. Just people living their lives in their own way. She secretly hoped for their happiness because she was a living testimony to how convoluted it can be to live in two different worlds.

She saw familiar faces. There was Sir Flex-a-Lot beside a lovely older woman that Gale presumed was his doting mother. Standing to the left was Sir Michael, surrounded by other kids his age. Sir Reginald and Sir Knoxville shining brightly in the afternoon sun with Sir Robert and Sir Hunk. Edna, the seamstress, nearly bursting at the seams with joy, overwhelmed with pride for her son. Woltz stood by Gale's cousins, near Hans and Franz, smiling and waving at the stage. They were part of the sea of faces without a title or station or rank among them. Classmates and children with people of every land and every age, shoulder to shoulder.

William was right. It didn't matter what she said she was or wasn't: she was Nightingale, royal title or not. Whether she wore an ancient crown or one twisted from a balloon made no difference. Gale was just one of a sea of people, and all that mattered was who she was inside of herself. Reginald wasn't dirty or clean. He was a knight. Woltz could ride for her or her father, and he would still be the best horseman in the land. As a royal trebuchet mechanic or a miller, Ed was still a loving father and husband. His daughter, Lorynn, could be whatever she wished. So then could Nightingale.

"Thank you, everyone, for coming to my eighteenth birthday," she started. Her hands nervously squeezed her thumbs as sweat rolled down her back.

"I know that you have all heard the rumors regarding my renouncement..."

The crowd mumbled and rumbled at the acknowledgment of the elephant in the room. The royals seated on the stage passed troubled looks to one another and toward the king and queen seated behind her. She was relieved that they were out of sight because she didn't want to see their faces. She needed to make this decision without their influence.

"The fact of the matter is..." She stammered a bit as she searched her brain for the right words to say. Isn't that just like a brain? Shutting off when you need it the most?

"The fact is... that..."

Just as Gale was about to finish that rather weighty sentence, her worst fear came to fruition.

Her crown fell off.

Gasps and laughter rolled through the crowd as the crown bounced along the floor at her feet. Quickly, she bent down to snatch it, nearly knocking over the podium in the process. The urge to run started in her legs and welled up in her eyes disguised as teardrops. Feedback from the jostled microphone squealed through the castle and down the main street, causing some discomfort to the crowd.

Gale angrily picked up her tiara and briefly considered hurling it against a wall. Closing her eyes, she took a cleansing breath to collect herself. When she opened them again, Gale stared at the embarrassing piece of

Chapter 18

metal in her hands. It would never fit. It did not sit right on her head, and she felt as if this unfortunate incident would now be the defining moment in her life. Ex-Princess Nightingale the Clumsy. Who bravely fought the microphone of despair. Dropper of crowns and disappointer of parents.

So instead, she bent it.

If she wasn't right for the crown, she would make the crown right for her. Giving it a twist and a squeeze, Nightingale changed the crown and defiantly placed it on her head. It fit perfectly.

"How do I look?" she asked the crowd with a smile. They all enjoyed her playful joke, and the tension flew away, lifted up by the laughter of hundreds.

"After all… isn't this where it truly belongs?" Gale said, spreading her arms wide for acceptance. "People, I would never leave you. Just as you have never left me these eighteen years. As I rode through the kingdom, I saw so many familiar faces and smiles that only a fool or a coward would leave such a wonderful and warm place as this. As my father, King Killian the Stout-hearted has taught me, 'be neither a coward nor a fool.'"

Applause filled the air as Gale turned to smile at her parents. They were beaming with joy. King Killian gave her a nod of approval at her choice. The princess knew that they would have supported any decision that she had made. She was grateful to be given the freedom to make the right one.

"I love you, Princess!" came a shout from the crowd.

"And I love you, whoever you are!" she said as she pointed toward where she believed the comment originated. The crowd laughed and looked around to find out who the culprit was.

"I'd like to take a moment to introduce my escort today. Ladies and gentlemen, this is William, the son of our royal seamstress, Edna. Take a bow, kid."

William, face red from nervousness, took a deep bow to the applause of all. Gale clapped as well.

"Isn't he cute? I could not have asked for a finer person to escort me today. You see if you want to garner a girl's attention, you don't need to show off or act tough or cool. Just pick some wildflowers and act like a gentleman. You'd be surprised at the results, boys."

More laughter from the crowd was sprinkled with a smattering of applause.

"I'd also like to take a moment to acknowledge a group of girls who could not make it here today. Lorynn, Alicyn and Emylee Miller. Their family was stricken with the pox, and they chose to stay home to tend to their ailing mother. We all wish you a speedy recovery and, as I promised, some cake and food will be sent following my speech. Folks, I can't implore you enough. We need to take care of each other. In times of need, please reach out to your neighbors to see if they're doing well. A little goes a long way when it comes to kindness."

Nightingale was calmer now and in complete control, which is exactly how she liked it. The crowd was applauding, and she let it fill the castle walls. Now all she had to do was stick the landing, and in about ten minutes, she could dive into some much-needed pizza. Time to address her suitor situation.

"So... I don't know if you heard about this or not, but I had a little trouble in the suitor department lately," said Gale as the crowd roared with laughter.

"Yeah, I guess it has been well documented. It's not often a girl's dating habits become a news scroll on major networks. As you may know, my father graciously lifted the tradition of marriage by my eighteenth birthday. It seemed a little outdated. You see, someday, that choice will be made by me and me alone. I may choose to take a husband, or I may not, and I reserve the right to make that decision on my own. But now and forever after, I will always be married to you, the wonderful people of This-And-That."

That was the hint that Mittens had given her when she gave her the crown as a gift. Elizabeth was called the Virgin Queen because she never took a husband. Instead, she pledged her devotion to the people of England. As for actually being a virgin, there has been some speculation on this. It has been considered a falsehood since the queen had many friends who were of the male flavor. I tried to ask her myself, but she's not answering any of my calls. Probably because she's been dead since 1603.

"But know this," Gale continued, "that, as your spouse, I promise to never treat you with disrespect," Gale said as she looked directly at Sir Chad.

Chapter 18

"Never need to make time for you," she said as she stared at Sir Flex-a-Lot.

"Never be lured away by promises of fame and fortune," the princess then turned her eyes to Michael. "And never become so comfortable that I lose my focus." She gave him a look that begged forgiveness. His smile and nod said that he understood.

"Now, let's all have a great time and enjoy my party!"

The crowd went bananas. They cheered, threw balloon hats in the air, whistled and screamed. Then, the strangest thing happened. Everyone out in This-and-That started singing. The crowd of hundreds spontaneously sang "Happy Birthday" to her as they rocked back and forth, some clasping hands and others arm in arm. At that moment, she could not fight the tears any longer. Two weeks' worth of stress and anxiousness ran slowly down her cheeks, and she struggled to wipe them away.

The king and queen walked over to give their princess a hug that only moms and dads could give, and she welcomed them both. When the song had ended, the royal family held hands and took a bow in unison, and when they rose, their arms were thrust jubilantly into the air. Just then, Chad whipped up some appropriate music from the DJ booth. Hand in hand, the dad, the mom, and their eighteen-year-old daughter walked off the stage to cheers and applause from everyone.

Once out of view and safely inside the palace, Gale took a deep breath and tried to stop shaking. She instructed William where to meet up with Wrathnarok and her basket of cheer for the farm girls and, with a smooch of gratitude on his freckled cheek, sent him off to his liaison. Now that the royal family was alone, Gale peeled off her crown and wiped her brow. Flop sweat is a real thing, folks, and it's nothing to scoff at.

"How did I do?" asked the princess.

"Honey, you were wonderful!" said the queen.

"We never doubted you for a minute. We knew that if given the chance, you would make the right decision," said the king.

"Are you saying that my staying a princess was the right choice?" asked Gale with a hint of skepticism in her voice.

"No, not at all," said the king as he held her by the hands and looked into her eyes. "I knew if you were given the chance that you would make the right decision for *you*. Now please explain to me why I have been delivered hundreds of broken clocks and your mother was given enough art supplies to fill the Bauhaus?"

"A little gift from me to you. I can't have you working all the time and not enjoying yourself. You told me that you missed tinkering with things and that mom hasn't painted in ages. Well, it's about time you start again. Spend some time doing something you love so that you won't regret doing the things you must," said the princess.

"She is a wise one, Killian," said the queen.

"Yup. She takes after her mother."

"Do you mind telling me where you got all of these supplies in such short a time?" asked the queen.

"Uhh… Internet?" replied Gale. That was the mission that Gale had given to Reflexa and Mittens. Reflexa scoured the internet for donations, and Mittens delivered them all to the castle under cover of darkness. People from all over the land sent information on how to pick up old broken clocks and donations of art supplies. The response was overwhelming. After a few days, Reflexa had to refuse the gifts because there were just too many to bear. Never underestimate the kindness of people, kids. They will surprise you every time.

"Speaking of gifts, how's the carriage? Pretty sleek, right?" asked the king.

"Mom. Dad. It's wonderful! I love it so much. The horses are beautiful, and I think we hit it off well. I love the red interior! And the sound system rocks!" Gale found herself babbling about the carriage, and who wouldn't.

"Well, just be careful. Woltz is an old man, and he doesn't move too fast, so be patient with him if he's not speeding along like a maniac."

Gale thought about the breakneck rate at which they made it to the Castle and said that she would try to keep the king's advice in mind. After a few more hugs and "Love! Love! Love!" shouted back and forth, the princess changed into her casual wear and made her way to the back courtyard for the party.

Entering the rear courtyard of the castle revealed hundreds of kids, ranging from some William's age to others in their mid-twenties. Gale

Chapter 18

knew a few familiar faces but had no idea who the vast majority of them were. She recognized a few princes and princesses from neighboring lands and respectfully thanked each and every one of them for their attendance.

The courtyard was alive with music and a forest of purple and gold balloons. Banners that announced her birthday flapped in the light breeze. Huge tables filled with food and beverages lined the wall next to the castle stairs and came in every tasty variety from burgers to pizza, lasagna to fried chicken strips, along with some healthy alternatives sprinkled in for effect like vegetable platters and enough fruit to start an orchard. Confections lined a different wall, complete with sugar plums, cakes, tarts, cannoli, cupcakes and the lot. You have a favorite dessert? It was there. That thing you haven't tried in years? It was there too. Your grandmother's special brownie recipe that she won't share with Aunt Jill, no matter how many times she's begged for it? A whole platter full right there on the table.

The princess mingled around for a while, hugging her cousins and giving fake cheek kisses to old classmates and people she knew from town. The whole courtyard was a beehive of excitement, and it nearly took Gale's breath away. Circles of people dancing and another huddled near the food table. She looked through the countless faces and wondered if any of them were PizzaBoi. The thought of him being here and not knowing her identity enticed her in a devious manner. Every girl needs a little mystery, and now that she had found hers, the princess was going to relish it.

She wished Mittens would come back and hang with her. Although they had only known each other for a short time, Gale cherished their awkward and flawed friendship, and without her friend nearby, she felt lonely and adrift in the sea of people. Many of her friends stood near her, and they all joked and laughed, but it wasn't the same as when Mittens was close. The princess just wanted to find a nice quiet place to relax and decompress without the constant barrage of pseudo-friends and sycophants that were circling her at the party.

Lucky for her, a familiar face was walking toward her at that very moment. Michael was heading her way with a plate of your grandmother's brownies. He was flanked by a new face, a boy about her age that she had never seen before. He was cute, with a short cut of sandy hair on his head.

Very Bradley Cooper. Not A Star is Born Bradley Cooper, but more of a Limitless Bradley Cooper.

"I've come to rescue you," said Michael as he handed her a brownie.

"Do I look like a girl who needs rescuing?" asked Gale, taking a healthy bite of her gift.

"Never. Did I say rescue? I meant feed. I've come to feed you. Stupid autocorrect."

"Well, thank you in either case. Is this your date?" asked Gale, motioning to the new boy.

"Nah, I could never land a guy this hot. This is Pat. Pat, this is Princess Gale, Eater of Cheeses."

"My pleasure," said Pat with a brilliant smile. Gale found something odd about Pat. Immediately she felt that something somewhere was awry with the way he spoke. Something weirdly familiar.

"Have we met?" asked Gale.

"Doubtful. I'm kind of new in town, and I'd think I'd remember meeting the princess."

"Well, welcome to This-and-That. I don't know how to put this, but… I'm kind of a big deal around here," joked the princess.

"I'll ask around and see if anyone's heard of you," said Pat. Again, there was something about that voice.

"You do that. Meanwhile, I'm dying to grab some pizza. It smells amazing."

"Sit tight, and I'll grab you a slice," said Pat as he headed towards the buffet.

Now that they had a moment, Gale felt the need to set things straight. She felt awful about the way Michael left the tower and didn't want any animosity between them. She liked Michael. He was handsome and witty and carried a kind soul, but the magic that was there was not the type that she was looking for. Not like the magic of the late-night chat that she had with PizzaBoi.

"So… are you mad at me?" asked Gale.

"No. Why would I be mad?"

"Well, things kind of ended weird, and I didn't want there to be any ill will between us."

Chapter 18

"Oh, you mean the part where I was going to escort you, and you decided to blow me off and take a ten-year-old in my place? That part?"

"Yes, that would be the part in question."

"Princess, I thought I'd made a better impression than that. That's not me."

"I know," said Gale, looking at her feet. "But I want you to know that I really enjoyed hanging out with you. I got a lot going on."

"Is 'I got a lot going on' code for 'I met another boy?'"

"No. Well... no. It's weird and complicated. *I'm* weird and complicated. Is that OK?"

"I would expect nothing less. We're good, Princess. Maybe we'll watch a movie together or something. Think you can keep in touch?"

"You can't shake me that easy," said Gale. She was relieved that this was going well. Michael really was a great guy and hurting him was the last thing that she wanted to do.

"Great. Now tell me your joke. You said that the next time I see you, that you'd have a new joke for me. Fire away."

"Man! I was hoping that you forgot about that. OK, let's see. This guy walks into a dentist's office and says, 'Doc, I think I'm a moth. All I want to do is flap around and—"

Before Gale could finish that rather comical anecdote, her cousins arrived and cut her off. Cierra (or was it Starr?) was eating the cream out of a cannoli using her well-manicured fingernail as a spoon.

"Hey, Nightingale! We were thinking of heading over to the dock. The royal trebuchet is on the edge, and guys are diving off and swimming. Wanna go?"

"I'm gonna pass. I'm just going to hang here for a while. Maybe I'll head over in a little bit. Michael, want to go with my cousins? This is Starr, and the girl harking the cannoli is Cierra."

"Nice to meet you. What do you say, hotness, wanna go for a swim?" asked Starr.

"Sure. Is that OK, Gale? You can finish your joke when I come back."

"Have fun. And be careful. These girls are nothing but trouble."

"They never proved anything. C'mon Michael. If you're nice, I'll let you watch me put on suntan lotion," said Cierra.

As they left to go to the pier, Pat returned with an entire box of pizza and a soda in each pant pocket. The name on the box read "Three Guys from Nowhere Pizza." Pat opened the box and offered Gale a slice of pepperoni. Gale graciously accepted and took a healthy bite.

"How is it?" asked Pat.

"Amazing! It's probably the best pizza I've ever had. I should ask my father to name them the royal pizza makers."

"He already has."

"Really? That's incredible. How did you know that?"

"Because, Queenie, I own it."

Queenie. He called her Queenie. It was at that moment that it hit her right between the eyes. She knew that there was something familiar about that voice. It should be recognizable since our princess spent hours upon hours talking to him about everything and nothing. Standing before her, finally in the flesh, was PizzaBoi.

"Holy Panini! You're PizzaBoi??"

"And you are KillaQueen. It's a pleasure to finally meet you."

Our princess was mayonnaised yet again.

"I can't believe it's you!" She reached over and gave Pat a warm hug that, in my opinion, may have lasted a second or two too long.

"How long have you known that I was me? That Queenie was me? How long have you known that I was KillaQueen?" The princess was stammering again, and she hated it. Gale liked to be in control, but this revelation really knocked her for a loop.

"I honestly just figured it out today. When I heard you talking to the crowd, I had a hunch. But when I saw you up close for the first time, I knew it was you."

"You knew just by seeing me? How does that work?"

"I'm not sure. If I ever figure it out, I'll let you know."

His smile seemed to reach out and touch Gale on the cheek. She couldn't believe that he knew her secret identity just by seeing her. The princess wasn't sure how that worked either, but she kind of liked it. Gale felt that she needed to change the subject and fast. *Remember, stick to your plan*, she thought.

Chapter 18

"So, you guys are from the Kingdom of Nowhere. What brings you to my neck of the woods?"

"My brothers and I always wanted to open a pizza place. My older brother, Lance, loves to cook, and my middle brother Rico runs the business side of things."

"Tell Lance he has outdone himself. He gets the princess' seal of approval. So, if they handle all that, what does PizzaBoi do?"

"PizzaBoi delivers food and helps with the dishes. And the cleaning. And the garbage. I do whatever they don't want to do mostly."

"And you guys are part of the royal clique now. So, there's Sir Lance, Sir Rico and Sir Pat. Sir Pat doesn't have that cool of a ring to it, does it?"

"Yeah, it's pretty annoying when your name is a verb."

"Do you have a title yet or are you still waiting for one?"

"Oh no, I've had one bestowed upon me." Pat put the box onto a nearby table and presented himself royally to the princess. He cleared his throat and put his left arm up in the air, crossing his right arm at his waist.

"M'Lady, may I humbly present to you… Sir Patience the Swift." Pat took a deep royal bow.

"Wait… what did you say your name is?"

"Patience. Pat is short for Patience. My mom was a bit of a hippy."

Patience. There was that word again. The word that her mother had said and that song that Reflexa had played. Everyone was telling her to try a little patience. Gale never understood what they meant until now. Here it was, standing right in front of her. Could they have known that Patience was a real person? Absolutely not. But the karma of the universe loves to play tricks on us all, so why question it?

"Well, Patience the Swift, it is an honor to meet one of my royal subjects. Are you aware that your name is an oxymoron?"

"Yes, since I am the youngest of three brothers, they have made it painfully evident," said Pat.

"Still, it must be nice to have a title. I haven't gotten mine yet. I'm scared that I will be Princess Nightingale the Musty or Princess Nightingale the Window Licker."

"You already have a title, princess. Didn't you know?"

"I do? No, I had no idea. Is it awful? Spare me the indignity if it's awful."

"No, it's fine. I like it a lot. You are known as... are you ready?"

"Lay it on me."

"You are known as Princess Nightingale the Self-sufficient. You like?"

"Seems a bit wordy. What do you think?"

"I think it's nice and accurate. As for wordy, your dad is Killian the Stout-hearted. I think wordy titles will become all the rage."

"Ah, look at me. I'm trendy."

And so it was said. Nightingale, the Self-sufficient princess. I'm sure you all saw that coming from about a mile away since it's on the cover of the book and all. Gale enjoyed it as well and felt it accurately described her. It's your deeds and actions that define you, not who you say or think you are. There's an old joke about a bricklayer named Morris who was never called Morris the Bricklayer. If you don't know the joke, go ask a cool uncle to tell you. Wait, on second thought, maybe not. The joke *is* rather salty.

"Wait a minute, I just thought of something. YOU!" gasped Gale, pointing an accusing finger. Her pretty little face turned into a leer as she looked sideways at Pat.

"Uh-oh. I think I'm in trouble here. What did I do?"

"We spoke online for hours the other night. Some things were said. Some horrible, nasty, evil, wickedly decadent things. You're a sleazebag!"

"If I recall correctly, M'Lady, you did the same. You're just as sleazy as me. Gonna have to change your title to Nightingale the Dirty Sleazeball. I told you that things get a little funky after two a.m. You said bring it on."

"Oh, and you brought it on, all right. And I don't recall saying any such thing."

"Are you calling me a liar?" asked Pat with feigned surprise.

"Well, if the sleazebag fits," said Gale through a smile.

"Then I must apologize to Her Royal Sleaziness."

"Well, she doesn't forgive you. You said some horribly inappropriate things," Gale said as she playfully crossed her arms and acted offended.

"Completely inappropriate," agreed Pat.

Chapter 18

"Totally unbecoming a young lady such as myself."

"I don't know what I was thinking."

He paused. Then said, "Want to do it again?"

"Oh, yeah," said Gale. "As soon as possible."

"Cool, give me your number, and I'll call you for real. Maybe this time, we can have some fun without the headsets. How about another slab of pizza?" said Pat as he reached into the box to extract two more slices. Gale was glowing from ear to ear. Patience may be a virtue, but he was definitely not virtuous. She gave him the number and chomped on a sausage slice.

The party went on for hours. Pat and Gale stayed side by side for most of the night, talking about nothing and everything all at once. Music blared through the courtyard, with Sir Chad rarely taking a break from the DJ booth. There was dancing and singing and swimming and eating. The bash was considered a great success by all.

Michael returned with the twins, and the five of them spent the rest of the night together. It seemed that there was some magic in Michael after all, and he seemed to hit it off well with Starr (or Cierra. Who can tell anymore?). William had returned from his charity mission and said that he received a peck on the cheek from Alicyn for bringing her the promised cake. Gale outed the poor boy as N00bmaster on Scabs of Destiny, much to the chagrin of all parties present. Apparently, they all played the game under different names and never knew that any of the others were playing as well. They promised to form a team the next time that they played and vowed vengeance on the evil William.

As the day rolled into the night, the party never wavered. Usually, there is an ebb and flow to long parties, with people coming and going and pledging to return. Some do, some don't and sooner or later, it peters out and dies. Not this one. By the time that bonfires were being lit on the shoreline, it seemed that more people had arrived than before. Even some of the younger parents had drifted in to join the rave that was thriving in the courtyard. Foam-like suds were sprayed over the crowd, and thousands of glowstick bracelets and necklaces were handed out to everyone.

Gale was exhausted and was ready for bed. She wanted to head out before the party got out of control, which they usually did. Her group

The Self-Sufficient Princess

had settled down in a far corner of the courtyard, and all sat in a circle on the lawn. Pat sat next to Gale as Michael lay his head on Starr's lap. She was playing with his hair as Cierra put her chin on one of his bent knees. Maybe he had hit it off with *both* of the twins at the same time. Gale didn't care. No judgey, remember?

The princess whispered into Pat's ear that she was going to dip and head back to the tower.

"Come on, I'll walk you out," said Pat as he stood up and extended his hand to Gale.

"Where are you crazy kids off to?" asked Cierra.

"I'm gonna whelp. Mum's the word," Gale said and bent down to give all three of them a hug goodnight.

"Happy Birthday, Nightengirl!" said Starr as Gale made her way into the crowd.

"Love! Love! Love!" said the princess as she followed Pat through the darkness.

Electric laser lights filled the sky, but still, the ground was dark and hard to navigate. Pat acted as a fullback and cleared a path for the princess. He must have said excuse me about a hundred times as they weaved their way across the court. Gale was scared that she would lose sight of him, so she reached down and grabbed his hand. Holding his hand made her smile like a schoolgirl. I guess some things never get old.

Finally, after dodging one way and dodging some more, they emerged on the other side of the courtyard where only a few stragglers were lingering about. Gale did not stop holding Pat's hand. Pat didn't pull away, either.

"Where are we headed now?" asked Pat.

"I have to walk down to the stables where my coach is. You can go back to the party if you want," said Gale.

"I'm going to head to the pizzeria and help my brothers clean up. They must be done by now. I was hoping that they would have made it to the party."

"So, if they're all working, how did you get off?"

"After seeing your speech, I told them that I was going to meet you. They know me well enough that they weren't going to stop me, so they

Chapter 18

told me to have fun. I've known Michael since we were kids, so I asked him to bring me to the party and introduce us."

"He's a good friend," said Gale.

"He really is. He told me how special you were, and yet he still helped me meet you. You can't find a guy like that just anywhere."

As they made it to the stables, Gale saw her coach but no Woltz. She figured she'd give him a call when she was ready. Pat turned to her and took her hands in his.

"Can you give me a call when you get home?"

"Easy, tiger. You're doing fine. Don't blow it. Self-sufficient, remember?"

"Very well, I can accept that. Then in lieu of a call, can I ask for a kiss?"

"You may indeed," said Gale.

Pat took his hand, touched her gently on the cheek, and kissed her. It was a toe-curler. The princess felt fire race through her veins and, after a moment, gently pushed Pat away. No need to rush into things. You know how if you eat ice cream too fast and you get a brain freeze? It was something like that. Gale did not want to get a brain freeze. At least not yet.

There's something decadent about a first kiss. You can taste promise and hope on your lips when you're done. The look. The smile. The blush of innocence coupled with the flush of desire. Everything is suddenly new and possible. Gale so wanted it to last, but smartly knew that she needed to be patient when it came to Patience.

With a wave, Pat said goodnight and drifted off into the darkness. Gale watched as long as she could until he slowly disappeared out of sight. One thing she knew was that this would be a birthday to remember. The other was that she would be calling the new number on her phone very, very soon.

"Goin' somewhere, Princess?" asked a voice from the other side of the coach. Gale walked around to see Mittens. She was leaning her back on the coach with her eyes closed.

"Oh, nowhere special," answered Gale.

"Nowhere special. That sounds wonderful," said the dragon. "Can I give you a ride?"

"You mean, like, a *ride* ride?" asked an excited Gale.

"Yup, it's your birthday, and I thought I'd give you one last present."

"Like on your back? Like William?"

"Absolutely."

Gale flapped her arms in an excited squeal.

"Then let's do it."

Black smoke filled the stable area and rose alongside the dragon in a whirlwind as Wrathnarok appeared before her eyes. She landed on all fours and bent down so that Gale could climb aboard.

"OK, what do I do?" asked Gale as she settled in.

"Hold onto my hair, and don't slip off. I don't wish to explain away a princess puddle. Ready?"

Before Gale could answer, the dragon rose high into the night and above the stable. The great wings flapped behind her, and with a flick of the dragon's tail, they were off. They soared above the rear courtyard, swooping and rising to the cheers of the crowd and then headed off over the sea. Exhilarated, Gale bathed in the wind and the salty air, letting her hair dance as they flew through the night.

"Did we have fun, Smootchy McSmootchface?" asked the dragon.

"Oh, you saw that, huh? Yeah, I'd say it was pretty, pretty,… pretty cool."

"Glad to hear. When we get home, you can tell me all about it."

"And you can explain to me how Sir Chad was miraculously regurgitated. Thank you, by the way."

"Not a problem. Like I've said, you're not my first princess."

Gale wanted to tell the dragon that she loved her but instead settled on an affectionate squeeze as they flitted through the air. *No reason to make it weird,* she thought.

"Say, before we get home, do you want to say the word?"

"What word?" asked a windswept Gale.

"C'mon, you're a princess riding a dragon. Say the word, and I'll breathe fire, and it'll look super cool over the water."

"I am Nightingale the Self-sufficient. I don't use other princess' words."

"You're just scared of copyright infringements," said Wrathnarok.

"You're damn straight I am."

Chapter 18

"Then make up your own word."

Gale thought for a minute and then said the only word that had made any sense since this whole adventure had started.

"PATIENCE!" she screamed.

The dragon let loose with an enormous ribbon of flame that lit up the sky and danced along the waves below. They circled back towards the crowd and illuminated the night above the revelers in the rear courtyard. The birthday girl waved to all as the princess and her dragon escaped through the darkness and headed back home.

Epilogue

In the land of This-and-That, there lived a princess named Nightingale. She lived in a wonderful tower with great Wi-Fi, satellite TV and a wonderful mini kitchenette. She played video games and talked to her friends. On her eighteenth birthday, instead of getting married, she met a boy named Pat. He was known as Sir Patience the Swift of Nowhere, and they chatted about scones and dancing for about three paragraphs. After which, they had a beautiful wedding, happily ever after. The end.

They have twenty-seven kids, all gorgeous and none of their children suffer from anxiety and can totally get into all the good clubs without calling ahead first. All the boys were named Pat, and all the girls were named Patience. They lived happily ever after. The end.

Yeah, none of that happened. Our heroine did not get married nor spawn a litter of tricycle motors. Instead, our fair princess went back to her tower and was her own self-sufficient person. She and her new housemate, Mittens, spend their days doing the least amount that they could possibly do without creating cobwebs. They ate, played games and danced. Because that's what princesses do.

After turning eighteen, nothing much had changed except for the calendar page. No magical transformation, no inner sense of being, no third-eye revelation. She was still the same girl as she was before the party,

The Self-Sufficient Princess

and she kind of liked it that way. The only major issue was that Mittens clogged the garbage disposal with mac and cheese, except replace "disposal" with "toilet" and "mac and cheese" with "seven balls of yarn." They didn't even have disposal. Oddly enough, they didn't have any yarn, either. None of this makes sense, so I'll just move ahead.

Patience and Gale became good friends, and the door is wide open to become more than that if the need or desire arises. For now, they hung out together when there was time and kept in touch on the phone or sometimes online. Since Pat is a small business owner, time was scarce, so they were taking it slow. It wasn't fair to either of them to want more just yet since he was delivering pizza and she was busy being a princess. Don't worry, the late-night phone calls continued, with varied results and more than once, they fell asleep while chatting.

Michael also remained friends with Gale and was sort of dating both of the twins at once. Remember, no judgey. Nothing super serious, but they all seemed to have a good time and as long as they were smart about it, no one should get hurt. Once a week or so, the group of them would end up at the tower to play Kattan or Dummikub or just to chill with a movie. I'll keep you all posted on how that turns out.

William was never vanquished at Scabs of Destiny. The little jerk was amazing at the game and was accused of cheating more than once, but no one could ever prove it. One night, a group of twenty, including KillaQueen, PizzaBoi, DeathBlade, and a few others, set out to slaughter him in a 20v1 match. The bloodbath was legendary, and the twenty were sent to an early grave. We can only hope that Alicyn, his new sweetheart, can appreciate his prowess.

Sir Chad is now making the circuit as DJ DragNFyre. He has a following of over a million and performs concerts around the globe. His live feed at Electric Mayhem had over five million subscribers, and he is raking in stupid money. No one has heard from the bookends, but rumor has it that they started a conspiracy podcast about the evils of dragons and how to avoid them. It's not very popular, but since they both refuse to step outside, it pays the bills.

Sir Flex-a-Lot works at the gym, lives with his mom, and is completely saturated and well-hydrated.

A low tide and a high rock shipwrecked Captain Anton Neal. He landed on an island and was eventually rescued by a certain concerned dragon who got wind of his unfortunate event from a forgiving and gracious princess. As the knights had attested to, he had changed his ways and stopped preying on girls with low self-esteem. He is married to a woman close to his age bracket and is presently the postmaster in Truro, Massachusetts. His smee became a cook at an all-inclusive resort somewhere in the Bahamas.

Pop quiz, students: what have we learned from this silly parable besides the fact that I'm a terrible narrator and that this book was probably written in crayon? Well, we learned to be true to yourself. Don't feel the need to bend to pressures just to feel accepted. Dating for the sake of dating is a ridiculous, time-wasting notion. Trebuchets are fun, and a dragon is a splendid metaphor for your inner confidence. Mirrors are terrific for self-reflection. We learned that we are all princesses if we choose to be and that our choices are ours and ours alone.

We have also learned that the world is a terrifically mysterious place filled with all sorts of surprises and characters. We aren't going to like them all, but we do need to experience as much as possible. The good comes with some bad, and vice versa. It's the yin-and-yang of life. Enjoy the treasures of a good time, for they rarely last but can be sustainable with a little effort. And when the bad times come around and the world gets cold and lonely, always remember to bring your Mittens.

About the Author

Why are you reading the author page? You really don't care about the author. You're only here to be polite. Well, the joke's on you because this isn't a picture of the author. This is a title agent from Pennsylvania. She's a mother of three and married to a railroad conductor. Don't you feel silly for wasting your time? I thought so. Now, either go read the book or have a snack. Do something productive.

Made in the USA
Middletown, DE
21 July 2024

The Self-Sufficient Princess